The Armageddon Script

BY THE SAME AUTHOR AND
PUBLISHED BY ELEMENT BOOKS

The Great Pyramid Decoded
Gospel of the Stars
The Endless Tale

Peter Lemesurier

The Armageddon Script

Prophecy in Action

St. Martin's Press
New York

Library of Congress Cataloging in Publication Data

Lemesurier, Peter.
    The Armageddon script.

    1. Prophecies—History.   I. Title.
BF1791.L45   1983   133.3   83-9791
ISBN 0-312-04922-6

First published in Great Britain by Element Books Ltd.

Contents

Acknowledgements

For permission to reproduce copyright material I am grateful to the following: W. H. Allen & Co., Ltd. and Harcourt Brace Jovanovich, Inc. for the extracts from Brad Steiger's *Gods of Aquarius*; William Collins, Sons & Co., Ltd. for those from P. Teilhard de Chardin's *Let Me Explain*; and The Thule Press, Findhorn for the extract from my own book *The Cosmic Eye*, due to be published in 1982. The extracts from the Dead Sea Scrolls are taken from pages 72, 85, 86, 87, 88, 90, 91, 92, 116, 121, 164, 165, 166, 167, 168, 171, 172, 227, 229, 236, 239, 240, 241 and 242 of Geza Vermes's *The Dead Sea Scrolls in English* (Pelican Books, Second Edition, 1975, Copyright © G. Vermes 1962, 1965, 1968, 1975), and are reprinted by permission of Penguin Books Ltd. The layout and outline of the map of Jerusalem are based largely on Hugh J. Schonfield's map on page 56 of his *The Pentecost Revolution*, published by Macdonald. Unless otherwise stated, biblical quotations are taken from the New English Bible, Second Edition, © 1970, by permission of Oxford and Cambridge University Presses.

I am indebted to Johann Quanier and Ursula Whyte for drawing my attention to the verse-epilogue which concludes the book, and tender my grateful acknowledgements to its author, whom I have unfortunately been unable to identify. My thanks are also due to Ray Smith for making presentable the three maps and the table of Old Testament prophets; to John Moore, Alun Owen and Rosemary Russell for reading and commenting on the manuscript; and to Michael Mann for his thoughtful and constructive editing.

P.L.

List of Illustrations

Jesus said: I have cast fire on the world, and see,
I guard it until the world is afire.

The Gospel according to Thomas

The truth has to appear only once, in one single mind,
for it to be impossible for anything ever to prevent it
from spreading universally and setting everything ablaze.

P. Teilhard de Chardin

The Armageddon Script

I
The Prophetic Gift

From time immemorial there have been those who have claimed to foretell the future. Sages, mystics, astrologers, clairvoyants, fortune-tellers — all have apparently displayed some sixth sense, some intuitive presentiment of things to come.

The phenomenon is not confined to human beings. The whole animal kingdom seems able in some measure to sense the future, and particularly impending disaster — whether the rats which are said to desert the doomed ship in advance, or the beasts and birds whose behaviour is even now beginning to be taken seriously as an indicator of imminent earthquake.[14] For centuries, too, the countryman has seen the comings and goings of the creatures of the wild as harbingers of the seasons, or of weather fair or foul, without the slightest suspicion that his attitude might be seen by others as superstitious or unreasonable.

It is almost as though the future casts its shadow before it as it comes, or as though the impact of impending events sends out a psychic shock-wave which precedes the actual news of their occurrence. Or perhaps it is the other way around. Since the future is the cumulative result of a flood of present causes, possibly the sensitive arrives at his prognosis by somehow tapping-in to the flow of events before its movement becomes apparent to his less aware contemporaries. The prophet's role, in these terms, would actually seem to be to feel the pulse of the *present*.

But analysing the mechanism of the process is not necessarily of first importance. True, many would-be explanations have been put forward, particularly in recent years. The electromagnetic vibrations so beloved of nineteenth-century pseudo-scientific speculation have jostled for approval alongside predestination, Divine inspiration, telepathy and a variety of exotic theories of time. But most of the intended explanations have testified more to their authors' scientific ignorance and philosophical naiveté than to the actual validity of the theories themselves. That validity, indeed, has seemed to retreat almost as the square of the number of rational arguments advanced to support it. The premonitive faculty and established wisdom, it seems, just do not mix.

Yet if explanation is difficult, it is at least possible to gain some idea of the nature of the prophetic process on the basis of simple observation. It is not long, for example, before it becomes clear that there are at least two, and possibly three, distinct types of prediction. These we could label, respectively, *rational*, *intuitive* and *creative*.

The *rational* form of prediction is that with which we are familiar on the lips of weather-forecasters, economic and social planners, market analysts and members of government think-tanks. It involves little more than a logical extrapolation of existing tendencies into the future, and the construction on this basis of a tentative model or scenario for a given future date. The fatal weakness of this form of prediction — which ought strictly to be described as *forecasting* — is that it can base itself only on *known* quantities and tendencies, and is therefore liable to be undermined by the operation of tendencies which were unknown or unrealised at the time when the original forecast was made. The deliberate run-down of the British coal-industry prior to the world oil-crisis of 1973–4 was a case in point, since it had taken as its basic premise that oil would continue to be both cheap and plentiful for years to come. The simultaneous run-down of Britain's rail-system on the grounds that road-transport would remain economically more viable may yet prove to have been another. And the inaccuracy of official weather-forecasting has by now, if somewhat unjustly, become almost proverbial.

The *intuitive* form of prediction, by contrast, has an entirely different *modus operandi*. Its practitioners seem able to glimpse, as though in a flash, disconnected but often vivid scenes from other times in a way which, as we have already suggested, defies all rational explanation. Nor is it confined to the professionals. Whether through dreams, visions, premonitions or a variety of physical 'omens', ordinary people with no pretensions to psychic powers — and women particularly — persistently report cases of foreknowledge which have enabled them to sense, predict and in some cases avoid potential disaster to themselves or those close to them.[15, 19, 46] This form of prognostication, in consequence, deserves to be filed under the blanket-term *clairvoyance*.

For this phenomenon the nature of the evidence points a strong finger of probability towards a source deep in the human unconscious, whether individual or collective, to which both dreams and visions are, of course, germane. The modern use of tea-leaf patterns, the configurations of the stars and planets, the lines on the palm or chance sequences of cards or coins represents a direct continuation of the age-old processes of divination which formerly involved the reading of sheep's entrails or of patterns of rune-sticks thrown up into the wind and deciphered as they lay scattered on the ground. All such processes depend for their operation largely upon the 'seeing' of order in chaos. All provide — like the glowing embers of a fire, the shapes of clouds in the sky, the patterns on the wallpaper or, for that matter, the psychologists' Rorschach test — endless opportunities for the unconscious mind to project its contents unwittingly on the world 'out there', where the conscious mind can then read them and, hopefully, learn from them. And if women — traditionally (in Western societies, at least) more responsive to the promptings of the unconscious than men — seem more prone to such experiences, then that is, perhaps, further evidence in favour of our supposition.

A further characteristic of this type of foreknowledge is that it often seems to depend heavily on emotional content or involvement, and upon fear in particular.[15] We might suspect this purely on statistical grounds. The great bulk of such predictions, after all, seem to refer to death and disasters. 'Doom' is possibly the word most closely associated in the public awareness with prophecy. It is to catastrophic future events, similarly, that animals seem most prone to react. And since conscious mental activity is not widely ascribed to animals, at least of the wild variety, this fact would add further weight to our theory of unconscious origins, as far as clairvoyance is concerned.

Such scientific research as has been carried out into the phenomenon lends even further weight to such a view. J. B. Rhine's experiments using pictorial 'Zener' cards at Duke University, North Carolina, from 1927 onwards[15] tended to show that his subjects' clairvoyant success-rates fell off noticeably with declining interest. An emotional spark, in other words, was necessary to kindle the clairvoyant faculty. Mere conscious attention was not enough; indeed, it sometimes proved counter-productive. Not surprisingly, therefore, Rhine's laboratory experiments, while distinctly encouraging from the psychics' point of view, did not always produce the overwhelming statistical evidence which might have been expected of a supposedly 'real' faculty, precisely because their nature and subject-matter were *too* scientific and emotion-free.

The major evidence for clairvoyance, consequently, is anecdotal rather than experimental. But that is not to say that such evidence is invalid. Exactly the same consideration applies to evidence in court. The case for clairvoyance, in other words, is potentially as strong as the case for crime.

The major difficulty affecting clairvoyant prediction, in fact, is not its operation but its application. Whether among ordinary people, with their occasional and inexplicable flashes of insight, or among the full-time professionals who somehow seem able to turn the prophetic faculty on and off at will, the business of relating glimpsed future to known present constantly presents all but insuperable obstacles. It is almost as though the two modes of cognition were mutually incompatible — as though conscious and unconscious were unable to speak the same language. Weather-forecasters, after all, are not renowned for their psychic gifts; nor do psychics generally make good weather-forecasters. Clairvoyants, in fact, seem to be the last people who should attempt to interpret their own insights. A division of labour therefore seems to be indicated — between the prophets on the one hand and their interpreters on the other. Esoteric wisdom has it that the ancient Egyptians observed just such a dichotomy: the Christian New Testament suggests that St Paul took a similar view.

Not that the dichotomy is particularly surprising. It merely reflects the by-now well-known division between the two hemispheres of the human neocortex. The left hemisphere of the brain, it is now widely accepted, is predominantly analytical and sequential in operation; it deals with language and logic; and it is intellectual in function. The right hemisphere, by contrast, takes a more holistic view of reality; it specialises in the instantaneous perception of relationships, in music and movement; and it is highly intuitive in function. The two halves of the brain thus correspond to two entirely different world-views — views which correspond to a remarkably large extent with those of the conscious and unconscious minds. And such is the human tendency to specialise in what we are best at that most of us side mainly with one or the other. The dialogue which is basic to our inner wholeness is broken off. Only in dreams or meditation is contact re-established via the so-called *corpus callosum* (the 'bridge' between the two hemispheres of the brain), and the imbalance re-adjusted. And so, inevitably perhaps, we live — both outwardly and inwardly — in a divided world.

It is this same division that seems to be reflected in the difficulty which the clairvoyant tends to experience in interpreting and communicating what he sees. And consequently the seer who is inwardly balanced and whole enough directly to relate the present to the future and, on this basis, to lay down firm guidelines for action, is a rare breed indeed. He it is who corresponds to our third category of prediction, and who alone strictly deserves the title of 'prophet'.

For prophecy in this sense is a truly *creative* act. The true prophet does not merely sense the future; in the light of his people's present circumstances he posits an ideal. He is both clairvoyant, forecaster and social catalyst. And, taking on the nature of a political plan of action, his ideas (often as interpreted by others) then become the matrix for the actions of entire peoples. To an extent, then, those ideas are self-fulfilling. On the prophet's shoulders, consequently, a heavy responsibility rests.

Not all so-called prophets necessarily measure up to this exacting standard, however. To many people, for example, the name 'Nostradamus' immediately springs to mind as soon as the word 'prophet' is mentioned. Certainly the ancient seer's fame is considerable. But did Michel de Nostradamus really measure up to the standards of a true prophet? And, in particular, do his still-outstanding predictions offer us any reliable guide for action during the coming years?

The bulk of the prophecies of this mysterious sixteenth-century Jewish-French physician and occultist are contained in a massive volume of verses known as the *Centuries*, which he produced towards the end of his life. Never out of print since, they were to exercise a persistent, almost hypnotic influence on ruling circles in France right up to the present century, as well as on the leaders of the German Third Reich. Based on a mixture of clair-voyance, divination and astrology, they are claimed by Erika Cheetham, author of *The Prophecies of Nostradamus*[5], to have successfully predicted an enormous range of historical events from the seer's own day to our own. The Great Fire and Plague of London, the execution of Charles I, the rise of Oliver Cromwell, the French Revolution, Napoleon's campaigns, both World Wars, the ravages of Hitler and even the deposing of the Shah of Iran in 1978 are all included. And if she is right, then Nostradamus was not only a notable clairvoyant, but also something of a prophet, in that he contrived to make the all-important link between present and future — even if not actually to propose an ideal to be achieved.

Yet this is to beg a great many questions. The language of the *Centuries*, for a start, is often exceedingly obscure, with words drawn from a mixture of French, Provençal, Italian, Latin and Greek, and with a syntax which is often virtually non-existent. Proper nouns abound, but these often take the form of allegorical references to classical and other sources, and frequently appear as anagrams into the bargain. Nostradamus, meanwhile, claimed to be able to put a date to each of his predictions: yet not only did he not do so, he actually shuffled the order of his quatrains, lest (it is said) their startling prophetic accuracy should prove too obvious. This may seem a strange piece of reasoning, until it is realised that Nostradamus, though a faithful second-generation Catholic, spent much of his life under threat from the Inquisition for suspected heresy. The 'shuffling' story, consequently, may have some truth in it.

Yet the outcome is inevitable. Any would-be interpreter of Nostradamus has not only to apply his intellectual faculties to matching the predictions with known and anticipated events; he also has to exercise considerable powers of intuition in deciphering the seer's intended meaning in the first place. The result is precisely that incompatibility of function to which not only interpreters, but also prophets, as we have seen, too easily fall prey.

Nostradamus, in other words, may well have *foreseen* the events to which he refers. But what he failed to do was to *forecast* them. They exist in a kind of premonitory limbo, awaiting the advent of an interpreter with sufficient prophetic ability to make the all-important link between present and future.

It is this role which Erika Cheetham, in her book, endeavours to fulfil, as others have done before her. Time alone will be the judge of her efforts. By the same token, however, her interpretations need to be regarded with great caution until the answer is known, one way or the other. And, in particular, it would be inadvisable to take at their face value — whether in the French original or in Miss Cheetham's English version — such major predictions as, it seems, still remain to be fulfilled, especially in view of their apparently doom-laden content.

For at this point a further potential threat to prophecy and its correct interpretation starts to become apparent, in addition to the observed incompatibility between intellect and intuition, between forecasting and clairvoyance. And that is the influence of prior assumption. Consideration of a few of Nostradamus's major outstanding predictions, as interpreted by Miss Cheetham, should demonstrate this point.

Perhaps the best-known of these is to be found at x:72:

L'an mil neuf cens nonante neuf sept mois,
Du ciel viendra un grand Roi deffraieur.
Resusciter le grand Roi d'Angolmois.
Avant que Mars regner par bonheur.

In the year 1999, and seven months, from the sky will come the great King of Terror. He will bring back to life the great king of the Mongols. Before and after War reigns happily.[5]

Apart from remarking that 'Roi deffraieur' could, as printed, equally well mean 'redeeming King' (quite conceivably Nostradamus actually intended the ambiguity), it is worth noting that at least one word appears, on metrical grounds, to be missing from the last line of the French text as quoted. Inevitably, meanwhile, the quatrain conjures up for Miss Cheetham visions of Antichrists and Armageddons.

x:74 and 75 both seem to have similarly millennial themes, with their apparent references to the raising of the dead and to the appearance either of a great spiritual leader or of an Antichrist in Asia (the reference is once again ambiguous). The latter figure is mentioned specifically in the horrific viii:77:

L'antechrist trois bien tost anniehilez,
Vingt & sept ans sang durera sa guerre.
Les heretiques mortz, captifs, exilez.
Sang corps humain eau rougi gresler terre.

The antichrist very soon annihilates the three, twenty-seven years his war will last. The unbelievers are dead, captive, exiled; with blood, human bodies, water and red hail covering the earth.[5]

Here, as Miss Cheetham points out, 'l'antechrist trois' could equally well mean 'the third Antichrist' — for Nostradamus apparently foresaw three of them.

Further horrors are portrayed at ii:46:

Apres grand troche humaine plus grand
   s'appreste,
Le grand moteur des Siecles renouvelle:
Pluie, sang, laict, famine, fer & peste,
Au ciel veu feu, courant long estincelle.

After great misery for mankind an even greater approaches when the great cycle of the centuries is renewed. It will rain blood, milk, famine, war and disease: in the sky will be seen a fire, dragging a trail of sparks.[5]

This apparent reference to a comet is taken up again at II:62, which places its appearance shortly after the death of one 'Mabus'. If we were to take the liberty of identifying this figure with *Mao* (the Chinese revolutionary leader Mao Tse-Tung, who died in 1976), the comet in question could be taken as due to arrive some time between the years 1976 and 2000, and Miss Cheetham herself is not slow to identify it with Halley's Comet, which is due to return next in early 1986. She thus places herself in a position to prophecy, in the somewhat uncertain light of II:41, a Third World War at or shortly after this time:

La grand estoille par sept jours brulera,
Nuée fera deux soleils apparoir:
Le gros mastin fera toute nuict hurlera,
Quand grand pontife changera de terroir.

The great star will burn for seven days and the cloud will make the sun appear double. The large mastiff will howl all night when the great pontiff changes his abode.[5]

Yet Halley's Comet returns every seventy-six years. The assumption that its *next* reappearance will somehow be especially significant may be correct — but such notions are all too familiar an aspect of prophetic interpretation where cyclic events are concerned.

Throughout, it is clear that Miss Cheetham relies (as any translator and interpreter has to) on her own preconceptions and received ideas as a framework for decoding Nostradamus's quatrains. She assumes, for example — partly on the basis of Nostradamus's own predictions and partly on that of current world-wide fears — that there will have been a Third World War and at least three Antichrists before the end of the present century. And who is to say that she will not be right? Two of the latter, indeed, she already identifies with Napoleon and Hitler. These ideas she then naturally superimposes upon the rest of Nostradamus's predictions, with the result that almost any major future world-leader, especially of oriental origin, tends to be tarred with the brush of the Antichrist, while almost any world-wide disaster acquires a hitherto unsuspected nuclear dimension.

The seer himself also has his own prior assumptions on the matter, meanwhile. They clearly derive from the biblical prophecies, in particular those of the Revelation of St John. And these received ideas he in turn has evidently superimposed on his own prophetic insights. How far, then, should we associate such notions with Nostradamus himself? If a prophet bases his predictions on the assumption that the earth is the centre of the universe, should his writings modify our attitude to that assumption? Or should that assumption in turn qualify our assessment of the prophet himself?

Clearly, the influence of received expectation on prophecy and its interpretation is considerable. It is therefore something which we shall need to examine with some care before presuming to settle, on the basis of available unfulfilled prophecies, the likely shape and scope of future events. For preconception, once again, has to do with an intellectual assessment of current circumstances, while prophecy of the clairvoyant kind that we have been discussing is essentially intuitive in nature. And the two, as we have seen, do not necessarily mix.

On the one hand, then, the difficulty of relating clairvoyantly-glimpsed future to known present, of turning premonitions into forecasts; on the other, the influence of preconceived ideas on the exercise of the clairvoyant faculty — these are among the perennial problems involved in putting prophecy to practical use. And they apply as much to the prophets' would-be interpreters as to the prophets themselves.

An instructive case in point is my own experience with the predictions of Ireland's St Malachy, sometimes known as Pseudo-Malachi. This eleventh-century Archbishop's chief claim to fame rests on having bequeathed to posterity a purported list of the last 111 popes, starting in the year 1143 and first published in 1595. The pontiffs were not specifically named, but identified via a series of cryptic, Latin tags — subsequently identified by interpreters as referring to the various popes' geographical origins, their policies or even their coats of arms. Yet it has to be admitted that, seen in this light, Malachy's predictions have turned out to be almost unerringly correct.[13, 48]

In my book *The Great Pyramid Decoded* (published in 1977) I summarised the remaining prophecies, which indicated at the time that there would be only four more popes. At the same time I took into account the comments of one of St Malachy's interpreters, the so-called Monk of Padua, Arnoldo de Wion, which were first printed in 1890. In the event, the latter's predictions proved less than accurate, but Malachy's continued to prove as reliable as ever.

First, according to his list, would come *De Medietate Lunae* (of a half-moon, or of the middle of the moon). The description, I suggested, might refer to 'his physical features, his coat of arms, the length of his pontificate . . .', though privately I considered this last suggestion to be perhaps the least likely.

In the event, John Paul I, elected on 26th August 1978, was to gain immediate world-wide renown for his toothy and, it has to be said, distinctly half-moon-like smile. But Malachy's prediction was to prove even more deadly. For John Paul's reign was to last only a month. Elected the day after half-moon (i.e. the lunar 'last quarter'), he died on 28th September 1978, only four days after the next lunar 'last quarter'. His pontificate had thus neatly bracketed a single full moon: it had coincided, in other words, with Malachy's 'middle of the moon'. Oblivious of the preconception that popes normally reign for years, not months, the least likely interpretation had, in the event, turned out to be the right one.

Next on Malachy's list was *De Labore Solis* (from the toil of the sun). Putting two and two — or rather, 'toil' and 'sun' — together, I suggested that he might prove to be the descendant of former negro slaves. Preconception, once again, had put in its appearance. Events, naturally, proved that this was to read altogether too much into the prophecy. Yet the 58-year-old John Paul II was still to fulfil it in the most literal way. For, almost alone among the 111 cardinals who formed the electoral conclave, he was a man who was familiar with hard manual labour in the open air — as a wartime stone-quarry worker during the Nazi occupation of Poland.

Even during the preparation of this book, however, John Paul was severely injured by a Turkish would-be assassin, thus apparently fulfilling one of the predictions made by the modern American seeress, Jeane Dixon, in respect of the last few popes. One of them, she had warned, would be injured in office, another dismissed by the cardinals to whom he would have delegated increased powers, a third assassinated after confounding his early critics.[9, 55] This last calamity, she had hinted, would spell the end of the autonomous papacy as such. Since Malachy likewise foresees only two popes after John Paul II, allocating Mrs Dixon's remaining predictions ought not, on the face of it, to be too difficult. Yet attempting to square her premonitions with what are now, in effect, Malachian preconceptions may still lay us open to some worrying surprises, as my efforts in *The Great Pyramid Decoded* may well yet demonstrate.[28]

John Paul's successor, according to Malachy, will be *Gloria Olivae* (the glory of the olive). This expression immediately suggests a peaceful and glorious reign, as the Monk of Padua is quick to point out — naming him Leo XIV and anticipating a period of Christian unity. Here once again, however, the word 'olive' can have more meanings than one, not least among them being the possibility of a black skin . . .

And so Malachy's list concludes with the figure whom he describes as *Petrus Romanus*. The expression may mean either 'Peter the Roman' or 'the Roman rock'. And at this point Malachy suddenly becomes more loquacious. 'During the last persecution of the Holy Roman Church,' he writes, he 'shall feed the sheep amidst great tribulations, and when these are past, the City of the Seven Hills shall be utterly destroyed and the awful Judge

. . . will judge the people.'[13]

The end, it would seem, of Rome and of the Roman Church amid a period of great calamity. Malachy does not date the event, but by the law of averages a total of two more popes should bring us to around or shortly after the end of the present century. During this final pontificate the Monk of Padua foresees the eventual burning of Rome.

Yet in all this, as in the case of Nostradamus, some very large questions remain. Did Malachy really intend his cryptic Latin tags to mean what his later interpreters have made them out to mean? Were they, in other words, true forecasts, or mere, disconnected snippets of clairvoyant information? Were they, for that matter, nothing more than shots in the dark which subsequent commentators have contrived to make accurate by, so to speak, interfering with the targets? How significant is it that in my own experience, as apparently in that of others, the eventual outcome has always been the one which no interpreter seems to have thought likely? And what explanation shall we advance if it eventually turns out that Malachy actually got his sums right after all, and *Petrus Romanus* — whoever he may be — is indeed the last pope?

Could it be in this case that the electoral conclaves, notwithstanding the official denigration of Malachy's predictions as fraudulent or, at any rate, as not by St Malachy, have consistently been at pains, whether consciously or unconsciously, to fulfil them? Have the former monk's intuitive insights — in their day, perhaps, no more than clairvoyant hunches — been turned into veritable prophecies and guides for action by subsequent generations? If so, then we may well posit the existence of a mysterious, hidden law of prophecy, operating at a deep level in the collective unconscious, which conspires to ensure that predictions — or at least those that are well-known and widely believed — actually tend to fulfil themselves. In which case, how sure can we be that that law will not likewise bring to pass the dire events apparently foreseen by St Malachy and Nostradamus for the end of our own century?

Such possibilities may well give us pause for thought. For if there is anything in them, then we may be forced to conclude that prophecy, far from merely foreseeing the future, actually conditions it, whether intentionally or otherwise. And if so, then discovering the laws by which it operates, and learning to manipulate them wisely, may be of crucial importance to the very survival of contemporary man, increasingly obsessed as he currently is with the conviction that he has no future at all.

2
The Rules of the Game

As we have already seen from Nostradamus and St Malachy, it is only in retrospect that the prophecies of a seer can be seen to be correct. That, one might think, is simply common sense.

But there is more to it than that.

Conventionally, a prophecy is formulated in terms of everyday words (though words, as we shall see, are not the only possible prophetic vehicle). But words, contrary to common assumption, do not have simple, fixed meanings. Every word, as students of linguistics are well aware, has a whole range, or spectrum of meaning, and its precise interpretation therefore depends to a very large extent on the context in which it is uttered. That context in turn comprises not only the rest of the utterance in question, but the circumstances in which that utterance is made and to which it is intended to apply.

Now, in the case of prophecy, the circumstances to which the words refer often lie far in the future. Except, possibly, to the prophet himself, they therefore represent an unknown. As a result, a vital key to unlocking the true meaning of the prediction is missing.

And so it comes about that each prophecy can have any one of a number of possible meanings. Indeed, it is almost axiomatic in prophecy-interpretation that the most obvious meaning — derived, as it almost inevitably is, from *present-day* attitudes and habits of thought — is likely to be the wrong one.

Or rather, *one* of the wrong ones.

A glaring example of this 'inverse' law of prophecy is supplied by the history of Bible-interpretation. Here, the application of a whole succession of everyday preconceptions to the text has resulted in the calculation of an almost equal number of different dates for such events as the Second Coming and the end of the world. On such data the perennial prophets of doom have thrived. Yet, to date, all of them have been wrong.

That is not, of course, to say that they will always be wrong. Until the Wright Brothers managed to coax the first powered, heavier-than-air flying machine off the ground on December 17th 1903, all their predecessors had, similarly, turned out to be 'wrong'. But that, of course, proved nothing. No doubt there were many, though, who thought that it did, and who warned the two unrepentant bicycle-mechanics repeatedly of the folly of their ways. Fortunately or unfortunately, the laws of aerodynamics were deaf to their warnings, and so we have aeroplanes today.

Similarly, in the field of biblical futurology, somebody will eventually be right — or so the apparently self-fulfilling nature of prophecy would suggest. When that will be we can but guess. But what is certain is that, when they actually occur, both the long-awaited Second Coming and the long-dreaded 'end of the world' will turn out to take a form which no fundamentalist Bible-interpreter has ever either thought of or even imagined to be within the realms of possibility.

Such, it seems, is the nature of prophecy.

Already, then, we can start to formulate — at least on a hypothetical basis — the first of the laws which seem to govern prophecy and its fulfilment. What I propose to call the First Law of Prophecy, applicable to all predictions that offer the slightest possibility of doubt, will run as follows:

> *The most likely outcome is the one that nobody has anticipated.*

We may term this law the *Law of Surprise Fulfilment*. And there is, of course, a corollary, which I propose to call the Second Law:

> *The most obvious interpretation is likely to be the wrong one.*

This law, in turn, begs to be called the *Law of Thwarted Expectation*.

The extraordinary prophecies of St Malachy, as we have seen, are innocent of datings. Moreover, like those of Nostradamus, they are expressed in terms which are capable of a number of possible interpretations. Applying the first of our two new-found Laws, therefore, we should expect to find that their apparent fulfilments — insofar as it is possible to identify them — have taken forms so far removed from prior expectation as to have been virtually unforeseeable. Applying the Second Law, moreover, we should expect to discover that the literal application of the prophets' words has been an unreliable guide to what appears to have been their true meaning.

In both cases, our expectations are amply justified.

The language of both seers, after all, is so cryptic as to demand considerable intuitive powers of the interpreter. But such an interpreter, as we have already seen, is unlikely, by the very nature of things, to be equally skilled in assessing the predictions from the intellectual point of view. To demand, in effect, that he should act both as psychic and as forecaster is to impose upon him a prophetic role to which only a handful of people in history have proved equal — if, indeed, anybody has done so. Small wonder, then, that the application of the two seers' predictions to future events has so far turned out to be a distinctly unreliable business.

Yet it has to be said that Malachy's predictions do have both a known sequence and a known starting-point. As a result, they can still shed, if valid, useful light on the shape of future events, even if exact dates are lacking. Indeed, if we could find other predictions that refer to those same events in more explicit terms, we might hope to integrate the two and so, little by little, build up a composite picture of things to come. We might even find that the Nostradamian predictions then start to fit in with the resulting scenario.

Were its origins not so dubious and its language so vague, for example, we could correlate with Malachy's predictions the so-called 'Prophecy of the Flowering Almond Tree', purportedly found in 1944 inside a lead tube in the ruins of a Berlin church. Its cryptic predictions, after all, bear specific dates. As quoted by Woldben in his *After Nostradamus*[55], those from 1972 to the end of the century run as follows:

1972	Triumph of the pilot	1987	Glade of crosses
1973	Light in the night	1988	Madness on Earth
1974	Road of the stars	1989	Expectation by men
1975	Storm of the crosses	1990	A sigh in the sky
1976	Love of the moon	1991	Light in the darkness
1977	Terrestrial dizziness	1992	Fall of the stars
1978	Forbidden dreams	1993	Death of Man
1979	Death of Judah	1994	Roar of a wild beast
1980	Rome without Peter	1995	Sob of the mother
1981	Triumph of work	1996	Flood on Earth
1982	The New Man	1997	Death of the Moon
1983	Hosanna by the people	1998	Glory in the Skies
1984	Ravings in Space	1999	The new Peter
1985	The voice of Antichrist	2000	Triumph of the olive
1986	Fire from the Orient		

Clearly, it should not be beyond the wit of man to link each of these predictions with some event or other during the year in question, though whether this would testify more to the ingenuity of the interpreter or to the accuracy of the prophet (ostensibly a nineteenth-century Benedictine monk) is open to question. Certainly, on the basis of the listed predictions to date, our First and Second Laws of Prophecy would seem to apply with a vengeance.

In view of the fact that several of the above entries seem to refer to events in the religious sphere, there appears at the same time to be a strong possibility — as in the case of Nostradamus and his interpreters — of interference between received expectation and the exercise of prophetic intuition. Indeed,

St Malachy too, as a fellow-Catholic, clearly shared Nostradamus's apocalyptic convictions. Consequently, arriving at a composite picture through a comparison of the various prophecies mentioned thus far may turn out to be less easy than expected. What the prophets concerned actually agree on, after all, is likely to consist mainly of the prejudices imposed upon them by the Catholic orthodoxies of their day.

But at this point it may be that we have stumbled upon an important key to unlocking the whole mystery of prophecy-interpretation. A would-be prophet, after all, whose work is devoted largely to fleshing-out an already-existing prophetic pattern is liable to fall into exactly the same trap as the clairvoyant who also tries to be a forecaster. He is endeavouring to mix his intellectual assessments of received preconceptions with his intuitive insights into future events. He is attempting to bring into double harness the normally disparate twin hemispheres of his brain. And that, as we have already suggested, is a feat which only a prophet of almost transcendent inner wholeness is likely to prove capable of achieving, at least in man's present state of evolution.

So important does this fact turn out to be for prophecy-interpretation that it deserves to be stated in the form of a Third Law of Prophecy:

Preconception and prophecy do not mix.

We may term this the *Law of Prejudicial Interference*. And nowhere is this law better exemplified than in the sphere of religion.

A religious prophet, after all, already has an axe to grind. His religious convictions, whether Christian or non-Christian, are likely to stem less from any genuine prophetic insight into the truth than from his upbringing and culture — whether by direct absorption or, of course, by reaction. And so he is liable to see the future in terms of those convictions — with an eye, in other words, at least partially blinded by prejudice. Indeed, no prophet can be totally absolved from this potential human failing.

In the religious sphere particularly, however, the speck of prejudice is liable to turn into a mighty beam of delusion. Perhaps this is because a religious prejudice is, by its very nature, a pre-eminent prejudice. In other words, we tend· to attach to our particular religious preconceptions an importance which transcends all other considerations — including, if need be, even the truth itself.

And again and again, it seems, prophets fall foul of this fact.

Nostradamus, St Malachy and the author of the Almond Tree Prophecy, after all, alike bear witness to a profound conviction of a coming period of cataclysm. By the very nature of the faith which all three shared, it is axiomatic that they also looked forward to a future Antichrist, a Second Coming, a Last Judgement and the ultimate dawning of the Kingdom of Heaven. It is these same assumptions that continue to underlie their major prophecies for the remainder of the present century. To an extent, then, their predictions are merely variations on a theme. They are the tinsel on the Christmas-tree, the icing on the cake. And, by the same token, they may actually serve to disguise, rather than to clarify, the prophetic message on which they are based.

For that underlying core of predictions, too, is a prophetic creation in its own right — a creation, moreover, which so much devotion on the part of so many latter-day seers shows to have been of major, even over-riding importance in the development of modern man's view of his own future.

Curiously enough, then, by studying the genesis, development and present-day significance of the ancient Bible-prophecies from Moses onwards, we are actually likely to get closer to the prophetic heart of the matter than by analysing the pronouncements of their later elaborators. The future reality to which the writings of seers such as Nostradamus and St Malachy refer is likely to emerge less from their own writings than from the ancient biblical texts themselves. The further back we can go in our researches, the closer we are likely to come to the true prophetic sources, less adulterated by preconceptions and subsequent misunderstandings.

As far as prophecy is concerned, in fact, the real future is actually most likely to emerge from the most distant past.

If evidence were needed for this proposition, one would have no further to look than the offerings of the more modern prophets themselves. For they inevitably carry with them not only a range of preconceptions culled originally from biblical sources, but also further sets of preconceptions based in turn on Nostradamus and St Malachy. Their very cultural background makes this virtually inevitable. Indeed, many of the prophets of our own day have long since superimposed on these preconceptions even further layers of assumption based on such sources as the revelations of twentieth-century America's 'sleeping prophet', Edgar Cayce.[3]

The individual prophetic insights of such seers (to whom we shall be referring later) may well be quite valid. Yet, if our Third Law is to be believed, the probability is considerable that, in general, the added layers of preconception will have taken them not nearer to, but further from the truth, and this fact should be evident from their pronouncements.

A. Woldben's extraordinary book *After Nostradamus*[55], of 1972, for example — one of numerous recent attempts to assess man's likely future by assembling and comparing the testimonies of a number of different psychics — provides clear evidence of this tendency. Even leaving aside his report on the 'Monk of Padua' already referred to above (whose work, of course, represents nothing less than a commentary on the received Malachian and Nostradamian preconceptions), the results can only be described as disastrous. Paris and Marseilles have not been invaded by the Muslims, as predicted by E. M. Ruir for the late nineteen-seventies, apparently on the basis of Bible-interpretation. Italy and much of Europe were not submerged by the sea during the same period, nor was over half the world's population wiped out, as deduced by Karmohaksis, again under more than a hint of biblical influence. A Third World War of unprecedented destructiveness did not break out in 1972, nor did Bolshevism, aided by the Arabs, completely take over the world, nor did a Fourth World War commence in 1980, as forecast by the obviously Armageddon-minded A. Barbault. Even P. Innocent Rissaut's prediction of a Third World War starting in or shortly after 1980 and won by the Russians in 1983 seems most unlikely to be fulfilled. As for the multiplicity of Antichrists likewise envisioned — clearly after the pattern apparently laid down by the Bible — these have simply failed to materialise in any identifiable form consistent with the title.

Not that biblical eschatology and Nostradamian gloom-mongering are the only preconceptions that can warp the prophetic gift, however. American prophets, for example, often display a tendency to assume that the American, capitalist way of life is some kind of God-given ideal, while foreign, socialist tendencies are, almost by definition, of the Devil. The result is an almost obsessive concern with the state of American democracy, and notably with the Presidency. This bias almost inevitably, therefore, tends to distort their prophetic judgement. The tendency is observable, for example, among the seers mentioned by Herbert B. Greenhouse in his immensely informative and thoughtful *Premonitions: A Leap into the Future*[15] of 1971. Edward Kennedy did not become president in 1976, as forecast by Alan Vaughan, nor does a US war with China seem likely for 1981. But then the English Malcolm Bessent was equally incorrect in predicting the same event for 1979 and in forecasting that Senator Muskie would become President in 1972. Again, it is difficult to justify in terms of administrative effectiveness Jeanne Gardner's forecast that an era of 'good government' would start in 1976, the date of Jimmy Carter's inauguration as President. And one-third of the world was not devastated in 1974, nor was Nixon the last US President, as predicted by Paul Neary.

Nevertheless it has to be said that most of the modern American seers mentioned by Greenhouse, while often vague in their pronouncements, are less prone than many of the latter-day European prophets mentioned by Woldben to make wild and totally inaccurate forecasts. More often than not, in fact, they have been remarkably successful. Their main weakness seems to lie mainly in the field of relationships between the USA and the communist world — which, in view of our Third Law, is precisely what one would expect. The greater accuracy of Greenhouse's forecasters seems to be almost entirely due to the fact that they refuse to allow themselves to be blinded in advance by a superstitious commitment to ideas such as those of

Nostradamus — or, indeed, by an equally superstitious devotion to what purports to be biblical eschatology. While emotional involvement can help to 'spark' the prophetic process, objectivity seems, as Greenhouse himself points out, to be vital for reliable prediction — and this view is entirely in line with the Third Law as proposed.

To sum up our conclusions thus far, then, the more religious and nationalistic preconceptions a prophet has, the more likely it is that his clairvoyant faculties will be swamped, distorted or in other ways adversely affected. Total freedom from prior assumptions is, it seems, an essential prerequisite. Moreover, like other faculties of an extra-sensory, intuitive nature, clairvoyance tends to work spontaneously or not at all. Its insights derive from deep, unconscious levels which are not amenable to conscious control. It works best when the seer is in a relaxed, even meditative state. It expresses itself through sudden 'knowings', through pictures or symbols, even through snatches of music — only rarely through words, and even then just as likely in pictured, printed form. In many respects it pertains to the world of dreams, a denizen of the pre-linguistic right hemisphere of the human neocortex. Small wonder, then, that it resents the imposition of constraints from outside, and even finds language at best an inadequate tool for expressing itself.

Perhaps inevitably, therefore, most attempts to tame the prophetic gift have been less than successful. Hans Holzer's attempt to arrive at a prophetic concensus of sixteen psychics for the nineteen-seventies (reported in his *The Prophets Speak* of 1971[19]), for example, has proved less than conclusive. Nor is this any more than one would expect in terms of our Third Law (of Prejudicial Interference). The sixteen psychics interviewed were, after all, presented with two sets of prior assumptions — that they would have something to say when interviewed by Holzer, and that such insights as they had would refer specifically to the nineteen-seventies. Given their alleged psychic abilities, indeed, there is no guarantee that they were not also picking up Holzer's own prior expectations regarding the years in question, whether telepathically or otherwise. And so, not surprisingly perhaps, the prophetic faculty, denied its crucial spontaneity, proffered only grudging co-operation.

The likelihood of telepathic interference is even stronger in the case of Jeffrey Goodman's well-meaning attempt to amplify the Cayce predictions for the period from 1980 onwards, reported in his dramatic, if sometimes naïve *The Earthquake Generation* (1978).[14] Indeed, he himself repeatedly attests to the presence of telepathic contact. And so, when the likely deleterious influence of prior expectation based on the Cayce data is likewise borne in mind, it is likely that the predictions of Goodman's psychics for the 1980s onwards will prove as unreliable as those of another group of would-be seers who, according to Greenhouse, got together on one occasion in an attempt to 'date' Cayce's prediction of the destruction of San Francisco by earthquakes. Their answer, possibly influenced by a current wave of hysteria on the subject, was unanimous: April, 1969. Needless to say, nothing of the kind happened. Greenhouse takes such damp squibs, with all their prior associations with the traditional biblical prophecies, as a salutary warning to mistrust sweeping forecasts of cosmic upheaval.

Which is not, of course, to say that they will always be wrong.

Religious preconceptions, nationalistic leanings, experimental expectations, telepathic conditioning and the influence (thanks largely to the communications-revolution) of earlier prophets — all tend to make it even more difficult for the modern prophet to make reliable predictions than for his ancient predecessors. And the more determined the attempts by well-meaning prophetic middlemen to capture and tame the clairvoyant faculty, the more determinedly it flies away, leaving its pursuers with only a few token tail-feathers of random prediction on purely peripheral matters. The big guns of science — and not least Francis Kinsman's attempt to 'democratise' the clairvoyant faculty by means of what he calls *TAROT* (Trend Analysis by Relative Opinion Testing)[23] — threaten to kill the precious quarry altogether: and even the toy guns of pseudo-science merely serve to frighten it away.

But of all the preconceptions which persistently warp the modern prophetic faculty, none is more all-embracing in its effect than received religious dogma. We have already seen how it lies, as a common denominator, within the basic frame of reference of religious prophets such as Nostradamus, Malachy and the author of the Almond Tree Prophecy. But it also underlies Woldben's various sources and influences the *lay* psychics interviewed by Greenhouse, Holzer, Goodman and Kinsman. As Westerners, all the latter-day psychics involved have at some time or other been exposed to the historical world-view proposed by Christianity and its Judaic antecedents, and later taken up by seers such as Cayce. Itself a product of the prophetic faculty, this overriding set of prior assumptions has been imposed on generation upon generation of Western thinkers — and by them, over the last few centuries, upon the rest of the world as well — to the point where it has become enshrined in man's very view of his world, reflected (as we shall see) in his whole cultural pattern and enthroned at the heart of his future expectations. We can no longer escape it. Even those who have long since rejected Christianity and all that it stands for continue, unknown even to themselves, to reflect its assumptions at every turn. It is almost inevitable, therefore, that the original eschatological prophecies, already powerful enough in their day, have gained immeasurably in potential effect over the centuries as they have been repeated, elaborated and given credence by growing millions of believers. Even their rejection by unbelievers has, one may assume, merely added further to their power through the renewed attention which that rejection and the ensuing controversy have tended to draw to them. Any publicity, it has been said, is good publicity.

And so our next conclusion is inevitable. While the modern-day seers may well have some useful light to throw on peripheral matters — such as isolated political, climatic, scientific and personal events — the Third Law of Prophecy (that of Prejudicial Interference) will tend to ensure that any prophetic attempts which they may make to flesh out such vital matters as the familiar future-paradigm traditionally expressed in terms of Antichrist, Armageddon, Second Coming, Day of Judgement and Kingdom of Heaven are likely to be sadly unreliable.

By contrast, however, the original biblical predictions themselves, perhaps paradoxically, are potentially even more valid today than when they were first formulated by the Old Testament prophets over two thousand years ago. For, if there is a tendency for prophecies to be self-fulfilling — and it is increasingly difficult to avoid this view — then that tendency has been immeasurably reinforced by their constant repetition from generation to generation, and by the fervent — even rabid — belief which has often attached to them during much of that time. Their potential impact, in consequence, is enormous. Their power to influence the human psyche, and thus the future course of history itself, cannot be overestimated. The very fact that scarcely any major modern prophet can resist incorporating them into his predictions is itself a measure of their continued influence. In a myriad unsuspected forms, as we shall see, they continue to cast an almost mesmeric spell upon a humanity which imagines that it has long since progressed beyond such childish and superstitious notions. In a real sense, indeed, it is those same ancient prophecies that have largely created our world of today, and which will go on to mould the world of tomorrow unless we ourselves decide that things should be otherwise. For we, too, can prophesy. We, too, can create visions. Given the knowledge of how to ground and manifest those visions, we ourselves are capable of creating a new, alternative future which has little in common with the ancient and — it has to be admitted — somewhat terrifying biblical picture.

Yet the chances that we shall ever be able to compete with the former vision, to match its power and authority and so, in the end, to overcome it, are extremely slight. The ancient prophecies have too much time and too many devotees on their side. Moreover, there is more than a little evidence that the scenario mapped out by the scriptural predictions corresponds in some deep way to an underlying evolutionary dynamic within the human psyche itself — one dubbed by Jung the *archetype of initiation* — which it could be dangerous, even fatal, to resist. The very fact that the vision has gained the strength it has may be due, indeed, to repeated attempts throughout history to do just that. Again and again the Old Order has re-asserted itself instead of giving way to the New, deliberately institutionalising the seers' insights into religious dogmas and rituals rather than physically and psychically deferring to them. The flow of history has repeatedly been blocked instead of facilitated, the prophetic forces for change have built up to ever-increasing heights, until it becomes inevitable that the dam will eventually burst, allowing the psychic floodwaters to thunder down upon an all-but-unsuspecting world, and leaving little but chaos and destruction in their wake.

Exactly, in fact, as the prophecies themselves have always predicted . . .

Rather than attempt to create a new vision, therefore, the task which presses most urgently upon us at the present time would seem to be to investigate those ancient prophecies which seem to swamp our world of modern vision, to research their origins and implications, to observe their extraordinary effects throughout history and above all to watch the successive efforts of those concerned to control and cope with the forces thus unleashed. In this way we may hope to gain some understanding of the laws and processes involved and the ways in which they can be applied responsibly for man's ultimate benefit. Learning by the historical mistakes of others, in other words, we may finally find ourselves in a position not merely to anticipate the likely flow of future events and to assess more accurately the efforts of more recent seers to predict it, but actually to exercise a conscious control over those events by co-operating with, rather than opposing, the prophecies.

Only then, perhaps, having, as it were, exorcised the former visions, shall we be in a position to create new visions of our own, and thus go on to create a 'new heaven and a new earth' of our own devising.

The prospect is an awesome one. It promises, as we shall see, to place man in command of almost magical powers over his own destiny and that of the planet on which he lives. For that very reason it is full of dangers. Such powers, once acquired, can be misused. The unleashing of what, in effect, are the hidden powers of the unconscious can have devastating effects. Equally, they can, if used wisely, be immeasurably creative — for those powers are also the powers of Creation itself.

Thus, we have the option of learning to release the enormous, accumulated prophetic pressures gradually, under a measure of conscious control, or of resisting them until, in a paroxysm of violence, they take matters into their own hands. Seismologists will already be familiar with the dilemma which, curiously enough, is just as much a matter of the moment in their field too.[14] The result of the second alternative can only be disaster.

And so our investigation leads us back inexorably once again to the beginnings of the process in the utterances of the Old Testament prophets. As the *Tao Te Ching* puts it, 'Knowing the ancient beginning is the essence of Tao.' Incredible as it may seem, it is only by tracing the archetypal story of

Moses and his people, the warnings and predictions of the Israelite prophets, and particularly the extraordinary attempts of the later Essenes to turn them into actuality — with all the consequences which that dramatic act was to entail for Christian belief and expectation — that we may actually hope to discover not only the true meaning of the prophecies of Nostradamus and his successors, but also, as it happens, the likely pattern of our own destiny in the years to come.

That ancient story, as we shall see, actually revolves around prophecy itself. Ostensibly so familiar to us already, it may well turn out to be far stranger and more disturbing than we had suspected, once we have succeeded in laying aside the religious blinkers which have hitherto obscured our view of what really happened. But then, in history as in prophecy, it is only by discarding our preconceptions that we are in any case likely to discover the truth.

The greatest barrier to finding the answer to a question, after all, is assuming that you know it already.

3
Prediction and the Bible

Among Jews and Christians at least, the names of the Old Testament prophets have long been regarded as by-words for reliability. Because they spoke with the voice of God, it is claimed, their prophecies were one hundred per cent accurate.

Logically, of course, the argument ought to be the other way around. Having once established that the prophecies were one hundred per cent accurate, one might then be justified in assuming that their authors were divinely inspired. Moses himself is said to have suggested this very approach. 'When the word spoken by the prophet in the name of the LORD is not fulfilled and does not come true, it is not a word spoken by the LORD.'[a]

We shall be well advised to examine that proverbial accuracy impartially for ourselves.

It was Moses, the Egyptian-trained hierophant who led the tribes of Israel out of Egypt to their Promised Land during the fifteenth century BC[b], who first laid down and codified the religious and social system of the new Hebrew theocracy — a system now known as the Jewish Torah, or Law. But he was more than just a leader and legislator. At the same time (if we are to believe the texts) he also made a series of far-reaching predictions to the assembled tribes, predictions which were to provide a general conceptual framework for all the prophets that followed. And, in particular, he warned of what would happen when, as he foreshadowed, Israel forsook the system that he had laid down. For that Law was a Divine Covenant, a bargain struck with YHWH (Yahweh, or Jehovah) Himself. Observing it would bring peace and lasting prosperity to Israel. But forsaking it would bring down on Israel's head all the fury of the Divine wrath.

So, at least, we are assured.

Accordingly, he predicted, their land would be invaded, devastated and

[a] Deut. 18:22   [b] Biblical dates based on Rutherford[38], whose proposed chronology seems as watertight as any.

settled by foreigners. The Israelites themselves would be deported, enslaved and dispersed among foreign nations. Large numbers of them would be put to death. Only after this time of terrible disasters would they be allowed to return to their ancestral homeland. And there, as the fairy-tale ending has it, they would at last live happily ever after, in eternal peace and prosperity.*

The list of prophesied disasters is certainly disturbing. With hindsight, moreover, it is extraordinarily impressive. For nearly all the predictions were to come true. And not just once, but many times. Not only did the Israelites fall repeatedly for the seductive snares of foreign religions and rival cultures. During the succeeding centuries a whole succession of invaders duly swept in a grisly train across the land of Palestine. Between them, the Egyptians, Philistines, Assyrians, Babylonians, Persians, Greeks and Romans repeatedly laid waste the land, devastated the cities, decimated the population and deported the survivors. And in it all the prophets saw the vengeful and dreaded hand of Yahweh Himself.

There was only one thing to be done. Israel must repent, renew its ancient Covenant, devote itself to the strict observance of the Mosaic Law. And so, when the Jews of the Babylonian exile returned to a ruined and deserted Jerusalem in 534 BC, that was precisely what they did. Solomon's Temple was rebuilt, the people were reminded of their solemn bargain with Yahweh, and the laws of Moses, together with his dire warnings and predictions, were written down in their present form in the books of Exodus, Leviticus, Numbers and Deuteronomy.

And so written, it has to be said, *for the first time.*

The implications of this fact — nowadays accepted by all but the most blinkered and partisan of biblical scholars — are, of course, more than a little worrying. We may accept that Moses existed, that he led the Israelites out of Egypt, and that he laid down the basis of their religious and social Law. But if his alleged predictions were not written down until nine hundred years later, *after* they had already started to be fulfilled, what guarantee do we have that Moses himself ever made them at all? Could well-meaning scribes have been putting words into Moses' mouth in order to reinforce the need to raise the national standards and stress the dire consequences of their neglect? Were the Assyrian and Babylonian invasions and exiles being adduced as supporting evidence only after the event?

Perhaps we shall never know.

There is a curious sequel, however. For, although two exiles had already come to pass, the world-wide Jewish Dispersion of more recent centuries had not yet occurred. Events during the first and second centuries AD, and even more during our own times, have fulfilled the prophecies of Moses in ways far more drastic and far-reaching than anybody could have imagined at the

---

* Compare chapters 27 to 31 of the book of Deuteronomy.

time of the local, and relatively insignificant, skirmishes between Israel and Babylon in the sixth century BC.

Moses' prophecies, in the event, have indeed turned out to be evidence of forethought, not afterthought. Whether 'genuine' or 'false', they have actually been fulfilled.

All, that is, except the last one. For eternal peace and prosperity have not yet come to Jewish Palestine, and seem most unlikely to do so in the foreseeable future.

There may be good and valid reasons for this distinct lack of interest in genuine authorship on history's part. For it becomes increasingly clear that an idea that we have already tentatively advanced on more than one occasion is nothing less than a basic law of prophecy — our fourth, in fact, to date:

Prophecies tend to be self-fulfilling.

We may describe this Fourth Law as the *Law of Self-Fulfilment.*

Moses, after all, had told the Israelites that they would break their Covenant. So, at least, the pre-scriptural tradition asserted. Therefore, in a sense, they could regard their action as inevitable. It had been predicted, decreed, fated by God. It was henceforth part of their destiny.

But with the breaking of the Covenant, a collective guilt would naturally have set in. The Divine bargain had been broken. It was now but a simple step for Israel and Judah (the northern and southern kingdoms respectively) to provoke the wrath of their imperial overlords. The unconscious desire for self-punishment can be a powerful force in human affairs. In due course the Big Powers duly reacted, and the rest of Israel's prophesied destiny could thus be set in train.

So that, in the end, what happened to the Israelites was what they always believed would happen to them.

Who can be sure, then, that the same process will not produce even more astonishing results in the future? For Moses also saw for his people a role as a 'kingdom of priests', a 'holy nation'*a* that would eventually lead the whole world to the knowledge and obedience of the True God . . .

The case of Moses is instructive. It reminds us both of the power of prophecy and of the care that needs to be taken in interpreting it. One question in particular, it seems, needs to be asked where biblical prophecies are concerned:

Did the prophecies precede the events, or vice versa?

Bearing in mind the difficulty of identifying any given prophecy-fulfilment

a Ex. 19:6

SUMMARY OF THE LAWS OF PROPHECY
as proposed in this volume

1. *The Law of Surprise Fulfilment* (p. 22)
   The most likely outcome is the one that nobody has anticipated.

2. *The Law of Thwarted Expectation* (p. 22)
   The most obvious interpretation is likely to be the wrong one.

3. *The Law of Prejudicial Interference* (p. 24)
   Preconception and prophecy do not mix.

4. *The Law of Self-Fulfilment* (p. 34)
   Prophecies tend to be self-fulfilling.

5. *The Law of Diminishing Accuracy* (p. 46)
   A prophecy's accuracy decreases as the square of the time to its fulfilment.

6. *The Law of Divided Functions* (p. 70)
   Prophecy and interpretation are incompatible activities.

7. *The Law of Prophetic Foreshortening* (p. 217)
   Clairvoyance foreshortens the future.

8. *The Law of Non-Existent Impossibility* (p. 226) — rider to Law Four
   If it can happen, it will; if it can't happen, it might.

— especially when that prophecy is expressed in general terms — a further question might be:

Did the prophecies really refer to the events with which they subsequently became associated, or to other people, times and places entirely?

This question is perhaps even more applicable to such extra-biblical sources as Nostradamus and St Malachy than to the Bible itself.

In view of our newly-formulated Fourth Law, and the apparent role of expectation in prophetic fulfilment, we might also ask:

Were the events either deliberately or unconsciously engineered in order to fulfil the prophecies?

And finally, it is important to establish the true answer to the question:

Did the events really occur at all, or were they 'invented' subsequently in order to 'prove' the prophecies?

'Proving' prophecies, after all, is important to the committed Bible-enthusiast, and especially to the Christian Evangelical. The prophecies are 'of God' because they have been fulfilled: the events are 'of God' because they have been prophesied. This neat, if slightly incestuous argument ought not to blind us to the facts or to inhibit our enquiry. Commitment is admirable, but unhelpful where establishing the truth is concerned. An assumption that cannot stand investigation may rightly be suspected of standing on shaky foundations.

In the chapters which follow, then, we shall need to leave behind any religious preconceptions we may have, and stay alive to the four time-honoured tricks of the prophetic trade outlined above. For ease of reference, we may summarise them as (a) retrospective prediction, (b) prophetic transference, (c) deliberate fulfilment and (d) wishful hindsight. Our investigations are likely to be that much more fruitful as a result.

And the study of one prophet in particular handsomely repays such an approach.

Among the Jewish exiles in Babylon during the sixth century BC was a young man called Daniel. Esoterically trained by the local Chaldean Magi, he was, we are told, consulted by King Nebuchadnezzar himself as an interpreter of dreams. He was still there when the Persian King Cyrus overran Babylon in 537 BC, and he subsequently became the latter's friend and confidant.

Daniel's insights seem, on the face of it, to have been extraordinary, if not unique. The second chapter of the book of Daniel recounts how he interpreted one of Nebuchadnezzar's dreams to mean that his empire was to be the first of a series of four great empires. Of these the second would be inferior to Babylon, the third would dominate the known world, and the fourth would shatter the whole earth. This last would, however, be a limited empire, its power and alliances unstable and dependent on intermarriage. And it would be during the final empire that Israel's God would at last take control of man's affairs, setting up an everlasting kingdom on earth.

Commentators have not been slow to identify these various empires. It may be doubted whether Persia, Babylon's successor, was in any way inferior to it. In fact, its power was immeasurably greater and its international conduct, if anything, more civilised. But the succeeding empire, the Greek one of Alexander the Great, is well described, as is the subsequent division of world-power between the Seleucid empire of Syria and the Ptolemaic empire of Egypt, who indeed endeavoured to patch up their long-running international dog-fight with occasional intermarriages.

But the final establishment of God's dominion on earth clearly failed to occur as predicted during this late Hellenistic period. Perhaps inevitably, therefore, commentators have been tempted to 'adjust' the obvious interpretation. The fourth empire, they have suggested, was really that of Rome, the 'division of the kingdom' its split into eastern and western empires in the fourth century AD.

Yet even during this period the expected kingdom of God failed to take over the earth, even if Christians could claim to see an unmistakable manifestation of it in Jesus of Nazareth. Even according to Jesus, that culminating event still lay at some distant time in the future, at 'the end of the age'.[a]

Accordingly, the interpretation has had to be stretched yet again. The latter part of Daniel's vision of the fourth kingdom, it is alleged, actually refers to a kind of 'fifth kingdom', a nondescript and fragmented successor to Rome. And so the analogy is pursued right through the Holy Roman Empire to the European Common Market of our own day, whose founding charter is, of course, the *Treaty* of Rome.

And so the expected coming of the kingdom of God is deferred — as it has always been deferred — to a time just in advance of the time of the interpreter himself.

Needless to say, Daniel's original meaning has long since been stretched far beyond breaking-point in the process. His power of foresight may, on the face of it, have been remarkable, but the scale of the suggested interpretation is clearly out of all proportion to the scope of the prophecy as recorded in Daniel's second chapter.

As it happens, Daniel himself confirms this. In chapter 8 he describes how the Persian Empire would be shattered by the Greeks under Alexander, and how on the latter's death his empire would be divided into four.

[a] Mt. 24

Subsequently one of these sub-empires (the Seleucids) would bear down on Israel from the north, abolish 'true religion' and desecrate the sanctuary of the Temple at Jerusalem by setting up there what Daniel calls 'the abomination of desolation'.[a] Finally, after '2300 evenings and mornings' — or just over six years — 'the Holy Place shall emerge victorious.'

The expected events duly occurred. In 169 BC the Seleucid king Antiochus IV, fresh from his bloody conquest of Ptolemaic Egypt, plundered the Jewish Temple and stripped it of its treasures. Two years later, he caused Jerusalem itself to be ransacked and set ablaze, and took many of its citizens captive. Then, in 167 BC, Antiochus took the final and decisive step. He officially abolished the Jewish religion and decreed death for anybody who continued to practise it. Having destroyed any copies of the sacred scriptures that he could lay his hands on, he then turned over the Temple to the worship of Olympian Zeus, rededicating the altar to the pagan cult. The First Book of the Maccabees itself records the event. 'On the fifteenth day of the month Kislev in the year 145 (167 BC), "the abomination of desolation" was set up on the altar.'[b]

And so the crucial event in Daniel's prophecy had, by the scriptures' own admission, duly taken place. The Divine take-over could thus be expected within 2300 days — or, at the latest, by the year 160 BC.

At this point the nation, perhaps in consequence, became gripped by a sudden messianic fervour. A violent revolt was organised to such good effect that, by 164 BC, the celebrated guerrilla-leader Judas Maccabeus was able to rededicate the Temple in Jerusalem. In accordance with other prophecies, it now needed only the advent of a royal leader of the line of King David to seal the deed and usher in the everlasting Kingdom of God. But no such leader materialised. The promised Divine Kingdom still failed to overwhelm the earth. And by now the advancing troops of the rising Roman Empire were already on the northern horizon . . .

Once again, then, it became necessary to 'stretch' the prophecy. Perhaps Daniel had written 'days' when he really meant 'years'? Such symbolic substitutions were a well-known feature of the established prophetic tradition, and the prophet Ezekiel had specifically sanctioned this particular one with the words 'I count one day for every year.'[c]

But 2300 years from 167 BC brings us to the year 2134 AD, which appears, once again, to be totally out of kilter with the general scale of Daniel's predictions. A mere thousand years, after all, was currently regarded as being virtually synonymous with eternity.

So perhaps the prophet had been referring to some *other* 'abomination of desolation'? The vision of four beasts emerging from the sea in chapter 7 offers little help either way in answering the question. Ostensibly dating

a Dan. 11:32 and 12:11   b 1 Macc. 1:54   c Ez. 4:6

from near the end of the Babylonian captivity, it appears to be a description of the four empires into which the dominions of Alexander the Great were to split at his untimely death. The fourth beast has ten horns which, according to Daniel, indicate that the empire in question will have ten kings; a further horn then 'humbles' or 'replaces' three of these, according to the translation used — apparently indicating that the last king would actually be the eighth, but that he would be worse than any three of the others put together. The description once again fits the Seleucid empire, whose eighth king was the hated Antiochus IV.

The vision concludes with the killing and burning of the fourth beast, while its companions are allowed to survive for a short time. The Seleucid empire, in other words, would suddenly be destroyed. Then Daniel sees 'one like a man coming with the clouds of heaven; he approached the Ancient in Years and was presented to him. Sovereignty and glory and kingly power were given to him, so that all people and nations of every language should serve him; his sovereignty was to be an everlasting sovereignty which should not pass away, and his kingly power such as should never be impaired.'[a]

The expected final saviour was thus, as the other prophets also suggest, to be a great and everlasting World-King. In token of that fact, he would be anointed with oil, in common with all Israelite kings since the time of David. He would thus be a royal Anointed One — a term for which the Hebrew is *mashiach* (Messiah) and the Greek is *christos* (Christ).

But once again, the event failed to happen, the Kingdom of God declined to materialise. Since, however, Daniel had not, this time, given any indication of a timescale, 'stretching' the prophecy was not particularly difficult. True, chapter 11, like its predecessors, makes it quite clear that the expected Kingdom would begin with the demise of the Seleucid empire.[b] Almost the whole chapter is given over to a remarkably detailed description of its continuing wars with Ptolemaic Egypt. But in chapter 9 Daniel had produced figures which were, in the event, to give heart to the inveterate 'prophecy-stretchers' . . .

It is in this chapter that Daniel offers the famous 'seventy weeks' prophecy. As interpreted in late Old Testament times, it was seen to predict that the Kingdom of God would supervene 'seventy weeks of years' (i.e. 490 years) after Cyrus's decree that the Jewish exiles should return home from Babylon to rebuild Jerusalem. Seven weeks (i.e. 49 years) before the New Order was finally inaugurated, an Israelite king would be deposed or killed, and a brutal invasion would lay waste both city and Temple. Within 3½ years all sacrifice and offering would cease, but after a further 3½ years 'everlasting right'

---

[a] Dan. 7:13-14   [b] Consequently modern attempts to fit this particular prophecy to a twentieth-century European Common Market comprising ten sovereign states (thus 'ten kings') stretch not merely the prophecy, but also credulity somewhat.

would be ushered in, and Daniel's 'vision and prophecy sealed'.

The figures are further refined at the end of Daniel's last chapter. 1290 days (3½ years) would elapse between the setting up of the 'abomination of desolation' and the end of the age. But within 1335 days (3 years 8 months) the new Kingdom would finally begin.

Cyrus's celebrated ordinance is known to have gone out in 534 BC.[a] Among the Jews of the first century BC, Daniel's prophecy was accordingly taken to mean that the promised reign of Yahweh, the new social and religious order which would take over the whole earth, would commence in around 44 BC. The disappointed 'prophecy-stretchers' of 160 BC accordingly had another 120 years to play with.

And so, in due course, the year 44 BC finally arrived. We shall eventually be examining some of the extraordinary effects which the passing of this date had in contemporary Palestine.

Meanwhile, it was just possible that the prophecy's starting-date had really been 520, 458 or even 445 BC, when first Darius I and then Ataxerxes I had issued further decrees along the lines of that of Cyrus.[b] Indeed, the last-mentioned order is the only one which specifically mentions the rebuilding of the city of Jerusalem itself. This would give alternative datings of 30 BC, 33 AD and 46 AD respectively. The 'prophecy-stretchers' could thus comfort themselves that they had two or three reserve dates up their sleeves, should the new era of everlasting righteousness fail to materialise in 44 BC.

As, indeed, it did, and continues to do to this very day . . .

And so the book of Daniel constantly confronts us with a mystery. How was it that a man who had accurately predicted the succession of Middle-Eastern empires up to four hundred years ahead, and even the precise sequence of the campaigns between Seleucid Syria and Ptolemaic Egypt towards the end of that time, could suddenly start to prove so wrong as soon as King Antiochus IV appeared on the scene? Why did the years 167-161 BC not produce a seven-year holocaust, followed by the inception of the promised Kingdom? And, in particular, what was it that apparently enabled the prophet to 'see' the disastrous year 167 BC, but not the more hopeful 164 BC or the progressive disappointment of the ensuing decades? What, in short, caused his prophecies to start falling apart after the year 167 BC?

The answer is a strange one, if also, in retrospect, rather obvious. For Daniel's purported biographer makes a number of curious factual errors. He describes Nebuchadnezzar as going mad for seven years (the text uses the expression 'seven times', but there is no real doubt that here, as at the end of the book, the word 'time' is intended to represent a year), when in fact his

---

[a] As dated by Rutherford.   [b] A transcription of the earlier decree is given in Ezra, chapter 5, and the later one is reported in the second chapter of Nehemiah.

bout of insanity is known to have lasted only four. Again, Belshazzar is described as Nebuchadnezzar's son, when he was in fact his grandson, and as king, when he was merely crown-prince. To top it all, the author has the Babylonian court specifically speaking Aramaic, which was the language of its Persian successor.[a] And such veracity as the book possesses is not improved by the inclusion of an adulatory chapter allegedly contributed by Nebuchadnezzar himself.

The inaccuracy of the book regarding the earlier period, and its uncanny accuracy in respect of the later, Seleucid era — the reverse of what one would expect had it genuinely been written in Babylonian and Persian times — thus suggest an obvious conclusion. The book's author was writing retrospectively, rather after the style of one who purports to have discovered a 'lost gospel'. Indeed, his apparent knowledge of the events of 167 BC, and his ignorance of those following the year 164 BC, suggest a date somewhere between the two. Accordingly the majority of reputable Bible-scholars nowadays date the book to around 165 BC.

In retrospect, then, we can assess Daniel's predictions for what they are — for the most part, prophecies after the event. Even the remainder, not having been fulfilled, turn out not to have been true prognostications at all — notwithstanding persistent efforts at prophetic transference by later devotees. As prophecies, therefore, Moses' own yardstick condemns them as being 'not of the LORD'.

That is not to say, however, that Daniel himself never existed, or that he did not produce valid prophecies in his day. What it does suggest is that his biographer embroidered and overworked whatever source-material he may have had to hand, in a deliberate effort to 'validate' Daniel's word as a prophet. In this way his (or the author's) 'Kingdom of God' predictions could be given added force, and the beleaguered Jewish people, believing their fulfilment to be imminent, would be inspired to rise as one man and take the promised Kingdom by storm.

The author, in other words, was well aware of our Fourth Law and the self-fulfilling nature of prophecy. Only convince enough people that the Kingdom of God was about to be inaugurated, and they themselves would see to it that it was. In this way, the end could be seen as justifying the means. Skulduggery it may nowadays seem to us to be, but anything that helped to usher in the new age of righteousness was at any rate worth a try.

In the event, it nearly succeeded. The Maccabean revolt which managed to re-institute the Temple worship in 164 BC went on to achieve astonishing successes against the Seleucid overlords. It even contrived to produce at least one priest-king (John Hyrcanus I) of sufficient stature to make people wonder whether the promised Messiah had at last arrived. Even when that hope was

[a] Dan. 2:4

dashed, the 'seventy weeks' prophecy succeeded in producing a renewed frenzy of messianic expectation in the following century — a frenzy whose effects culminated at the time of Jesus of Nazareth — not to mention a further spasm of national liberation-fever during the second century AD.

And if the promised Kingdom of righteousness failed, even then, to put in an appearance, there is no cause for despair. Thanks partly to the effects of generations of Christian and pseudo-Christian 'prophecy-stretchers', the Fourth Law will continue to apply — almost, it seems, on a cyclic basis.

And one day, no doubt, much to everybody's surprise, and in ways that are totally unexpected, the prophecies of Daniel — faked and retrospective though they may have been — will be shown to have been right after all.

4
The Law and the Prophets

By comparison with the vast timescales apparently envisaged by Moses and Daniel, the other Old Testament prophets seem positively parochial in their scope. But then it should be borne in mind that mere prediction was never in any case their primary concern. Their function, as they saw it, was limited to warning their compatriots and contemporaries when they departed from the Law as laid down by their ancient Covenant, and to forecasting the consequences if they persisted.

Now, whatever the context, there is a limit to the length of time for which the direct consequences of a particular action can be either predicted or traced. It is not long before the consequences of quite other actions start to impinge upon the process, so that in the end nobody but a politician can pinpoint a *single* cause for anything at all — be it inflation, unemployment, poverty, war, plague, famine, exile or national decline.

There is a verse in the book of Exodus in which Moses appears to define a time-limit for regarding any particular state of affairs as the direct consequence of any given past action. It occurs in the course of the third of the Ten Commandments in the form: 'I punish the children for the sins of the fathers to the third and fourth generations of those who hate me'.[a]

Now, whether or not there is any scientific basis for the religious view of things represented by this statement, it is a fairly safe assumption that the view was also shared by the later biblical prophets. And from this it follows that they would be unlikely to see any form of Divine retribution lasting for much more than a hundred years or so. Thereafter, the following verse of Exodus would start to apply, a verse whose well-attested variant reading runs: 'But I keep faith for a thousand generations with those who love me and keep my commandments.'[b] Following the period of retribution, in other words, a virtually everlasting era of justice, peace and prosperity would

---

[a] Ex. 20:5 [b] Ex. 20:6. This reading is known to have been the one adopted by the later Essenes of Qumran, for example.[51]

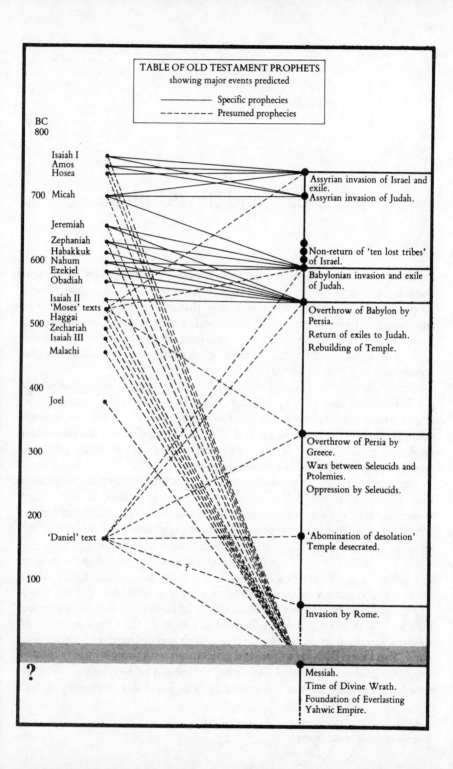

TABLE OF OLD TESTAMENT PROPHETS
showing major events predicted

————— Specific prophecies
- - - - - Presumed prophecies

BC
800

Isaiah I
Amos
Hosea
700 Micah

Jeremiah
Zephaniah
Habakkuk
600 Nahum
Ezekiel
Obadiah

Isaiah II
'Moses' texts
Haggai
500 Zechariah
Isaiah III
Malachi

400
Joel

300

200

'Daniel' text

?

100

?

Assyrian invasion of Israel and exile.
Assyrian invasion of Judah.

Non-return of 'ten lost tribes' of Israel.

Babylonian invasion and exile of Judah.

Overthrow of Babylon by Persia.

Return of exiles to Judah.

Rebuilding of Temple.

Overthrow of Persia by Greece.

Wars between Seleucids and Ptolemies.

Oppression by Seleucids.

'Abomination of desolation' Temple desecrated.

Invasion by Rome.

Messiah.
Time of Divine Wrath.
Foundation of Everlasting Yahwic Empire.

ensue, given only a renewed and lasting adherence by Israel to its founding Covenant — for these very terms were made explicit by the Covenant itself.

It is no surprise, therefore, to find that the prophets' warnings and predictions closely follow this general scheme of things. Isaiah, Amos, Hosea and Micah, who lived shortly before the Assyrians finally overran the northern kingdom of Israel in 722 BC, all forecast this dread event. They went on to describe how the land would be laid waste and its inhabitants deported *en masse* to foreign lands. All this was to be the Divine punishment for Israel's religious and moral backsliding, its flirtation with the ancient idol-worship of Canaan, its shabby treatment of its neighbours.

But in due course the Divine anger would be spent, Israel would repent and reform. And so the exiles would be rescued and eventually return to their homeland, there to live in everlasting peace and prosperity under the benevolent rule of a king of the line of David, or even of the reborn David himself.

About the invasion, deportation and exile the prophets were, of course, totally right. But then the Assyrian empire had been threatening to undertake just such an action for at least the past century-and-a-half. It had already mounted military campaigns against Palestine in 853, 848 and 841 BC, and a new bout of armed expansionism had followed under Tiglath-Pileser III around a hundred years later. For a while Israel succeeded in buying off the invaders. But with the accession of the Israelite king Pekah in 740 BC, the almost inevitable tax-revolt eventually set in. Angered at the consequent loss of tribute-money, the Assyrians duly waded in to the attack. Israel had, in effect, called down judgement on its own head.

By 731 BC, only the capital city of Samaria had still not been subdued. For a while the invaders withdrew and the ruined country's tribute-payments recommenced. But then, with the connivance of Egypt, the tax-revolt was resumed. And so, predictably, the Assyrian hordes returned to finish off their grisly work.

By 722 BC it was all over. The countryside was laid waste, the cities devastated, the entire able-bodied population deported to other parts of the Assyrian empire. In their place, foreigners were brought in to settle the empty lands.

Yet even this final act of vengeance was totally predictable. For the splitting-up and resettlement of subject-populations was actually a known part of official imperial policy.

So far, then, the prophets' predictions had not, perhaps, been particularly extraordinary. Isaiah, Amos and Hosea were all operating in around 750 BC, while Micah's probable dates place him no earlier than the beginning of the exile itself. All had merely made a reasonable assessment of the current situation and, sensing the 'hand of the LORD' in the general drift of events, had duly intuited the outcome in terms of the overall predictive framework laid down by Moses.

At this point, however, all of them seem to have fallen foul of the Third Law of Prophecy: *Preconception and prophecy do not mix.* Intuition, after all, comes from a largely unconscious level of the psyche. Awareness of Moses' predictions, on the other hand, was a purely conscious, mental matter. Mixing the two was, and still is, liable to produce what one can only call 'psychic interference'. And in the process the message was liable to become garbled.

Certainly something of the kind seems to have happened, since all four prophets, as we have seen, went on to predict that Israel would in due course return from its exile and re-occupy its homeland. A golden age of righteousness would then ensue.

In fact, however, nothing of the kind happened. The ten tribes of Israel disappeared totally from the pages of history. Probably through social mixing with other subject-populations, they were never heard of again. Indeed, in due course, they were to become retrospectively known as the celebrated 'Lost Tribes of Israel'. Meanwhile the aliens who had occupied their ancient homeland came to be known as 'Samaritans'. And it was with this mixed and much-maligned immigrant population of as long ago as the seventh century BC that the now notorious Palestinian problem of our own day first arose.

The prophets, then, had in this case accurately predicted the events closest to them. About the more distant events they seem, however, to have been almost totally in the dark. In part this may be simply due to the operation of the familiar first two Laws of Prophecy — those of Surprise Fulfilment and Thwarted Expectation. Certainly, too, the Third Law (that of Prejudicial Interference) had its part to play. But one may also suspect the existence of a Fifth Law of Prophecy which would run somewhat along the lines of:

A prophecy's accuracy decreases as the square of the time to its fulfilment.

In which case this Law deserves to be called the *Law of Diminishing Accuracy.*

At the time of Assyria's campaign against Israel, the southern kingdom of Judah was still living in peace as an Assyrian vassal-state. But the Jewish king Hezekiah was soon involved in plots against his overlords, both with Egypt and with the rising power of Neo-Babylon, especially after the assassination of King Sargon II of Assyria in 705 BC. Not a moment too soon, Jerusalem's defences were accordingly strengthened, its water-supply assured. By 701 BC, Sargon's successor Sennacherib was already on the warpath. All Judah's fortified cities except Lachish and Jerusalem were swiftly taken. Eventually Lachish, too, fell amid a bloodbath to the Assyrian war-machine.

Now all the invaders' fury was concentrated on Jerusalem. At the last

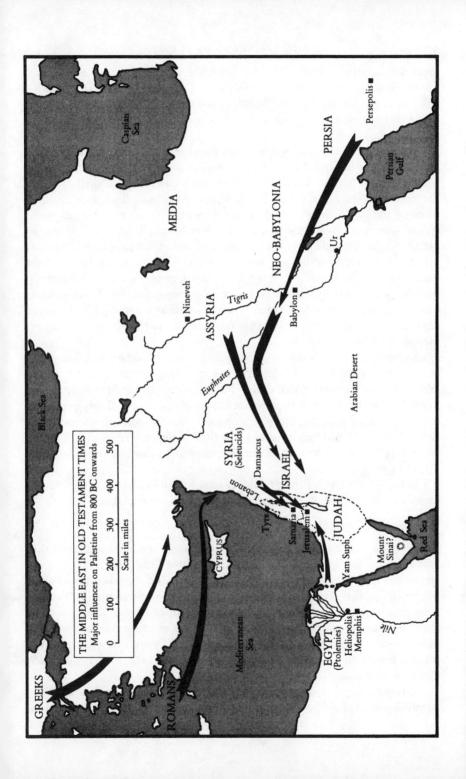

THE MIDDLE EAST IN OLD TESTAMENT TIMES
Major influences on Palestine from 800 BC onwards

Scale in miles

0   100   200   300   400   500

moment, however, some natural catastrophe seems to have overwhelmed the marauding alien hordes. Probably it was the plague.[22] At all events — and much against the odds — Jerusalem and its king, Hezekiah, were saved, the Assyrians withdrew, and the former overlord/vassal relationship was resumed.

To give them full credit, all four of the prophets already mentioned seem to have had some inkling that Judah, too, would in due course be devastated by the Assyrians. Amos had called down fire on Judah, 'fire that shall consume the palaces of Jerusalem'.[a] And indeed, the Assyrians did reduce to ashes most of the cities of Judah. But about Jerusalem, as we have already seen, Amos was wrong. So, for that matter, was Micah. Only Isaiah correctly predicted that Jerusalem would be spared at the last moment by an Assyrian withdrawal. But then this prophecy, by the text's own admission, was not made until the year 701 BC, when the great siege of Jerusalem had already begun. How far the prediction's success depended on Isaiah's well-established inside knowledge of his country's politics we shall probably never know. Certainly the plague-bearing rodents may not have been entirely to blame.

Curiously enough, however, Jerusalem was indeed to be destroyed — not once, but several times — during the succeeding centuries, much as the Fourth Law of Prophecy (that of Self-Fulfilment) would seem to require. Yet the question still arises as to whether the prophets had not dimly perceived the events of a far distant future which most of their contemporaries would never know. Or had they merely made the obvious inference that, if Judah were invaded, Jerusalem could not long survive against the overwhelming might of Assyria?

On the whole, the second possibility seems the more likely. It was simply easier to infer the fall of Jerusalem than the arrival of the plague.

And yet Micah at least also went on to predict the next major catastrophe that was to befall the surviving southern kingdom of Judah. For in 607 BC the Assyrian empire was at last itself overrun, at one and the same time, by the Medes from the north and the Babylonians from the south. Judah now became a vassal-state of the new Babylonian empire. Consequently the old tribute-problem remained. And in due course the inevitable happened. A new tax-revolt occurred in 596 BC, almost precisely after the pattern of the former one in the northern kingdom of Israel. And the results, too, were virtually identical.

Almost at once, the Babylonian king Nebuchadnezzar sent imperial troops to subdue the rebellious hill-province. The young Jewish king Jehoiachin, together with his family and retinue, were summarily deported to Babylon along with the Temple treasures, and a puppet-king, Zedekiah, installed in his place. But by 588 BC, egged on once more by Egypt and the neighbouring vassal-states, the new king was persuaded to stage a fresh revolt. This time Nebuchadnezzar decided to intervene in person. In no time his forces had overrun the whole of Judah — apart, once more, from the fortress of Lachish and Jerusalem itself.

Now the Babylonians deployed their secret weapon. Lachish was reduced by the expedient of building enormous wood-fires against the walls until they cracked and crumbled. Then Jerusalem in turn came under siege. Timber being scarce in the neighbourhood, the city held out for eighteen months. At one stage the Babylonians even withdrew, as a large Egyptian army passed by en route for an attack on the Phoenician ports. But any hopes that the defenders might have had for deliverance from that quarter were soon dashed. The Egyptians, having done their dirty work, withdrew again to their own frontiers, and the siege was resumed.

And so the end duly came. Jerusalem was ransacked, the Temple and palace put to the torch, the fortifications reduced to rubble. The renegade Jewish king, captured while attempting to escape, was made to watch his children being slaughtered before his very eyes. Then those eyes were in turn put out. The main Babylonian force withdrew, taking a large number of the native population with them.

Yet still the resistance continued. Guerrilla groups waged a continuing campaign in the hills. And at length, his patience at an end, Nebuchadnezzar decreed the final death-stroke. Between 586 and 581 BC the whole population of Judah was deported to Babylon, leaving only a desolate and uninhabited wasteland behind them.

And so Amos's prophecy of 'fire upon Judah' had been fulfilled yet again — this time, if anything, even more completely than before. More to the point, so had a prophecy of Micah's, to the effect that the inhabitants of Jerusalem would in due course have to leave their city and make the long trek to Babylon.[a] Quite when Micah made this particular prophecy is not known, but ostensibly it dates from even before the Assyrian conquest, and so seems to be evidence of a predictive ability capable of seeing at least a century into the future. This, if genuine, would be no mean feat, involving, as it does, an awareness not only of the future demise of Assyria at the hands of Babylon, but also of Judah's almost textbook repetition of Israel's experience of exile.

Not that Babylon's overthrow of Assyria was entirely unpredictable. As Assyria itself had done, Babylon had been posing a serious threat to the established order of the region since at least the time of the Babylonian ruler

[a] Mic. 4:9-11

Marduk-Aplaiddin, following the death of Sargon II in 705 BC. Yet the specific prediction that the people of Judah would eventually be exiled in Babylon still involved, if genuine, a remarkable feat of clairvoyance.

Meanwhile Isaiah, astonishingly, had apparently already foretold, in addition, the eventual fall of Babylon to the Medes[a] and this, it seems, without even predicting its initial rise to power in the first place. This particular prophecy, however, needs to be approached with some caution. For the prophet seems to be writing of a city that is already at the height of its power. It may be, in other words, that the prophecy was actually inserted into the text at a later date — or even that a prophecy originally relating to Assyria's capital city of Nineveh was 'edited' subsequently to apply to Babylon.

In Isaiah's case, such possibilities certainly cannot be ruled out. It is now accepted among most serious Bible-scholars that at least three different hands have contributed to the book of Isaiah. The later chapters, from chapter 40 onwards, make no secret of the fact that they were written at around the time of the Persian Empire in the second half of the sixth century BC. The book, in other words, may be regarded as the product of a whole 'school' of prophets in the tradition of Isaiah, rather than as the sole work of the man himself.

And in this case the insertion of a prophecy of the downfall of Babylon in 537 BC into the main text of 'Isaiah I' would not indicate such extraordinary clairvoyant abilities as might seem to have been in play if the text were to be taken at its face value.

But if there are doubts about the authenticity of Isaiah's prophecy relating to the fall of Babylon, there are no such doubts about the 'Babylonian' predictions of a whole constellation of later Old Testament prophets. During the latter part of the seventh century BC, Jeremiah, Zephaniah, Habakkuk, Nahum and Ezekiel had between them successfully predicted Assyria's downfall, the Babylonian invasion, the devastation of Judah, the deportation of its inhabitants and the exile in Babylon itself. The later Obadiah and 'Isaiah II' had joined them in forecasting, in addition, the subsequent fall of Babylon and the eventual return of the exiles to their homeland — though the prophecies of 'Isaiah II' seem to have been almost contemporary with the events.

Indeed, Jeremiah had even succeeded in putting his finger on the exact length of the exile. The Jewish expatriates would be released, he forecast, 'a full seventy years' after Babylon's rise to power[b] — i.e. in or just after 537 BC. In the event, this was the very year in which the Persians, under Cyrus the Great, finally laid Babylon low — and by 534 BC the Jews' long-awaited

[a] Isa. 13:17-22 [b] Jer. 29:10

homeward trek had indeed started, thanks to the Persians' enlightened and tolerant attitude to subject races and creeds.

The prophets, then, had scored a notable triumph. Events had unfolded much as they had foreseen, even to a multitude of smaller details not specified here. The only notable failure to date had been an apparent prophecy by Jeremiah of imminent war with the advancing Scythians in around 604 BC.[a] In the event, the northern invaders had merely swept harmlessly by on their way towards Egypt. But apart from this, the prophets had succeeded in foreseeing the shape of future events at a range of between 15 and 120 years — an achievement which has to be accounted remarkable, and which was entirely innocent of the dubious hindsight that we have attributed to the author of the book of Daniel.

Even more remarkable, however, is the almost exact correspondence between the sequence of events forecast in connection with Judah and Babylon on the one hand, and those involving Israel and Assyria on the other. Both sequences, in fact, follow precisely the pattern apparently laid down by Moses himself. When we consider that the major part of the process was in due course to be repeated yet again under the Romans, we may be tempted to deduce that the events involved actually represented the outworking of some kind of fixed paradigm, or archetype, within the Jewish soul — a psychic pattern which will actually ensure the continued repetition of such experiences until such time as the long-promised era of justice, peace and prosperity does eventually dawn. The events, in other words, have tended, as we suspected earlier, to be self-invoked. In each case, the errant Hebrew nation, perhaps out of feelings of collective guilt for its imagined misdemeanours and religious backslidings, seems deliberately — if unconsciously — to have called down judgement on itself. The prophets could see in their nation's very oppressors the vengeful hand of their God, Yahweh. And so the Fourth Law of Prophecy duly came into operation, and the prophecies fulfilled themselves. What eventually happened was what the nation had always believed would happen.

Perhaps the prophets were aware of the operation of this law. Even if they were not, it cannot have been difficult for them to sense the national mood, to savour current expectation. One expects nothing less of a prophet than that he should be responsive to the collective psyche of his people. And so, having rationally assessed the current international situation and deduced a number of possible outcomes, they could put those intuitions to work. In the light of the current state of national consciousness, outcome (a), let us say, was inherently more likely than outcomes (b) or (c). Call it intuition or 'the word of Yahweh' — it made no difference to the fact that the prophetic process indubitably worked.

[a] Jer. 1:14-19

Except, that is, where it was interfered with by the operation of the Third Law of Prophecy — *Preconception and prophecy do not mix.*

For all of the second group of prophets were to fall down badly when it came to predicting the events following the return of the exiles from Babylon. Apparently influenced, once again, by the overall predictive framework laid down by Moses, they went on, almost to a man, to predict the rebuilding of Jerusalem and the re-establishment of the ancient Covenant, closely followed by the appearance of a Davidic World-King and the final establishment of the promised Kingdom of God. In this they were also joined by Haggai, Zechariah and Malachi.

There is no question here but that the prophets were referring to events close to their own time. Ezekiel specifically quotes Yahweh as saying, of his own predictions, 'No word of mine shall be delayed.'[a]

Yet, in the event, the prophets' expectations were to remain largely unfulfilled. Jerusalem, certainly, was eventually rebuilt, along with its Temple, which was finally recompleted in 515 BC. The ritual sacrifices prescribed by the Covenant could thus now be reinstituted. By 445 BC the New Covenant had been inaugurated — in that the returned exiles were forcefully reminded of their ancient Law and obliged by their leaders to resume observing it.

Under the terms of the Fourth Law of Prophecy, we should expect no less.

Now, therefore, it lacked only the appearance of the promised king of the line of David for the expected New Age, the everlasting Kingdom of God, to begin. For a time, as Haggai and Zechariah both suggest, there was a feeling among the first settlers to return that Zerubbabel, governor of Judah, might fulfil this role, assisted by Joshua the High Priest. But their hopes were disappointed. Not only did the promised World-King fail to materialise, but conditions in the recovered homeland proved far from millennial. The impoverished settlers could do little more than scrape a precarious living from the long-neglected soil, while doing their best to restore their ancient capital city under their newly-installed priest-king.

What, then, of the promised Messiah? What of the long-awaited Golden Age? There were only two possible reactions to the apparent failure of the prophecies. Either the prophets had been wrong, or their predictions should be regarded as simply 'so far unfulfilled'. But the first possibility was simply unthinkable. In virtually all of their other predictions the prophets had proved that, according to Moses' yardstick, their words were 'of God'. The nation's whole destiny seemed to revolve around their prophecies. To reject the words of the prophets was to reject Yahweh Himself — and everybody knew what the results of that had been in the past.

Consequently there was only one possible alternative. The prophecies had,

[a] Ez. 12:28

it seemed, been delayed. Delayed, perhaps, by the Jews' own continued failure to measure up to the demands of their religion. Sooner or later, perhaps at a time when everybody least expected it, the great fulfilment would still come. 'If it delays, wait for it,' had written the prophet Habakkuk.[a] As soon as the remnant, the returned survivors, at last achieved a sufficient degree of righteousness in the sight of Yahweh, the Messiah would appear, the Kingdom of God be established on earth.

And from that conviction, zealously preserved by later Jews, were to flow consequences of the most extraordinary kind.

[a] Hab. 2:3

5

Taking the Future by Storm

By the first century BC, messianic expectation had reached fever-pitch in Palestine. Persia had fallen to Alexander the Great in 331 BC, yet still the promised Age of Righteousness had not dawned. The old imperial order had merely given way to another — and one which, in the form of the Seleucid empire of Syria, was in due course to threaten the very survival of the little Jewish theocracy's newly re-established religious ideals. Indeed, with the advent of the notorious Seleucid king Antiochus IV, events — as we saw earlier — seemed finally to have reached crisis-point.

In 167 BC the expected crunch finally came. Having already plundered the Temple, the Greek tyrant decreed the abolition of the Jewish religion and set up an altar to Zeus in the place sacred to Yahweh. The Jews were forbidden, on pain of death, to perform the traditional sacrifices, to circumcise their sons, to observe the Sabbath. The scriptures themselves were destroyed.

Clearly, then, the case had now become desperate. The People of God were being forcibly prevented from observing their ancient Covenant with Yahweh. And if the Covenant were broken, then their messianic World-King would never come, the long-awaited Golden Age would never dawn. And so all their centuries of hard work, of painful reconstruction, of constantly renewed devotion to the demands of the Law of Moses would have been in vain.

At once, a large body of devout Jews fled to the Judean desert in a desperate effort to preserve their religious traditions in the relative safety of its remote caves and ravines. But an armed force was swiftly dispatched in their pursuit. The expected attack was deliberately mounted on the Sabbath. The assembled Jewish devout, or Hasidim, preferring death to the profanation of their religion, offered no resistance. Over a thousand men, women and children were slaughtered that day, and thereafter large numbers of Hasidim, overcoming their Sabbath scruples in the interests of sheer survival (for how should the Covenant be invoked, they seem to have argued, if there were no righteous people left to invoke it?), flocked to join the growing resistance movement.

Other Jews, meanwhile, had already reacted in more predictable fashion. There had been a general call to arms. A violent revolt had followed. Under Judas Maccabeus and his successors, the Seleucids — much against all the odds — were successfully beaten back in a succession of bloodthirsty military engagements. Judas Maccabeus himself rededicated the Temple in 164 BC. Despite a temporary victory gained with the aid of elephants and cavalry by Antiochus V, the Jews' religious rights were officially restored. And by the year 142 BC an independent Palestine was once more in control of an area almost as large as in pre-exilic times.

Perhaps now the Messiah would come. For a time, under the priest-king John Hyrcanus I (134–104 BC), there were hopes that perhaps he had. The new ruler, if the historian Josephus is to be believed, was not only a king, but also a priest and something of a prophet. But his reign, as successive events increasingly showed, was not the expected thousand-year Kingdom. His successors proved ever more despotic, ambitious and unjust.

Clearly, then, something had gone wrong.

What could it be? It was unthinkable that the prophets could have been wrong. Everything else in the nation's history seemed to prove the contrary. But there was only one alternative. The new nation of Israel had still not succeeded in satisfying the full demands of the Divine Covenant.

The fault, in other words, was not in the prophets, nor even in the succession of foreign invaders who had laid waste their country. It lay firmly in the Jews themselves.

But if it took until the beginning of the first century BC for this realisation to become general, it had long been taken for granted by the more religious elements in Palestine. As early as 162 BC — only two years after the rededication of the Temple — when the pro-Greek Alcimus had secured the High Priesthood with armed Seleucid support, sixty of the Hasidim or 'Devout' had been promptly massacred. Nine years later, the Seleucid usurper Alexander Balas offered the High Priesthood to the popular Jewish war-leader Jonathan, brother and successor of Judas Maccabeus, as a bait to secure Jewish support in his political intrigues. In this he was certainly successful. But Jonathan's acceptance merely further scandalised the Devout since, although Jonathan was of priestly stock, he was not of the line of Zadok (High Priest in Solomon's time), to whom alone the office properly belonged.[51]

From the religious point of view, in short, things were already beginning to go badly wrong. Daniel's recently discovered forecast that the Kingdom of God would dawn within seven years of the Temple's desecration had come to nothing. Extraordinarily successful though the new Maccabean regime was proving both militarily and politically, its leaders were rapidly losing sight of the very religious ideals that had originally inspired them, and were increasingly using their newly-acquired power to line their own pockets.

The Devout, Pious, Holy Ones or Saints — all of them interchangeable renderings of the Hebrew word *Hasidim* — were in a state of grave bewilderment. As the years passed, remonstration was repeatedly tried, only to fall on deaf ears. The crisis came to a head when a particularly revered leader of the religious dissidents — whose name remains unknown to this day — apparently succeeded in staging a semi-public verbal confrontation with Jonathan Maccabeus himself.[52] In accordance with the traditional Jewish rules governing disputes, the complaint had thus been laid before witnesses — the essential preliminary to the passing of judgement by higher authority. But there was, of course, no higher authority to turn to, other than the scriptures and Yahweh Himself. And since it was the errant rulers' refusal to acknowledge that very authority that the religious dissidents saw as the basis of the whole dispute, there was only one thing to be done. The people themselves must exercise judgement, in accordance with the further tradition that, in matters of religious dispute, a majority decision constituted the will of God. The time had come to stand up and be counted.

Those who felt they could continue to live under the existing regime were, of course, free to do so. But all those who believed that Israel's religion was being betrayed, the strict observance of its Law allowed to disintegrate, the imminent fulfilment of the promises of the Covenant itself being threatened, must separate themselves from the whole ungodly society and retire to some desert place, there to act as the 'righteous remnant', the custodians of the Law on whose continuing faithfulness the very continuance of the Divine Covenant was repeatedly stated in scripture to depend.

But at this point dissension — never in any case far from the surface — broke out in the ranks of the Hasidim themselves. There were some of them, it seems, who felt that they could still best serve their religion by continuing to work under the existing authorities. Still others, mainly of priestly and aristocratic stock, insisted that they could actually combine the practice of true religion with support of the regime, even to the extent of identifying themselves with it.

And so it was only a relatively small group of particularly zealous sectarians who eventually set off into their self-imposed exile in an effort to preserve what they regarded as the precious flame of Divine truth.

It was these three basic groupings of would-be religious reformers who were eventually to give rise to the three celebrated Jewish sects now known to us as the Pharisees, the Sadducees and the Essenes. All three were groups of religious enthusiasts professing allegiance to the Law of Moses and dedicated to its strict observance. All three looked forward to the eventual fulfilment of the terms of the ancient Covenant.

But there all resemblance ended.

The Pharisees, who by the late first century BC numbered some six thousand[43], were far more than the mere religious nit-pickers so effectively caricatured in the Christian gospels. In essence, they saw themselves as the party of popular religious and moral reform. Somewhat analagous to the English Protestants of the nineteenth century, they were a largely lay movement dedicated to strict observance, not only of the written Law, but also of the ancient oral traditions which surrounded and, some would claim, preceded it. So keen were they on scriptural studies and exegesis that they came to be generally regarded as the acknowledged experts where matters of biblical doctrine were concerned. In their synagogues, or lay meeting-houses, they specialised particularly in the re-interpretation of the scriptures to meet contemporary conditions. As a result, they increasingly took on a role as the collective conscience of the nation, even occupying at various times both the presidency and the vice-presidency of the Sanhedrin, or Jewish Council, in Jerusalem.

But the Pharisees were not mere moralists and biblical scholars. On the one hand, they delved deeply into Jewish occultism. They believed, among other things, in angels and demons, Heaven and Hell, magic and astrology, predestination, the transmigration of souls, the resurrection of the body and everlasting life.[44] On the other hand, they also immersed themselves energetically in all kinds of practical social work. Tithing — the giving of one-tenth of one's income to charity — was a firm rule among them. Certain professions — notably tax-collecting on behalf of the later Roman occupying power — were barred to them. In these and other ways, despite occasional lapses into sanctimoniousness and self-righteousness, they achieved great popular respect as supporters of the people and upholders of their ancient religion against the now well-established priestly clique of the Sadducees.

The Sadducees, for their part, represented the aristocratic faction, and seemed imbued by the familiar conviction that they could somehow have their religious cake and eat it too. Not only could they enjoy all the practical advantages of priestly power and a share in the running of the government, but they could somehow combine this, by turning a suitably myopic eye on the scriptures, with the 'strict' observance of the Law. However, the idea of strictness can be interpreted in a number of different ways. To the Sadducees, it meant concentrating on the letter of the Law as recorded in the scriptures, rather than on its spirit as handed down orally or re-interpreted for modern conditions, whether by the former prophets or by their own contemporaries, the Pharisees. In consequence, their general attitude was rigid and ritualistic and — as ever with such attitudes — they consequently felt themselves free to adopt practical postures of quite astonishing religious incongruity. In the case of the Sadducees, this meant not only supporting a Temple-cult and a priesthood whose legitimacy was suspect, but also taking a pronounced pro-Hellenic viewpoint at a time when, among others of the original Hasidim, it was regarded as little less than sacrilege to have any truck with the pagan, Greek thinking that had lain at the root of the current religious crisis in the first place.

The Sadducees first emerged into the light of history as a distinct party during the reign of John Hyrcanus I (134-104 BC). Their name appears to derive from the word 'Zadokite', which by then had become a term indicative of priestly legitimacy — an idea having in this case more to do with wishful thinking and the needs of propaganda than with historical accuracy. They rejected the 'occult' doctrines espoused by the Pharisees, holding (no doubt with some relief) that nothing could be said about such ideas because nothing was definitely laid down about them in the Torah. Even the popular idea of a sudden Divine intervention leading to an imminent Golden Age they continually played down, admitting only that the Kingdom of God, when it finally dawned, would be ushered in (in accordance with scripture) by 'a prophet like Moses'.

Inevitably, then, Pharisees and Sadducees were continually at loggerheads not only in religious terms, but also politically and socially. Their power-struggle represented the familiar tension between lower and upper classes, between the forces of change and the supporters of the status quo, between would-be spirituality and dead ritualism, between lay freedom of thought and the dogma of the establishment, which has been characteristic of almost every developed human society before or since.

It would, of course, be aesthetically gratifying if one could say at this point that the Essenes neatly occupied the middle ground in the argument. It would, however, be totally misleading. The Essenes, as we have already seen, were in fact determined not to hold any of the ground at all while it was occupied by powers which they saw as inimical to the Divine Covenant. Even the Pharisees, in their valiant efforts to reform the nation, were, in the Essenes' view, merely flogging a dead horse. Only a reform-movement of quite extraordinary vigour and strictness, undertaken by an isolated and totally dedicated élite, could hope to succeed where previous attempts at reform had failed, and so finally usher in the Golden Age which was still hovering tantalisingly just out of reach.[a]

And so, while there is historical evidence of occasional mutual admiration between Essenes and Pharisees, the former determinedly embarked upon a separate course of their own devising, firmly believing that it alone stood any chance of achieving eventual success. However, the precise methods they chose to employ, and the precise ground they decided to occupy, are matters

[a] Compare *Community Rule*, v.[51].

on which historical and documentary evidence is as yet by no means complete. Even the question of their exact identity still leaves some room for speculation. Yet the amount of circumstantial evidence is now such that it is at least possible to put forward a comprehensive hypothesis based on the documentary and archaeological data.[35, 42, 43, 51, 52, 53] We may find it instructive to supplement this with the evidence of certain psychic sources[24], and even the results of our own native intuition.

And the upshot is a story of high drama, its subject an undertaking of do-or-die daring which is virtually unique in the history of human endeavour.

Unlike the Pharisees and Sadducees, the Essenes were not a political party as such. Indeed, they were not even a homogeneous group. At the time of the fateful decision to separate themselves from the existing social order, they were united only by their determination to achieve total religious purity, in a supreme effort to bring down the long-delayed Kingdom of Heaven upon earth.

To some of the Devout, this meant a life of extreme individual asceticism lived, as it were, on the very fringes of society. To such men, generally termed Nazirites, this meant imitating the revered 'holy men' of old — wild, long-haired hermits of the stamp of Elijah, who were often to be found wandering or living in caves in the wilder parts of the country, especially in the north. Of more recent years, some of them had taken to a more 'civilised' way of life, yet still they preserved the traditions of their spiritual ancestors. They never cut their hair, visited the public bath, oiled their bodies after the Greek fashion, touched alcohol or ate meat. Their highly eccentric ways and wild appearance helped to foster for them a certain reputation as prophets, healers and miracle-workers, and their highly original approach to their religion owed more to a deep, intuitive appreciation of its spirit than to any scholastic devotion to its letter.[42]

In consequence, therefore, the Nazirites were typically moralists rather than legalists, God-lovers rather than religionists, and they were much more anxious to obey the Mosaic Law's essentials than scrupulously to observe its minutiae — though their very piety often served to ensure that their religious observance was even *more* strict than that of the Pharisees. Individualists to a man, the Nazirites were consequently not the type to be regimented or subjected to the strict code of any religious sect. If they supported the Essene cause at all, it was out of sympathy with its ultimate aims, rather than out of automatic agreement with any fixed methods it might devise for achieving them.

But the Nazirites were not the only group of dissenters who chose to stay within Israel's borders — to remain, so to speak, in society but not of it.

There were many less strong-minded and individualistic men and women, for example, who yearned for the reassuring paternal discipline and security of some kind of controlling organisation. Their natural inclination, therefore, led them to form communities with other, like-minded people, and to submit themselves voluntarily to the sometimes exceedingly strict rules which tend to spring up within such religious groups. Initially, it seems probable that such communities were formed in the more remote country areas, where contamination by rival religious ideologies was least likely, but it was not long before communities of dissenters started to spring up in the towns and cities as well. This development would suggest that a fairly comprehensive and rigid set of rules had by this time been drawn up, such as to ensure almost total physical and religious segregation from the community at large, and strong enough to give the community-members full confidence in their ability to maintain their refined religious ideals in the very midst of a society that had been, they were convinced, seduced by paganism.

Thanks to the discovery of the celebrated Dead Sea Scrolls at Qumran in 1947, and their subsequent decipherment, we now know a good deal about the agreed rules which eventually sprang up to govern some at least of these communities. We know from the Qumran *Damascus Rule*[51], for example, that each community was governed by a hierarchy headed by the *mebaqqer*, or Guardian — either a priest or a Levite — who was specifically charged with ensuring that nothing beyond the minimum permissible contact (basic buying and selling, for example) occurred between community-members and the public at large. Total obedience to all 613 provisions of the Mosaic Law was enjoined on all members, and enforced by a tribunal for whom the Guardian acted as a kind of examining magistrate. The Sabbath laws were interpreted with especial severity (work was not even to be *mentioned* on the Sabbath), and dietary restrictions rigidly observed. Special stress was laid on observance of the solar calendar described in the sect's *Book of Jubilees*, rather than the lunar one adopted during the Babylonian exile and still observed by the rest of society. Thus, for members of the sect, the new year always fell on a Wednesday, as did the beginning of each subsequent season. So, for that matter, did the Passover and the Feast of Tabernacles. By the same token, the Day of Atonement, unlike that observed by the rest of society, always fell on a Friday, while the Feast of Weeks fell on a Sunday, the first day of the Jewish week. This particular festival, celebrating the reception by Moses of the original Covenant on Mount Sinai — and nowadays better known to Christians as Pentecost — was held by the Essene communities in especial reverence. On that day the communities assembled to hold what was, in effect, their Annual General Meeting, at which each member's spiritual progress during the year and consequent hierarchical ranking was re-assessed by his superiors, while new members — including non-Jewish converts — were examined and admitted.

Despite the apparently daunting demands placed upon their members, such communities seem to have flourished and spread throughout the length and breadth of Palestine during the last century-and-a-half or so BC, and for at least a further half-century thereafter.[35] By the time of the Jewish general and historian Josephus (37-100 AD), there was virtually no town or city without its Essene community, and there were many others besides in remoter areas. The sect had effectively created a nationwide network of religious communities, all offering free board and lodging to travelling members of the order, and had appointed guestmasters to minister specifically to their needs. Even Jerusalem apparently had at least one such community, and its typically white-clothed members gained sufficient general recognition to have the city's south-western gate named after them. Since, however, the Essenes' rules were so strict as to forbid sexual intercourse within the holy city itself[a], it seems likely that the Jerusalem community was an all-male one, and so was typical of a further, exceptionally strict wing of the sect — one which seems, in practice, to have provided its ideological spearhead.

For there were a few of the Essene dissidents (many of them priests) who seem to have seen themselves as the self-chosen elect of what was already an élite — the spiritual shock-troops, so to speak, of the whole movement. For them, prolonged residence within the borders of apostate Israel was altogether too much to contemplate, and so voluntary exile was decided upon. In order to keep themselves in a permanent state of ritual, priestly purity under the terms of Jewish Law during what they believed to be the brief period of the Last Days, they even went as far as renouncing marriage, and so became the first celibate monastic community in Palestine. This decidedly un-Jewish practice was flatly contrary to the convictions of the Pharisees, for example, who saw failure to marry as a violation of Yahweh's commandment in Genesis to 'be fruitful and multiply', and so as tantamount to murder.

Having formed their special, closed community, these Essene extremists proceeded to develop their own, secretive internal jargon, to devise exacting procedures for screening new members before admission, and to super-impose upon the Mosaic Law and the sect's general regulations a whole superstructure of special ritual and organisational requirements.

Thus, the group's *Community Rule*[51] refers to their original arch-enemy, Jonathan Maccabeus, merely as 'the Wicked Priest', 'the Liar' or 'the Spouter of Lies'; to the Pharisees as 'Ephraim' or 'the seekers of smooth things'; to the Sadducees as 'Manasseh' or 'the last priests of Jerusalem'; to the Seleucid Greeks (and later the Romans) as 'the Kittim'; and to the true Temple (temporarily represented by the community itself) as 'Lebanon'. 'The men of perfect holiness' is the document's code-expression for the sect itself

a Damascus Rule, XII[51]

(elsewhere referred to as 'the Poor' and 'the sons of Zadok'), while the revered founder of the whole movement is almost always referred to anonymously as 'the Teacher of Righteousness'.

The community's entry-requirements, meanwhile, involved a probationary period of at least two years, during the course of which postulants were admitted first to the sect's so-called 'New Covenant' (equally well rendered into English as 'New Testament'), and then, after further instruction and searching examination, into the monastic community itself. Here daily life involved a constant round of prayer, Bible-study and manual work, interspersed with ritually-organised meals. These were preceded by equally ritual purification, involving the donning of white veils or sheets and total self-immersion in clean water. All personal property was surrendered to the community and held in common, and a prescribed order of hierarchical precedence rigidly observed.

This ritually-sanctified way of life was seen as a kind of deliberate atonement for the nation's sins, temporarily replacing the animal-sacrifices of the Jerusalem Temple, which were in any case now seen as invalid since, according to the Essene calendar, they were performed on the wrong days, and by a corrupt priesthood headed by an impostor. Scrupulous observance by the community's members of all the remaining provisions of the Law was thus vital for — indeed, the only surviving guarantee of — the preservation of the nation's Covenant with Yahweh. The slightest deliberate infracture was consequently punishable by expulsion. On top of this, betrayal of the community's secrets to outsiders, covert retention of personal property, disrespect towards superiors, lying, gossip, avoidable nakedness or self-exposure, idle chatter, spitting in assembly, interruption of another while speaking and even gesticulating with the left hand were all punishable by various periods of penance, often involving living on reduced rations.

The Essene élite, it is clear, certainly meant business.

As for the group's organisation, this was always headed by a Zadokite priest, together with a figure known as the Guardian (*mebaqqer*), Master (*maskil*) or 'Interpreter of the Law'. The latter's job was constantly to study the scriptures and to extract from them, by largely intuitive means, practical and spiritual guidance for the community as a whole. He must also be especially well-versed in the sect's so-called *Book of Meditation*. Aided by a priestly chief supervisor, or Steward, the Master (who served, among other things, as master of novices) was supported by a General Council. This comprised twelve laymen and three priests, the latter probably being identical with the governing triumvirate itself. His responsibilities included all decisions involving doctrine, discipline and ritual purity, presiding over all meetings, blessing the community's ritual meals and assessing and ranking each member according to his spiritual progress. To aid him in this, he was expected to be especially proficient in the 'lore of the two spirits', a

Zoroastrian concept no doubt adopted (had the Essenes but known it) from the Persians during the late Babylonian exile and the subsequent period of Persian domination. In terms of it, each human being was seen to be governed by a given mixture of the 'spirits of truth and falsehood', and could be identified, in consequence, as a potential 'son of Light' or 'son of Darkness'. The whole of creation, indeed, was permeated by these two spirits in roughly equal measure.

As a result of its sheer dedication and purism, this extremist group of monastics naturally tended to represent itself — and to be seen by outsiders — as the sect's national conscience and driving-force, and in due course seems to have effectively taken over its leadership, in the Judean south at least. But it should always be borne in mind that it never represented more than an untypical minority of the sect as a whole. Even in its heyday during the first century AD, when the bulk of its members finally returned from their self-imposed exile to take up residence in the restored ruins of the desert-establishment at Qumran, by the western shore of the Dead Sea, this extremist wing numbered no more than 250 out of a total Essene population of some four thousand. The sect as a whole was always made up of a bewildering variety of sub-groups, in which we may possibly include, among others, the Nazirites (mentioned above), the Notsrim or Nazoreans ('preservers'), the Nazareans (from Aramaic *Natsaraya*, 'keepers'), the baptising Mandæans, and even possibly the Samaritan *Shamerine* ('custodians' or 'keepers').[42]

Such, indeed, was the devotion of each group to its particular beliefs and way of life that the one thing none of them ever seem to have called themselves was 'Essenes' — much as many Christians tend to identify themselves as 'Catholic', 'Baptist', 'Greek Orthodox' and so on, rather than using the wider blanket-term. 'Essene', 'Essean' or 'Hessean', in fact, is merely a Greek version of the Aramaic word *Chasya* (Saint), cognate with the familiar Hebrew *Hasid* already referred to above. As such, it was simply an umbrella-term used by the public at large to designate the whole body of 'Holy Ones', of whatever description, whom they knew to be active throughout contemporary Palestine. Like the word 'Christian' itself, it was a term originally applied *from without* on a disparate body of religious activists who seldom, if ever, cared to use it themselves, and who were often more prone to see the differences between themselves and the other sub-groups of their sect than the few, simple convictions that united them.

And prime among these, of course, was the need for national re-dedication to the Divine Covenant of which they saw themselves as the sole 'keepers' or 'custodians'.

Yet there does seem to have been a time, especially in around 160 BC, when all the religious dissidents of whatever persuasion agreed to sink their many differences in some kind of common effort at total reform. Even the precursors of the Pharisees seem, for a while, to have gone along with the new initiative. And out of the doctrinal confusion a charismatic reformer eventually emerged from among the ranks of the activists to forge a set of living ideals that were to inspire the whole Essene movement for two centuries and more.[51]

To this day we do not know his name. We can be certain, however, that he was a Zadokite priest, as well as something of a prophet. Described in the Dead Sea Scrolls as 'the Priest' and 'the Teacher of Righteousness', he saw with blinding insight that the time had come for a national re-dedication in the form of a New Covenant, as already foreseen by Jeremiah. 'The time is coming,' the prophet had written[a], 'when I will make a new covenant with Israel and Judah . . . I will set my law within them and write it on their hearts . . . No longer need they teach one another to know the LORD; all of them, high and low alike, shall know me . . .'

The Covenant, in other words, would be written indelibly in the consciousness of the faithful in such a way that they could henceforth act out of direct knowledge of the truth, rather than out of mere second-hand instruction. Intuition and Divine inspiration would once more come into their own, as the prophet Joel had long ago foretold: 'I will pour out my spirit on all mankind; your sons and your daughters shall prophesy, your old men shall dream dreams and your young men see visions . . .'[b] And the faithful would consequently be inspired by a positive, innate yearning for righteousness, rather than by negative fear of the consequences of its neglect. Imbued with this new spirit, they would then find within themselves sufficient strength and conviction to carry out an undertaking which went far beyond all previous attempts to fulfil the Mosaic Law.

For merely fulfilling the Law, it now appeared, was not enough. The contemporary Hebrew scriptures consisted not only of the Law (the first five books of the familiar Bible), but also of the more recently adopted collection of books known as the Prophets. It was in these latter texts that repeated references were to be found to a new Covenant, a fresh start for Israel. Further light was shed on this idea by a further set of texts known as the Writings, in which the Psalms and the book of Daniel were prominent. The new initiative must therefore take a new and perhaps surprising form.

The objective of the new reform-movement must be to fulfil not only the Law, *but also the Prophets, as supplemented by the Writings.*

The Dead Sea Scrolls testify repeatedly to this realisation. The sectaries must act 'according to all that has been revealed from age to age, and as the Prophets have revealed by His Holy Spirit'. And there is absolutely no doubt

[a] Jer. 31:31-34 [b] Joel 2:28

in the texts as to the source of that revelation. For the Teacher of Righteousness was held to have been instructed by the mouth of Yahweh Himself. In his heart 'God set [understanding] that he might interpret all the words of His servants the Prophets, through whom He foretold all that would happen to His people and [His land]'. To him Yahweh had revealed 'all the mysteries of the words of His servants the prophets', and it was therefore the task of the Teacher and his successors to 'measure out all knowledge discovered throughout the ages, together with the Precept of the age', and to 'do the will of God according to all that has been revealed from age to age.'[a][51]

The Teacher, in consequence, set himself the daunting task of studying and meditating upon all the prophecies relating to the current times, which historical events had convinced his compatriots were the long-predicted Last Times, the culmination of world-history, immediately leading up to the promised Golden Age. We may assume that the result was nothing less than a comprehensive 'book of oracles' — a kind of blueprint for action, detailing exactly how and in what order the sect must now address itself to *deliberately bringing about the fulfilment of all the outstanding biblical prophecies*. In this way all the conditions would finally be fulfilled for the inauguration of the long-awaited Kingdom which, as a result, could scarcely fail to materialise.

Everything therefore now hinged on the powers of prophetic interpretation of the Teacher and his successors. Prophecy had finally come into its own. With its aid there now seemed to be every prospect that beleaguered mankind could at last take the promised Kingdom of Heaven by storm.

[a] Square brackets indicate probable readings at points where the original scrolls are damaged or illegible. Compare also Josephus's description of the Essenes' prophetic activities in *Wars of the Jews*, Bk. II, viii.[35]

6
The Power of Expectation

The Teacher's book of oracles is not, unfortunately, among the Essene texts that have so far been rediscovered, though fragments of later scrolls of similar type have certainly survived.[a] Yet the Scrolls refer to it repeatedly, terming it HGW (*Hagu*), or the *Book of Meditation*. They insist, moreover, that the priestly leader of each Essene community must be thoroughly conversant with it. The children of Essene families must also be instructed in it from their youth up, as well as in 'the precepts of the Covenant.' It might thus be assumed that the Book of Meditation was in fact the sect's bible. In one sense it clearly was. But a moment's reflection reveals that the term *Book of Meditation* is unlikely to signify the scriptures themselves, since the contemporary Bible consisted not of one scroll but of a whole library of different texts. The Scrolls themselves, which include fragments of every book of the Hebrew scriptures, as well as many others besides, bear eloquent witness to the fact.

The *Book of Meditation*, then, seems to have been the Essenes' religious manifesto, their documentary *raison d'être*, their central blueprint for action. And in view of this, it is difficult to avoid identifying it with the precious document originally bequeathed to the sect by the Teacher himself, who was held to have been, through meditation, the recipient of Yahweh's latest and ultimate revelation to man.

It is therefore not too surprising, perhaps, that no copy of the document has ever been found. We may imagine that it was regarded as so vital to the sect, and of so potentially explosive a nature that, rather than hiding any copies of it along with the other Dead Sea Scrolls in a cave for safe-keeping at the time of the genocidal Roman War of 66-73 AD, the fleeing Qumran sectaries took all copies of the precious scroll along with them.

It is nevertheless possible to glean from the surviving Dead Sea texts a fairly clear idea of how the Qumranites in particular were prone to interpret

---

[a] Compare the *Midrash on the Last Days* and the *Messianic Anthology*.[51]

scripture and apply it to their own circumstances. Consequently it is by no means beyond modern human capability to attempt a reconstruction of the scenario envisaged by the Teacher, taking full account of the Essenes' known attitudes and habits of thought, the familiar scriptural background and the known history of the sect as revealed by textual and archaeological evidence.

We know, for a start, that one of the Teacher's first conclusions was that the sect must undertake an exodus to the 'Land of Damascus' — i.e. somewhere beyond Israel's northern borders. In view of the Essenes' typical way of thinking, it is axiomatic that this idea had been gleaned in some way from scriptural precedent. And here the obvious precedent was the Mosaic Exodus from Egypt and the subsequent forty-year journey through the wilderness to the Promised Land. For the name 'Egypt' was traditionally used by Jewish esotericists to symbolise any 'pit of iniquity' such as, in the Essene view, Israel itself had now become under the Maccabeans, while there was also a natural and well-documented tendency to link the notion of the Promised Land with the idea of the future Kingdom. Both traditions are still preserved today in the typical Negro spiritual. It is no surprise, therefore, to find numerous Exodus parallels in the Essenes' early thinking, together with the expectation — subsequently extended and de-literalised — that the exiles would at last return to cleanse their homeland of its enemies at the end of forty years.[52] The symbolic link was to be perfectly expressed by the later Paul. 'All these things that happened to them,' he writes of the original Exodus, 'were symbolic, and were recorded for our benefit as a warning. For upon us the fulfilment of the ages has come.'[a]

And so we may assume that Yahweh's command to Moses at Exodus 3:10-12 was immediately pressed into service by the Essenes' Teacher of Righteousness: 'I will send you to Pharaoh and you shall bring my people Israel out of Egypt.' Interpreted, this would have been taken to signify that the Teacher of Righteousness, acting in the capacity of a latter-day Moses, must first confront the current ruler, Jonathan Maccabeus, and then withdraw with all his followers across Israel's frontier. The words of Isaiah 62:10 would have been seen as supporting this interpretation: 'Go out of the gates, go out, prepare a road for my people; build a highway, build it up, clear away the boulders; raise a signal to the peoples.' So, too, as we know from direct evidence[51], was the text of Numbers 24:17: 'A star shall come forth out of Jacob, a comet arise from Israel.'

A similar interpretation would have been accorded to Isaiah 37:31-32: 'The survivors left in Judah shall strike fresh root under ground and yield fruit above ground, for a remnant shall come out of Jerusalem and survivors from Mount Zion.'

And the Teacher's own recapitulation of the role of Moses might have been

[a] I Cor. 10:11

seen as foreshadowed by the dual mention of the word 'prophet' at Hosea
12:13-14: 'By a prophet the LORD brought up Israel out of Egypt and by a
prophet he was tended. Ephraim has given bitter provocation; therefore his
Lord will make him answerable for his own death and bring down upon his
own head the blame for all that he has done.' 'Ephraim', it will be recalled,
had latterly become the standard Essene code-word for the dissentient
Pharisees, whose forerunners seem to have been in the throes of splitting
away from the Teacher's group at about the time their exile began. Possibly
the identification arose from this very passage.

At this point it may, of course, be objected that the Exodus extract in
particular was never intended as a prophecy, but as a simple order applying
directly to the biblical Exodus of over a thousand years earlier. The extracts
from Isaiah and Hosea, too, may be seen as having been taken out of context.
Yet the Teacher and his successors were totally unworried by such considerations. For them, the entire scriptures positively bristled with Divine
revelations, if only one knew where to look and how to interpret them. Such
revelations were as liable to be found masquerading as historical statements
and orders as spelt out overtly in words of prophecy. Indeed, it was held by
the Essenes that even the prophets themselves were often unaware of the full
import of what they had said — an observation towards which we likewise
have found ourselves led earlier in this book. In support of this view they
could quote, for example, Isaiah 42:19: 'Yet who is blind but my servant,
who so deaf as the messenger whom I send?' What counted above all was the
Divinely-inspired intuition of the acknowledged and accredited interpreter,
who was entitled to use the scriptures almost as freely as a diviner might use
sheep's entrails or a fortune-teller tea-leaves.

The scrolls of biblical interpretation discovered at Qumran testify
repeatedly to this approach. The fact that most of these commentaries date
from the community's later years suggests, furthermore, that it was not
peculiar to the Teacher alone — while also adding weight to the view that the
earlier commentaries, including the Teacher's own, were taken with them by
the fleeing sectaries in 68 AD. The commentary on the book of Habakkuk, for
example, interprets verse 2 of the second chapter, here quoted as: '["Write
down the vision and make it plain] upon the tablets, that [he who reads] may read it
speedily"', in the following way: 'interpreted this concerns the Teacher of
Righteousness, to whom God made known all the mysteries of the words of
His servants the Prophets.'[51]

The prophet Habakkuk, in other words, was held to have been unknow-
ingly prophesying that the sect's Teacher, born some four hundred years
after his own time, would alone be qualified to interpret the words of his
vision. And the text goes on: 'For there shall be yet another vision concerning the
appointed time. It shall tell of the end and shall not lie. Interpreted, this means
that the final age shall be prolonged, and shall exceed all that the Prophets

have said; for the mysteries of God are astounding.'[51]

Such exegetical gymnastics are comparatively tame by comparison with other examples, however. The promise at Isaiah 54:12 to '[make all] your pinnacles [of agate]' concerns, it seems, 'the twelve [chief Priests] who shall enlighten by judgement of the Urim and Tummim'. Yahweh's threat, at Habakkuk 1:6, to rouse 'the Chaldeans' is applied, of all people, to 'the Kittim' — either the Greeks or the Romans, but more likely the latter. And in the Messianic Anthology — a collection of proof-texts designed to show that the shortly-awaited Messiah must fulfil the roles of prophet, priest and king — Joshua's curse on the city of Jericho at Joshua 6:26 is actually treated as though it applied to Maccabean Jerusalem.[51]

Interpretation, then, was all. The second of our four original questions regarding the accuracy of biblical prophecies — 'Did the prophecies really refer to the events with which they subsequently became associated?' (p. 36) — must, in the Essenes' case, be answered with a resounding 'no'. Prophetic transference was rampant. And yet the case is not quite as open-and-shut as perhaps it seems to be. The Essenes, after all, were perfectly well aware of the third chapter of Ecclesiastes — the celebrated passage which begins: 'For everything its season, and for every activity under heaven its time: a time to be born and a time to die . . .' And in the course of it they would have found the statement: 'Whatever is has been already, and whatever is to come has been already, and God summons each event back in its turn.'[a] The implication is, of course, that history is basically cyclic in form, with events and tendencies liable to repeat themselves ad infinitum. This 'Law of Everlasting Return' would therefore tend to ensure that whatever was prophesied and fulfilled in respect of one generation was just as likely to be re-fulfilled in respect of another. We ourselves have already observed this tendency in respect of the Fourth Law of Prophecy. The interpreter merely had to divine exactly when and where the inevitable blow would fall. It was his task, in other words, to intuit, and to interpret for his times, the successive seasons of the national psyche, as it continually brought to pass the ancient prophecies over and over again.

Historically, however, few interpreters have had their intuitive gifts for biblical exegesis trusted so implicitly as the sect's Teacher of Righteousness. This undoubted fact suggests not only that he was a man of enormous presence and of overwhelming and contagious conviction, but that his prophetic interpretation had proved astonishingly accurate even during his own lifetime. It would certainly not be too surprising if the latter were the case since, as we have already suggested, his whole approach seems to have centred on the deliberate fulfilment of prophecy. This fact, plus the operation of the Law of Self-Fulfilment, would probably have been more than enough to

a Eccl. 3:1, 15

give rapid factual credence to his prophetic gifts.

Yet it needs to be borne in mind that the Teacher was still attempting to do two things at once — to interpret *and* to prophesy. This is by no means an easy task, even at the best of times. The mixture is liable to prove a heady cocktail all too befuddling to any but the most clear-headed. So often do both prophets and interpreters fall foul of this phenomenon that one might see fit to formulate a Sixth Law of Prophecy which runs:

Prophecy and interpretation are incompatible activities.

We could term this axiom the *Law of Divided Functions*.

But the Essenes clearly had good and cogent reasons for holding their Teacher's gifts in high regard. His successors, too — apparently the products of a veritable school of Essene prophetic science — were to become renowned throughout Palestine for their prophetic accuracy. Undaunted by the difficulties, therefore, the Teacher continued to pursue his awesome mission.

Having decided that the scriptures demanded a mass-exodus of the group, the next task was naturally to tackle the question 'Where to?' And here, with the aid of prophetic inspiration, the scriptures could once again be relied upon to supply the answer.

For a start, there was still the biblical precedent of the Exodus under Moses. For one of the Israelites' first acts on leaving Egypt had been to cross the Sea of Reeds — a shallow arm of the then Gulf of Suez whose name (*Yam Suph*) is often mistranslated as 'Red Sea'. Following this, they had made their way to a Holy Mountain (Sinai, or Horeb), where they had assembled to receive the original Divine Covenant.

The parallelism was, of course, totally apt to the dissidents' present situation. It was, as we have seen, the sect's central aim to reinvoke that ancient Covenant — or rather, as they preferred to put it, to establish a New Covenant. And so the other historical aspects of the pattern must also be reinvoked. The contemporary faithful, in other words, must once again separate and symbolically cleanse themselves from the polluted spiritual atmosphere of Maccabean Israel by crossing a body of water. Then they must make their way to a new Holy Mountain, there to rededicate themselves to the Divine will and so — on the strength of that fact — to hold the still-procrastinating Yahweh to His ancient promises.

A suitable body of water was not difficult to pinpoint. It was, after all, the river Jordan that Joshua and his followers had first crossed to enter the Promised Land all those centuries ago at the end of the same Exodus[a], and so it was the Jordan that the faithful remnant must now recross to leave it again.

[a] Josh. 3

Moreover, it was by immersion in the Jordan that the great prophet Elisha had successfully cured Naaman the Syrian of his leprosy.[a] The Jordan could therefore serve the same cleansing function now, as the body of religious reformers finally waded across it and headed into their self-imposed exile.

But where were they to make for? The text of Zechariah 10:10 offered the first important clue. 'I will fetch them home from Egypt,' it ran, and then went on, 'I will lead them into Gilead and Lebanon until there is no more room for them.' Now Gilead was the region of mountainous country lying, appropriately, on the opposite side of the Jordan from the original Israelite heartland of Judea, Samaria and Galilee. Thence it stretched northward as far as the Golan Heights and eastwards into the Mesopotamian desert. Lebanon, on the other hand, lay far to the north. It was the range of coastal mountains stretching northwards from the region of Tyre, in Syro-Phoenicia. By implication, however, the name could probably also be applied to the southern outliers of the range, no doubt as far south as the northern borders of ancient Israel itself.

Somewhere within these two hill-regions, then, the migrating Essenes must find their new Holy Mountain, and so fulfil the words of scripture at Exodus 3:12: 'When you have brought the people out of Egypt, you shall all worship God here on this mountain.' But which peak was it to be? The one of the original Covenant had of course been Horeb in Sinai. Yet locating it today is by no means easy. The mountain described in Exodus 19 is clearly a volcano, yet the peak traditionally identified as Mount Sinai has not been volcanic for millions of years. Perhaps the truth lies in the fact that the word *Horeb* was not originally a Hebrew word, but an Egyptian one (*Hor-'ib*) meaning 'heart of Horus' — i.e. 'heart of the sky'. The name could thus apply to any one of a number of mountains, and quite possibly to a whole succession of them. Any mountain could, if suitably sanctified, become a 'holy mountain'. Every hill was a potential 'hill of Yahweh'.

And so King David had sanctified Mount Zion, in Jerusalem, as sacred to his God, founding upon it a kind of royal chapel, the precursor of the magnificent Temple of Solomon which, as reconstructed after the Babylonian exile, the Essenes now saw as fatally profaned by the Sadducean priesthood. The Samaritans, likewise, had taken Mount Gerizim as their 'holy hill' and founded their own, alternative temple upon it. And now it was the turn of the Essenes to repeat the process yet again, and re-establish what they saw as the true worship of the New Covenant on their own sacred mountain, wherever that might be.

But the hill-country of Gilead was distinctly unpromising as a site. Most of it actually lay well within the traditional borders of Israel, and consequently might be expected to be incorporated into the steadily growing Maccabean

[a] 2 Kings :5

kingdom in the not too distant future. The text from Zechariah seemed to hint that Gilead was to be seen merely as a staging post on the way to Lebanon. And so, while a few of the exiles would go on to set up camp in the more inaccessible eastern desert regions, for the main body of believers it was the mountains of Lebanon and their southern outliers that must be combed for a likely site. Or rather the scriptures themselves must be combed for likely clues to one.

The text of Isaiah, for example, afforded to the Teacher powerful hints of the assembly of a warrior-host for Yahweh 'in the mountains' at 13:2-4. At 40:9 the same scroll urged the herald of the new Millennium, whether individual or collective, to make his voice heard from 'the mountain-top'. Nahum, too, at 1:15, gave expression to the theme in the celebrated words: 'See on the mountains the feet of the herald who brings good news.' The exiles, clearly, were doing the right thing. As they saw it, they were the collective herald in question. Yet they still needed clearer marching-orders.

Only with Ezekiel did the picture start to come into focus somewhat. 'I, too, will take a slip from the lofty crown of the cedar and set it in the soil,' ran the text of 17:22-3. 'I will pluck a tender shoot from the topmost branch and plant it. I will plant it on a lofty mountain, the highest mountain in Israel. It will put out branches, bear its fruit, and become a noble cedar. Winged birds of every kind will roost under it, they will roost in the shelter of its sweeping boughs.'

Here at last the Teacher could start to give full rein to his gifts of prophetic intuition. The mention of 'cedars' immediately suggested the region of Lebanon. The northern mountains, in other words, were to be the general assembly-area for the body of Essene refugees. And indeed, their own documents confirm that they were eventually to draw up their New Covenant in the 'Land of Damascus'. But out of their various groupings and ideologies a kind of 'core-group' must be formed to spearhead the movement. It must set up its base-camp on the 'highest mountain in Israel', where its 'tender shoot', planted in the new soil, would become first a sapling, then a great tree, cognate — even in the later gospels — with the coming Kingdom of Heaven on earth. Yet this core-group had to remain doctrinally broadly-enough based to permit 'winged birds of every kind' — i.e. members of all the various Essenic sub-groups — to give it their allegiance.

And so where was this 'highest mountain in Israel' that was to become the new site of the Essenes' general headquarters? Somehow it had to satisfy the apparently irreconcilable requirements of being both 'in Israel' and yet not in Israel. Perhaps the correct interpretation was that it had to lie beyond the borders of the contemporary state of Israel, yet still within the area traditionally regarded by the Jews as Israelite territory.

And there, almost miraculously, the answer suddenly swam into view.

Mount Carmel.

At a mere 1728 feet Carmel was not an Everest among peaks. It was not even necessarily the most lofty eminence in the region. But the Essenes' leaders were not in any case concerned with the niceties of modern surveying-techniques. Their aim was simply to pinpoint and to occupy the tallest mountain they could find — and Carmel, with its wooded slopes sweeping dramatically right down to the sea just south of the site of the modern Haifa, presented them with a mountain whose height, from top to bottom, clearly put all other peaks to shame.

But Carmel also presented them with all sorts of other bonuses. While well outside contemporary Israel's northern border, it nevertheless afforded vast vistas across the beloved homeland. Moreover, it had been widely regarded as by far the most sacred mountain in the region since early Egyptian times.[24] Far more than that, however, it had later become the headquarters of the great prophet Elijah, whose cave on Carmel can still be visited to this day. And Elijah, as we saw earlier, was the prototype and forerunner of all the subsequent Israelite prophets and holy men (Hasidim) right down to the Essenes themselves.

Elijah, indeed, had been one of the first to recall decadent Israel to the terms of its founding Covenant. And, like the Essenes, he had felt himself to be very much in a minority. 'I am the only prophet of the LORD still left,' he proclaims at 1 Kings 18:22. In an effort to restore the balance, he determines on a magical trial of strength between himself and the 'prophets of Baal'. 'Send and summon all Israel to meet me on Mount Carmel,' he orders.[a] And there the confrontation is duly staged and the discredited prophets of Baal, unable to call down fire from heaven, are finally put to death.

Whatever the pedigree of the story — and there are suggestions that the celebrated incident may have involved Elijah in the pretence that natural petroleum was really water[22] — there can be no doubt that the Essenes' Teacher saw in it clear parallels with the Essenes' own present circumstances. They, too, saw themselves collectively as the 'only prophet of the LORD still left.' As the sole true remnant of Israel, they too must now make their way to Mount Carmel. As a result of their initiative, their enemies — the 'prophets of Baal' in the ranks of the Sadducees — would finally be defeated. And just as the Elijah incident had involved the rebuilding by the prophet of 'the altar of Jehovah' on Mount Carmel with twelve stones — one for each tribe of Israel — so the Essenes likewise could hope to restore the true national worship there.

Yet even there the parallelism did not stop. For Moses had long ago promised that Yahweh would 'raise up a prophet from among you like myself,'[b] and the much more recent Malachi had even gone so far as to

---

[a] 1 Ki. 18:19 [b] Deut. 18:15

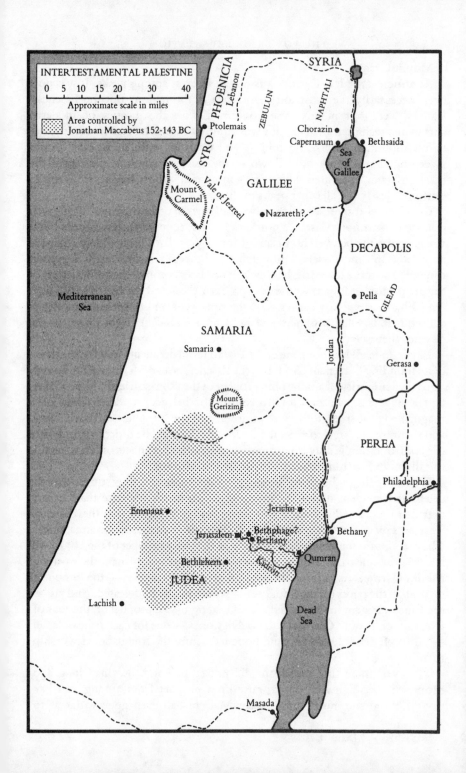

INTERTESTAMENTAL PALESTINE

0 5 10 15 20   30   40

Approximate scale in miles

Area controlled by
Jonathan Maccabeus 152-143 BC

SYRIA

SYRO-PHOENICIA

Lebanon

ZEBULUN

NAPHTALI

Ptolemais

Chorazin

Capernaum

Bethsaida

Sea
of
Galilee

GALILEE

Vale of Jezreel

Mount
Carmel

Nazareth?

DECAPOLIS

Mediterranean
Sea

Pella

GILEAD

SAMARIA

Samaria

Jordan

Gerasa

Mount
Gerizim

PEREA

Philadelphia

Emmaus

Jericho

Jerusalem   Bethphage?
            Bethany

Bethany

Qumran

Kidron

Bethlehem

JUDEA

Lachish

Dead
Sea

Masada

identify him. 'Look,' he had quoted Yahweh as saying, 'I will send you the prophet Elijah before the great and terrible day of the LORD comes'[a] — and this a great many centuries after the historical Elijah had already come and gone.

The Pharisees, followed in general by the public at large, took this prophecy — with which the then scriptures actually concluded — to mean that the advent of the future World-King or Messiah would be preceded by the re-appearance, or even the reincarnation, of the prophet Elijah himself — who had, it seemed, disappeared under mysterious circumstances after crossing the Jordan eastwards opposite Jericho.

The Essenes, as we shall see, shared this view. But a prophecy can be fulfilled on a variety of levels, and they were quite capable of seeing themselves collectively — or even their Teacher in person — as fulfilling the role of the returned Elijah. And if so, where better than atop Mount Carmel, Elijah's own ancient headquarters?

And so it must have been with profound satisfaction that the Teacher, turning to the end of the book of Micah, discovered the crowning passage — a rhetorical demand[b] that Yahweh should shepherd his own special flock which, in the familiar King James translation, 'dwells solitarily in the wood, in the midst of Carmel.'[c] 'Show us miracles,' the text went on, 'as in the days when thou camest out of Egypt,'[d] thus confirming the Teacher's conviction that the events of the Exodus must somehow be recapitulated. 'Who is a god like thee? Thou takest away guilt, thou passest over the sin of the remnant of thy own people, thou dost not let thy anger rage for ever but delightest in love that will not change. Once more thou wilt show us tender affection and wash out our guilt, casting all our sins into the depths of the sea. Thou wilt show good faith to Jacob, unchanging love to Abraham, as thou didst swear to our fathers in days gone by.'[e]

The passage could have been specifically written for the Essenes. Indeed, as far as the Teacher was concerned, there can have been no doubt that it actually was. And, in particular, there could no longer be any doubt among the Essene predestinarians that Carmel was their prophesied objective, marked out for them from even before time began. There they must now make a fresh start, continually purifying themselves with ritual ablutions in fulfilment of the passage just quoted, following to the letter the conditions imposed on Israel by Yahweh during their ancient Exodus, and thus holding Him finally to His promises.

To date, while there is certainly some psychic evidence of the Essenes' sojourn on Carmel,[24, 37] specific archaeological evidence of it is totally

[a] Mal. 4:5 [b] Mic. 7:14 [c] The New English Bible translators, apparently unwilling to believe that the text can mean what it says, here actually *translate* the Hebrew word *karmel* ('fruitful place'), thus giving the nondescript phrase 'on the heath and in the meadows.' [d] Mic. 7:15 [e] Mic. 7:18-20

lacking. The one expedition so far mounted revealed only Elijah's cave, altar and spring, and the remains of an ancient monastery of indeterminate date.[24, 37] This is entirely to be expected, however, since one of the conditions of the original Exodus was that the people must live only in temporary shelters or arbours until they reached their Promised Land.[a] Even the Divine sanctuary was to be no more than a 'Tent of the Presence' within its sacred enclosure. These provisions, entirely logical for the nomadic period of the Exodus, were almost certainly observed by the Essenes on Carmel as a strict ritual requirement, appropriately symbolising their determination not to rest until they had achieved their ultimate, spiritual goal. In confirmation of this, we know that the later Qumran Essenes lived in caves, huts or tents and constructed no solid dwellings — the Qumran ruins were devoted entirely to communal activities such as eating, ritual immersion and daily work and worship — and even the much later Carmelite monks, or Roman Catholic White Friars, were to continue this tradition when their order established itself on Carmel in the twelfth century AD. But then, the recorded history of the latter's predecessors suggests that there had in fact been an unbroken continuity of such monastic settlements on the mountain since well before the time of Christ;[24] and the only pre-Christian monastic communities in Palestine were, as we have seen, those of the Essenes.

While the world awaits the results of further archaeological investigations on Carmel, however, there is an interesting further piece of circumstantial documentary evidence to consider. The Habakkuk commentary of the Dead Sea Scrolls recounts how, at some stage during the earlier years of the Essenes' exile, the 'Wicked Priest . . . pursued the Teacher of Righteousness to his house of exile that he might confuse him with his venomous fury. And at the time appointed for rest, for the Day of Atonement, he appeared before them to confuse them, and to cause them to stumble on the Day of Fasting, their Sabbath of repose.'[51] Later, however, the 'Wicked Priest' was 'delivered into the hands of his enemies because of the iniquity committed against the Teacher of Righteousness and the men of his Council, that he might be humbled by means of a destroying scourge, in bitterness of soul, because he had done wickedly to His elect.'[51]

We have, of course, already identified the 'Wicked Priest'. He was the man whom the Teacher took to be his arch-adversary, the ruler Jonathan Maccabeus. Meanwhile it is clear from the Scrolls that the Essenes saw Jonathan's marauding expedition across his northern frontier as closely

---

[a] Lev. 23:43. Similar conditions are known to have been observed by the northern tribal sect of itinerant craftsmen known as the Rechabites, whom various commentators have associated with the Essenes.

connected with his eventual capture and death at the hands of enemy forces in 142 BC. The story of this event is recounted in 1 Maccabees 12 and 13. It tells how the Seleucid usurper Trypho lured Jonathan to Ptolemais, on the Syro-Phoenician coast, on the pretext of handing it over to him as a gesture of friendship, then seized him and slaughtered his followers. Jonathan himself was finally put to death the following year.

Since, prior to this expedition, Jonathan had been in southern Galilee, it is clear that his route to Ptolemais on this occasion must have taken him past Mount Carmel. If this was by then the site of the Essene headquarters, it is not difficult to imagine that the Jerusalem High Priest would have found the chance it gave him to turn aside in order to desecrate the dissidents' 'alternative temple' too good to miss. Jonathan and Trypho were, however, travelling northwards together, and it is possible that, in view of the supposed honour about to be bestowed upon him, the Maccabean felt somewhat inhibited in his actions. Trypho, after all, no doubt regarded the Carmel Essenes as friends, and would privately have admitted to seeing them as potential allies against Jonathan himself. The fact that the Essenes and their Teacher apparently survived the incursion thus adds weight to the view that this was the occasion of Jonathan's visit and that Carmel was its venue — since at any other time and place the sectaries would have been lucky to escape with their lives.

And so, in the event, Jonathan merely contented himself with an angry and possibly blasphemous confrontation on a day which, for him, was just an ordinary Friday but which, on the Essenes' solar calendar, was none other than the sacred Day of Atonement when, even had they been called upon to do so, they would have been unwilling to lift a finger to defend themselves.

The Essenes, then, had much to be thankful for, and their Hymn Scroll gives constant expression to that fact.[51] Their deliverance from Jonathan, much against all the odds, could be seen as a sign of Divine approval of their occupation of Carmel. It parallelled to a remarkable degree the Israelites' escape from the pursuing pharaoh's forces during the original Exodus. It might be expected, therefore, that the Divine blessing would also rest on their next great enterprise — the re-invocation of the ancient Covenant.

We have already referred to Jeremiah's planting of this concept in the national consciousness as early as the time of the Assyrian exile.[a] Its theme of inner renewal and intuitive knowledge of the Divine will had lain there dormant, just occasionally sprouting into fitful life, for the last five hundred years or so. Ezekiel had taken up the concept again[b] and had added further, specific provisions of his own.[c] Hosea, for his part, had foreshadowed the New Covenant in terms of a wedding between heaven and earth, between Yahweh and his people.[d] And now it had fallen to the Essenes to make an

---

[a] Jer. 31:31-40 [b] Ez. 37:26 [c] Ez. 40-48 [d] Hos. 2:18-23

all-out attempt finally to put the idea into practice.

We do not need to detail here the minutiae of what was involved. Suffice it to say that the exiles sought by every means possible to cultivate within themselves a direct and intuitive knowledge of the will of Yahweh — a knowledge which, inspired by love and religious fervour, transcended even the 613 provisions of the written Law, whose observance was regarded as a mere matter of course. Several hours of each day were devoted to prayer and to study of the scriptures. For it was by meditating on the scriptures that, guided by their Teacher, they sought to awaken their own intuitive prophetic powers to the point where they were totally inspired by what they termed the 'spirit of Truth'. From this point on, they could see themselves as acting as the vehicle of that spirit, and it followed from this that they could be quite sure of the rightness of any communal decision they might take. Wherever two or more of them met in the name of Yahweh, there — they could be assured — was He amongst them.

Thus, having meditated on Daniel 11:35, they took to wearing white clothes as a sign of ritual and moral purity. Following the prophecy of Malachi at 4:2, they devoted much study to the art of healing, subsequently becoming famed as herbalists throughout Palestine. They were not averse, in fact, to studying anything which might extend their knowledge and understanding of God's creation and of their own place in it. Thus, several fragments from Qumran attest a deep interest in astrology, and consequently it seems reasonable to assume that the sect's occult studies and beliefs were at least as deep and as wide-ranging as those of the Pharisees. These, as we have seen, included a belief in Heaven and Hell, in angels and demons, in human reincarnation and in eventual physical immortality.[44] The Essenes, too, believed in bodily immortality, but were inclined to see it in a somewhat spiritualised light, almost as though the whole physical world would in some way be transformed once the promised Kingdom had dawned.[a] This concept of bodily survival is not to be confused, however, with a further belief in the pre-existence and post-existence of souls, attested by Josephus.[b]

Meanwhile the Kingdom itself, the Essenes were convinced, was imminent, and in common with most of their contemporaries they expected it to take, in the initial stages at least, unmistakably physical form. Yet they were also prepared to admit of the possibility that it might be delayed in order, as it were, to test the zeal of the righteous to the limit. Thus, the Qumran scribe was able to interpret Habakkuk 2:3 to mean that the final age would be prolonged, 'exceeding all that the prophets have said.'[51] And so, as successive events unfolded, and the corrupt Maccabean regime eventually fell to the invading Romans under Pompey, with all the subsequent disasters

---

[a] *Community Rule*, IV.[51] Compare the later Paul at 1 Cor. 15:35-53.   [b] *Wars of the Jews*, Bk. II, viii[35]

which were to befall the nation as a result, the prophecies of Daniel had to be stretched and reinterpreted. What had formerly been seen as references to the Seleucids would have to be re-applied to the Roman Empire. The time of ordeal was far from over yet.

Nevertheless, the Teacher had long since made a whole set of contingency plans. As he continued work on his interpretation of the scriptures, his prophetic inspiration was by no means at an end. Far from stopping short at laying down the Essene community's rule of life and ritual requirements, he had gone on to lay down precisely what must happen next. It was not enough, as we have already seen, merely to fulfil the Divine Law. The writings of the prophets, too, must be deliberately fulfilled. Nothing which lay within the capacity of man to bring to pass could be left undone. Only when the powers of earthbound humanity had been stretched to their ultimate limit would the heavenly hand of God stretch forth to meet it and bring the new Kingdom into being.[a]

And so the Teacher's book of oracles went on to prescribe the next step towards finally taking that Kingdom by storm. When the signs indicated that the Last Times had truly reached their climax, a bold and extraordinary plan must be set in motion — a plan whose after-effects, in the event, were to reverberate around the world right up to the present day.

[a] Compare, once again, the imagery of Hos. 2:18-23.

7
A Boy is Born

If one thing was clear to the Teacher and his successors, it was that the New Age would not dawn until the promised Messiah had appeared to inaugurate it. As the Essenes originally conceived of the idea in their *Damascus Rule*, this awesome world-figure would fulfil at least a dual role, acting both as anointed High Priest and as anointed King.[51] Possibly under Pharisaic influence, however, some of the Essenes came to see the two roles as mutually incompatible, so that the Qumran *Community Rule* foresaw two separate figures — a kingly Messiah ben Israel and a priestly Messiah ben Aaron, the 'Interpreter of the Law' who, in true Essene fashion, would be the superior partner.[51]

Whatever the preferred schema, however, one fact was beyond dispute. The appearance of the Messiah or Messiahs was a quite separate matter from the expected semi-miraculous Divine intervention which would finally establish the New Age itself. The Messiah would not appear fully-fledged out of the ether like some angelic being from another world. Still less was he expected to be in any sense 'God in human form' — for the very idea would have constituted the most outrageous of blasphemies against the unknowable, unnameable Jewish Godhead. The very pronouncing of the name of God, it should be remembered, was still, under the terms of the original Law, punishable by stoning to death.[a] Equating Yahweh with a mere human being, apart from being manifestly ridiculous, would have seemed a hundred times worse.

Any Messiah, in consequence, whether priestly, kingly or a combination of the two, must be born an ordinary mortal. The title 'Messiah' merely indicated that he would subsequently be anointed with oil of spikenard[b], as kings and High Priests of Israel had been for generations, in symbol of the Divine power and authority that had been conferred upon him. Much hinged, therefore, on identifying the child virtually at birth. In this, the

[a] Lev. 24:16   [b] Heb. *mashiach*, 'anointed'

Essenes must of course be guided by their own visionary and psychic gifts. Their astrological knowledge, too, must be put to good account. Thus, the Qumran *Messianic Horoscope* specifies that the child must be red-headed, must have a birthmark on his thigh, and must already have reached years of discretion by the tender age of two.[52]

But mere identification was not enough. Since the child would have a whole series of exacting prophetic requirements to fulfil, he must be thoroughly educated and trained for the task. Throughout, his conduct must be blameless, a constant manifestation of the demands of the Divine Covenant. Yet where could he obtain such an upbringing? Where else could he find the strict conditions necessary for his education but within the only Israelite community that observed the Covenant correctly and completely?

The child, in short, must inevitably be trained and educated by the Essenes themselves. Rules, indeed, already existed for the upbringing of children in the sect's *Messianic Rule*.[51] But as he must also clearly be born of blameless parents, a further fact became obvious. Since no Messiah could be born amid the decadence of contemporary Israel, the earthly representative of Yahweh could appear only from among the True Elect themselves. And that, of course, could mean only one thing.

He must be born a member of the Teacher's own community.

But the prophecies also demanded that the Messiah, whether single or multiple, should be preceded by a forerunner, a reincarnation of the prophet Elijah. For the Pharisees, who held Elijah to have been a priest, it was this same figure who would also fulfil the role of Priest-Messiah and so prepare the way for what they saw as the much greater Davidic Messiah to come. Some of the Essenes, meanwhile, seem to have seen their original Teacher, himself a priest, as fulfilling the role of prophet and forerunner. Indeed, there are suggestions that they may even have expected the Teacher himself to re-appear as the promised King-Messiah. The Teacher, however, does not seem to have shared that view.[51] For him, Elijah was yet to re-appear, and therefore he, too, must somehow be identified and trained to fulfil the role laid down for him.

Once again, then, the visionary process must be allowed to take its course. It went without saying that the prophet, too, must be born of Essene parents, be brought up in an Essene environment, be instructed in how to fulfil the prophecies as interpreted by the Essenes' own experts.

And so all the Teacher's prophetic energies, we may be sure, were now turned to specifying every detail of the Divine Messianic programme. And, as luck would have it, the scriptures provided ample grist for his exegetical mill.

Manifestly the first problem was to identify the culmination of the Last Days — the age of national ordeal that had been starkly in evidence since at least the time of the infamous Antiochus IV. The Book of Daniel's expectation that the climax would occur within a mere seven years of 167 BC had already been cruelly dashed. The celebrated '490 years' prophecy, however, provided a distinct ray of hope. Counting 490 years from Cyrus's original decree of 534 BC that the Jewish exiles should return home to rebuild Jerusalem, this prediction seemed, as we have already seen, to pinpoint the year 44 BC as the vital year in question. As we also saw earlier, however, the years 30 BC, 33 AD or even 46 AD could, if necessary, be seen as potential alternatives. Adding to these facts the well-known general uncertainty among early Jewish commentators as to the precise length of the Persian period, it was clear, therefore, that the crucial moment would have to be identified more by the events which surrounded it than by any firm conclusions on the matter of dating. 44 BC was certainly to be regarded as the *terminus a quo* but, in the already-quoted words of the Qumran scribe, it could well be that the Final Age would be prolonged, and would 'exceed all that the prophets have said.'[51]

What, then, were to be the 'signs of the Times'? The scriptures provided abundant testimony of the events to be expected. To help them map out the course of future events, the later Essenes at Qumran were to make no less than eight copies of the Book of Daniel and of the so-called Minor Prophets, and as many as eighteen of Isaiah and twenty-seven of the book of Psalms. Between them, these revealed that there would be widespread wars, famines and pestilences, treachery in high places, persecutions and public disorder, a general falling-away from true religion, earthquakes and portents in the sky. And the crowning event would be the ultimate setting-up of the cryptically-named 'abomination of desolation' in the Temple at Jerusalem.[a]

It was clear that the process had long since started. Awareness of the fact had been general throughout Palestine ever since the time of Antiochus IV, and had lain at the very root of the Essene schism and exodus in the first place. After a brief spasm of hope at the time of the Maccabean rebellion, things had started to go from bad to worse under Jonathan and his successors, and the general awareness of crisis was to be given a powerful new boost when the Romans were called in to aid John Hyrcanus II in his dynastic squabble with his brother Aristobulus in 63 BC. Almost the first act of the religiously insensitive Roman general Pompey, following his successful siege of Jerusalem, was to commit the sacrilege of entering the Holy of Holies in the Temple — a privilege reserved for the High Priest alone, and then on only one day of the year (the Day of Atonement). Perhaps this event, then, represented the predicted 'abomination of desolation'?

Yet worse was to come. Not only were the Jews once more placed under a heathen yoke, but an alien king was placed over them. With the accession of Herod the Great in 37 BC, a period of growing public disorder began, and the

---

[a] Compare the selected texts quoted in chapter 12.

inherently able and even charismatic monarch was virtually forced by circumstances to act up to the image of tyrannical ogre projected on him by a public increasingly intoxicated with Messianic fervour. Having, for his own safety, murdered all the potential Hasmonean (i.e. latter-day Maccabean) pretenders to the throne, he proceeded to antagonise his subjects by deliberately adopting the role of 'friend of Caesar'. And so, when a massive earthquake struck Judea in 31 BC, killing 30,000 people, to be followed by persistent droughts and an outbreak of plague some six years later, the conviction became almost universal that the moment of crisis had finally arrived — with Herod a virtual reincarnation of the hated 'Pharoah of the Oppression'. And, that being so, surely 'Moses' must soon reappear to deliver his people?

It is, of course, most unlikely that the Essenes' Teacher of Righteousness had foreseen these events in any detail. Yet the situation that now obtained corresponded in astonishing degree to the prophetic blueprint for the Last Times that he had extracted from the scriptures. In this, the Fourth Law of Prophecy (that of Self-Fulfilment) may not have been entirely blameless. As the already neurotic king steadily sickened and became ever more irrational in his acts, widespread public disturbances threatened, and plots and counter-plots abounded. The tiniest spark could now set the whole situation alight. And out of the subsequent national tumult who could say what great New Order might not arise?

Yet, for the Essenes, it seems to have been the great earthquake of 31 BC that was the deciding factor. No event in nature, after all, has a more convincing feel of the overwhelming power of God about it. Again, 31 BC was only a year before one of the possible alternative dates for the inauguration of the expected Kingdom, in so far as anybody was aware of the fact. And, what is more, the earthquake, as we shall see, was to have the most direct of physical effects upon the Essenes themselves.

One of the facts originally deduced by the Teacher from the scriptures was that, even before the arrival of the Messiah and the inception of the New Age, a 'pioneer-force' of exceptionally 'strong souls' must be dispatched to the Judean desert, there to set up a preparatory community prior to the final *Putsch* on Jerusalem itself. The prophets were clear, even effusive on the topic. 'There is a voice that cries: Prepare a road for the LORD through the wilderness, clear a highway across the desert for our God. Every valley shall be lifted up, every mountain and hill brought down.' So had proclaimed Isaiah[a], and already there were hints in the text both of a desert mission and of a subsequent series of earth-movements. Three chapters later[b], the theme

[a] Isa. 40:3-4   [b] Isa. 43:19-20

was taken up again: 'I will make a way even through the wilderness and paths in the barren desert . . . I will provide water in the wilderness and rivers in the barren desert, where my chosen people may drink.' To the Teacher, the reference, redolent of the original Exodus-journey, was clearly to his own community of the Elect, still amid the throes of its own chosen exodus.

Meanwhile, in chapter 61[a], the same scroll offered the celebrated messianic passage beginning: 'The spirit of the Lord GOD is upon me because the LORD has anointed me; he has sent me to bring good news to the humble, to bind up the broken-hearted, to proclaim liberty to captives and release to those in prison.' 'Ancient ruins shall be rebuilt,' the text went on[b], 'and sites long desolate restored; they shall repair the ruined cities and restore what has long lain desolate.'

To the Teacher, it must by now have seemed that the Messianic initiative itself would in some way depend upon the rebuilding of some long-deserted site in the desert, and upon the establishment of the Essenes' own 'way of righteousness' within its walls. Amos 9:11-12 could be seen as confirming the connection: 'On that day I will restore David's fallen house; I will repair its gaping walls and restore its ruins; I will rebuild it as it was long ago, that they may possess what is left of Edom and all the nations who were once named mine.' The fact that the original reference was clearly to Jerusalem itself would have worried the Teacher and his successors not one jot, as we have already seen. If the unnamed, ruined desert-site was to be connected with the messianic initiative, then it too could justly be described as 'David's fallen house', and its rebuilding consequently seen as prophesied by the text.

Turning now to the book of Numbers[c], the Teacher could establish the expected length of the pioneers' desert-sojourn before the age of wrath reached its final climax. 'Your sons shall be wanderers in the desert forty years,' the text announced, referring to the original Exodus, 'paying the penalty of your wanton disloyalty till the last man of you dies there.' Two further facts, meanwhile, seem to emerge from the same text. The pioneer force must consist of 'sons' (*ben*) rather than daughters — i.e. it must be a celibate group of men, not a mixed community. And it would have, by its voluntary sufferings and self-denials, to perform an atoning function for the sins of apostate Israel. In this sense it could be seen as temporarily replacing the function of the now-invalid ritual animal-sacrifices at the Temple in Jerusalem, in fulfilment of Psalm 51:[d] 'My sacrifice, O God, is a broken spirit; a wounded heart, O God, thou wilt not despise. Let it be thy pleasure to do good to Zion, to build anew the walls of Jerusalem. Then only shalt thou delight in the appointed sacrifices; then shall young bulls be offered on thy altar.' Hosea, too, had taken up the theme at 6:6: 'Loyalty is my desire,

[a] Isa. 61:1   [b] Isa. 61:4   [c] Nu. 14:33   [d] Ps. 51:17-19

not sacrifice, not whole-offerings but the knowledge of God.'

Hence we find a great deal of emphasis in the later Dead Sea Scrolls on precisely this function of communal atonement. 'They shall be an agreeable offering,' decrees the *Community Rule* of its core-group, 'atoning for the Land and determining the judgement of wickedness, and there shall be no more iniquity.'[a] 'They shall atone for guilty rebellion and for sins of unfaithfulness that they may obtain lovingkindness for the Land without the flesh of holocausts and the fat of sacrifice. And prayer rightly offered shall be as an acceptable fragrance of righteousness, and perfection of way as a delectable free-will offering.'[b]

For forty years, then, the pioneer community must do penance for Israel in the remote fastnesses of the desert. Since the Dead Sea Scrolls reveal that the Essenes originally expected the same period to intervene between the death of the Teacher and the dawn of the messianic epoch[52], it therefore seems likely that the Teacher had specified that the pioneers should leave Carmel for the desert in the year of his own death.

The details of the desert-initiative were already starting to take shape. And the more the Teacher looked, the more the scriptures seemed to back up the idea. Indeed, the exultantly messianic passage at Isaiah 35 was quite specific about it. 'Let the desert rejoice and burst into flower . . . The glory of Lebanon is given to it, the splendour too of Carmel and Sharon.' Clearly, it was the best men, the 'glory' drawn from all the northern Essene camps — Carmel included — who must make up the expedition. 'Then shall blind men's eyes be opened and the ears of the deaf unstopped,' the text went on. 'Then shall the lame man leap like a deer, and the tongue of the dumb shout aloud; for water springs up in the wilderness, and torrents flow in dry land.'[c] Whatever else the text might have meant, physical healing must obviously be high on the agenda.

'And there shall be a causeway there which shall be called the Way of Holiness,' pursued the ancient scroll, 'and the unclean shall not pass along it.' The community, with its Essene 'Way of Holiness', must clearly be a strictly-enclosed one, separated from the rest of society. 'By it those he has ransomed shall return and the LORD's redeemed come home; they shall enter Zion with shouts of triumph, crowned with everlasting gladness.'[d]

The desert-community, then, must prepare the way for the sect's return to Israel at the dawn of the messianic age. But where exactly was it to take up residence?

It was the forty-seventh chapter of Ezekiel that supplied the final key.[e] In it, the prophet describes a vision of the new Jerusalem in which a torrent of water issues from beneath the eastern side of the Jerusalem Temple and flows,

a Community Rule, VIII[51]   *b Community Rule*, IX[51]   *c* Isa. 35:1-2, 5-6   *d* Isa. 35:8-10
e Ez. 47:1-12

ever gaining in strength, eastwards down to the Dead Sea. From it all the earth's living creatures draw life and healing; fruit-trees grow luxuriantly along its banks; and along the western shore of the Dead Sea, fishermen suddenly find innumerable fish to catch in their nets.

For the Teacher there was, of course, no difficulty in interpreting the passage. Fish and living creatures alike were human souls in need of salvation at the dawn of the astrological age of Pisces (the Fishes). In the spirit of Jeremiah 16:16, the fishermen were the Essene pioneer-force whose job it was to 'catch' them and persuade them to abandon the decadence of contemporary society in favour of joining their own order. The healing powers of the life-giving waters were the Essenes' own curative skills — not merely their physical knowledge of herbalism, but also the powers of spiritual healing which flowed, like the allegorical waters themselves, from the Jerusalem Temple, of whose original cult they believed themselves to be the sole true heirs. And the site of the new establishment was also finally and triumphantly fixed.

For there, far to the south, on the western shore of the Dead Sea, lay the ruins of a former settlement known — significantly — in Joshua's day as the 'City of Salt'. Not far from it, a small stream that had meandered all the way down from Jerusalem's Kidron Valley, directly below the eastern side of the Temple, finally emptied itself into the salt waters, providing a small oasis of trees and shrubs amid the hot, barren wilderness of the Judean desert. It was the lowest place on the planet, a veritable hell on earth, a truly fitting place for the Essenes to undertake their painful mission of atonement.

And so here, to Qumran on the western shore of the Dead Sea, the select few eventually came.

In all probability there were only fifteen of them at the outset. This would accord with the Qumran *Community Rule*, which lays down that 'In the Council of the Community there shall be twelve men and three Priests, perfectly versed in all that is revealed of the Law, whose works shall be truth, righteousness, justice, lovingkindness and humility. They shall preserve the faith in the Land with steadfastness and meekness and shall atone for sin by the practice of justice and by suffering the sorrows of affliction. . . When these are in Israel,' the text continues, 'the Council of the Community shall be established in truth.'[a]

After two years of faithful service, the document goes on to suggest, the new establishment would be confirmed as a fully-fledged Essene community, and entitled to share all the secrets of the prophetic wisdom of the Teacher and his successors. 'And the Interpreter shall not conceal from

a *Community Rule*, VIII[51]

them,' it ordains, '. . . any of those things hidden from Israel which have been discovered by him.'[a]

'And when these become members of the Community in Israel according to all these rules, they shall separate from the habitation of ungodly men and shall go into the wilderness to prepare the way of Him; as it is written, *Prepare in the wilderness the way of . . . make straight in the desert a path for our God*. This path is the study of the Law which He commanded by the hand of Moses, that they may do according to all that has been revealed from age to age, and as the Prophets have revealed by His Holy Spirit.'[a]

The Essene pioneers, in other words, were eventually to be invested with their own interpretative authority, free to enlarge and expand upon the original insights of the Teacher of Righteousness as local circumstances demanded, and as their own spiritual intuition guided them. From this development, as we shall see, important consequences were in due course to follow.

The immediate task for the newly-arrived sectaries of the late Second Century BC, however, was to plan and build the new desert-establishment by the shores of the Dead Sea, almost in the shadow, so to speak, of Jerusalem itself. At a time of scarcely-veiled hostility on the part of the ruling successors of Jonathan Maccabeus, it was a bold undertaking. Possibly because there was no attempt to set up any 'alternative temple' at Qumran, the sectaries were apparently left unmolested. Patiently they raised their new communal buildings atop the ancient ruins — a dining room and kitchen, workshops, a lavatory, a watch-tower, an assembly-room and a first-floor scriptorium for copying manuscripts, well out of the way of any possible flash floods. There were also two large baptismal tanks for the sectaries' purificatory ritual of self-immersion in clear water. This they collected in specially-constructed cisterns, chiefly from the waters of the Wadi Qumran itself.

Yet it seems that, even after they had finished building their fairly modest establishment, the Qumran Essenes, in token of the interim nature of their mission, continued to live either in caves or in tents or temporary shelters like their forebears of the Mosaic Exodus. But the end of the age was a long time coming. The expected forty years lengthened into fifty, sixty, seventy. All the original pioneers were long since dead and buried in the communal cemetery to the east of the monastery before the event occurred which finally spurred their successors into action.

For in 31 BC the great earthquake already referred to devastated Judea. Qumran, lying directly in the geological fault which had caused it, was severely affected. The tower was weakened to the point of collapse, the walls split apart, the baptismal tanks ruptured and useless. But for the fact that the sectaries had been strictly charged not to live in their permanent buildings,

---

[a] *Community Rule*, VIII[51]

they might have been killed. Perhaps regarding their escape as a Divine deliverance, they saw the earthquake as the direct fulfilment of Isaiah 40:4 (quoted above), and interpreted the event to mean that the remainder of Isaiah's further prophecy in chapter 13, already used by the Teacher as a pointer to the site of their original exile in the far north, was now about to be fulfilled. For the prophet had foretold a time of widespread terror, of horrors both natural and man-made. Then, following these signs that the 'Day of the LORD' was at hand, and at a time when true men were 'scarcer than fine gold, rarer than gold of Ophir', 'the heavens shall shudder, and the earth shall be shaken from its place at the fury of the LORD of Hosts, on the day of his anger.'[a]

To the Essene 'few' at Qumran, this great event, long awaited and even, perhaps, despaired of, had at last come to pass, and so the succeeding verse of the prophecy must now be invoked. 'Then,' ordained the text, 'like a gazelle before the hunter or a flock with no man to round it up, each man will go back to his own people, every one will flee to his own land.'[b]

The rest of the chapter made clear the reason for this. The Divine wrath was about to descend on Israel, which had now made itself into the 'Babylon' subsequently cursed by the text, and so it in turn must now be laid waste by a new generation of 'Medes'. The Teacher himself had possibly identified these expected invaders with the Seleucid Greeks, but to the Qumran Essenes of the first century BC the Divine judgement, it was now clear, was about to be executed by the dread hand of the Romans.

In the event, as we now know with the benefit of hindsight, the sectaries were anticipating events by almost exactly a century. But they were not to know this at the time. To the Essenes of Qumran, the final sign had indubitably come that they must quit their desert establishment and, leaving only a skeleton staff behind, return to the north while the Divine wrath passed over Israel. The monastery, as archeological evidence tends to confirm, was all but deserted.[51] The stage was set for the next great phase of the Teacher's plan. And its details were spelt out graphically in chapter 5 of Micah.

'Get you behind your walls, you people of a walled city,' the text commenced. 'The siege is pressed home against you: Israel's ruler shall be struck on the cheek with a rod. But you, Bethlehem in Ephrathah, small as you are to be among Judah's clans, out of you shall come forth a governor for Israel, one whose roots are far back in the past, in days gone by. Therefore only so long as a woman is in labour shall he give up Israel; and then those that survive of his race shall rejoin their brethren. He shall appear and be their shepherd in the strength of the LORD, in the majesty of the name of the LORD his God. And they shall continue, for now his greatness shall reach to

[a] Isa. 13:12-13   [b] Isa. 13:14

the ends of the earth; and he shall be a man of peace.'[a]

The message, give or take some free interpretation of pronouns, was unmistakable. The Qumran pioneer force must return to its northern fastnesses while King Herod was toppled from power. But they would remain in temporary exile *only for as long as it took for the Essenes to conceive the expected Messiah*. At the appropriate moment, arrangements must be made for the child to be born in King David's own native city of Bethlehem, while the pioneer-force returned once more to Qumran, ready to act as his spiritual shock-troops in the last battle that would usher in the final age of peace.

The Messiah himself, however, would have no direct part in the fighting. Repeatedly the prophecies insisted that he must be a man of peace. Isaiah's celebrated passage beginning 'The people that walked in darkness have seen a great light' described him as 'Prince of Peace'.[b] A subsequent passage[c] described him in terms of a ruler of immense wisdom and authority presiding over a peaceful world by the sheer power of his utterance.

But first the new leader must be conceived and born. Consequently the Essenes' attention must now be turned towards establishing the correct conditions for his birth. And we may assume that these, too, had been long since laid down by the Teacher of Righteousness himself. Specific echoes of his deliberations seem to surface in Hymn 4 of the Qumran *Hymn Scroll*[51] where, in a clear reference to Micah's 'Bethlehem'-prophecy above, the Essene community itself is likened to a woman in labour struggling to bring forth the messianic 'Man'-figure prefigured by the book of Daniel at 7:13 (see page 39).

Right at the outset, however, there had been a paradox to solve. In repeated references to the coming world-ruler, the scriptures apparently referred to him as a descendant of King David. Isaiah described him, for example, as 'a shoot' that 'shall grow from the stock of Jesse' (David's father), and as 'a branch' (*netzer*) that 'shall spring from his roots.'[d] Jeremiah likewise described him as 'a righteous Branch' who would 'spring from David's line',[e] and went on to promise, 'David will never lack a successor on the throne of Israel, nor will the levitical priests lack a man who shall come before me continually to present whole-offerings . . .'[f] The future king, then, whether himself a priest or merely accompanied by one, must apparently be of the line of David.

In another passage, however, Jeremiah reported Yahweh's promise that Israel and Judah 'shall serve the LORD their God and David their king, whom I will raise up for them.'[g] This clear suggestion that David would

---

[a] Mic. 5:1-5   [b] Isa. 9:6-7   [c] Isa. 11:1-10   [d] Isa. 11:1   [e] Jer. 23:5, 33:15   [f] Jer. 33:17   [g] Jer. 30:9

somehow be either resurrected or reborn as the new Messiah was further borne out by Ezekiel, who was likewise to refer to him directly as 'my servant David' and 'David their king'[a], adding, for good measure, 'My servant David shall for ever be their prince.'[b]

How, then, was the new leader to be both of the line of David and at the same time David himself? How, for that matter, was he to satisfy the popular — and unscriptural — expectation that he would actually be a 'son of David'?

The answer lay in the Essenes' own occult studies. For if, like the Pharisees, they believed (as now seems likely) in what the Greeks called metempsychosis, or the transmigration of souls — better known today as human reincarnation — the idea of 'sonship' could be understood in a spiritual, rather than a physical sense. Certainly they subscribed, if Josephus is to be credited, to the pre-existence of souls, which is basic to any such belief.[c] And so David, like Elijah, could be reborn in a contemporary human child, given only the right body and circumstances. In this case, it would be totally appropriate for the birth to take place in David's home-town of Bethlehem, as predicted by Micah. And these conditions it was therefore now the Essenes' pre-eminent duty to produce, thus providing a channel through which the coming Messiah could finally manifest.

But production of the 'right child' would, as we have already seen, depend upon the provision of blameless parents — a man and a woman who, from their youth, had been educated, trained and spiritually prepared for the role they would have to perform. Some kind of psychic selection-process must therefore now be set in train. A shortlist of potential husbands, in particular, must be identified at once since, if the thing were to be done properly, he ought already to have attained the age of at least 30 — the age of full adult male responsibility — before conception took place (sexual intercourse was in any case forbidden to Essene males below the age of twenty[d]). The timescale may seem to us an extraordinarily long one, but it should be remembered that the Essenes expected Yahweh's final judgement on Israel to last all of forty years.[e] The Messiah himself, in consequence, could be expected to have reached the age of at least ten by the time it was over, and possibly more if the as-yet unidentified father-to-be, somewhere among the northern camps, was already several years old.

Meanwhile, there was also the matter of the Messiah's priesthood to consider. The reborn King David would, of course, be king in his own right. His parents would not need to be of Davidic descent. But to qualify as a priest he would need to come of physical, priestly stock. And so it followed that the final selection of the father-to-be must be made from among a shortlist of the Essene priesthood. At least one source — albeit a psychic one[37] — actually

---

[a] Ez. 34:23-4   [b] Ez. 37:25   [c] *Wars of the Jews*, Book II, viii[35]   [d] *Messianic Rule* I[51]
[e] *Damascus Rule*, VIII[51]

affirms this to be the case.

Yet we have no reliable information on just how that final selection was made. Astrology may, on the evidence of the *Messianic Horoscope*[52], have played a part. Since the priestly *mebaqqer*, or Guardian of the community, was allegedly skilled in the art of assessing the spiritual make-up of individuals — i.e. the exact proportions within them of what the Essenes called the 'spirit of Truth' and the 'spirit of Falsehood' — this skill, too, may have come into play. Even the simple drawing of lots had a long pedigree among the Jews as a reliable indicator of the Divine will, and certain apocryphal sources go as far as to suggest that this was the method used.[a]

Meanwhile, a careful psychic watch must also be kept for the identity of the mother-to-be. As a first step, twelve young girls were selected from among families of exemplary religious uprightness to serve in the Essenes' temple on Carmel as 'handmaids of the Lord'.[a, 37] This was in order to comply with the passage in Psalm 116 in which the once and future Messiah was, it seemed, quoted as confessing to Yahweh, 'I am thy slave, thy slave-girl's son.'[b] As time went by and they reached puberty, these temple-virgins became ritually 'unclean' and were presumably replaced by others. And all the time the remaining group's ritual purity was maintained and their spiritual development carefully monitored, with particular attention to any visionary or mediumistic gifts which they might display. At length, it was believed, one of them would show unmistakable signs of Divine grace, and so be revealed as the Messiah's mother-to-be.

But there was also the question of the Messiah's prophetic forerunner to consider. The priestly Elijah, too, must be reborn amid the community. Admittedly, his role would be less exacting than the Messiah's. His task would be merely to preach repentance, to announce the Messiah and to proclaim the imminence of the Kingdom. For this he would need to be somewhat older than the Messiah himself, and consequently might well have to be born to parents who were already adult members of the community. But in view of his reduced responsibilities, this did not have to be seen as a drawback. It did not take semi-miraculous gifts, after all, to proclaim the good news of the Kingdom or to fulfil the semi-ritual role of messianic herald, and even the necessary prophetic gifts would be well taken care of by the training he would receive as a future priest in the Essenes' school of prophetic interpretation.

All that was required, therefore, was that the forerunner's father-to-be should be of priestly stock and, in common with his wife, upright and devout, a blameless observer of all the commandments and ordinances of Yahweh. Thereafter, psychic and visionary experiences could be relied on to

---

[a] Compare *Book of James*, or *Protevangelium*, IX; *Gospel of Pseudo-Matthew*, VIII; *Gospel of the Birth of Mary*, VIII; *History of Joseph the Carpenter*, IV.[20]   [b] Ps. 116:16

provide all the guidance needed.

And so the cast was gradually assembled. If we are to believe the scriptural records, the role of Messiah's father was eventually assigned to a carpenter called Joseph. This information, however, needs to be treated with caution, since the many apparent scriptural references to the sufferings of the expected Messiah (see chapter 11) were widely interpreted in terms of a 'Messiah ben Joseph', by analogy with the story of the earlier Joseph who was betrayed by his brothers and left for dead, eventually achieving a position of great power in Egypt. Again, while the trade of carpenter was certainly one of the main occupations practised by certain of the itinerant northern sects known as Rechabites and Kenites,[42] the word was also used in contemporary esoteric literature as a cypher for 'scholar', and thus for an interpreter of the scriptures.[53] One psychic source affirms that he was indeed of priestly descent.[37]

As for his abode, Nazareth actually seems unlikely since, although the modern town lies less than twenty miles from Mount Carmel, historical evidence that it existed at the time is entirely lacking. The tradition almost certainly goes back to the fact that the father-to-be was simply a member of the Nazarean or Nazorean sect of the Essenes; the two may have been either closely associated at the time, or even one and the same. This group seems to have become the dominant one on Carmel, to the point where the word later translated as 'Nazarenes' came to be applied to the northern Essenes in general. It is possible, of course, that the Essenes had a camp in the vicinity of the modern Nazareth. But the biblical use of the name, together with the reference to a non-existent prophecy that 'he shall be called a Nazarene,'[a] merely seems to represent a later attempt by ill-informed outsiders to explain how such a strange term came to be applied to the pan-Jewish World-Messiah.

There was to be a long delay, however, before the sign eventually came that was to identify the father-to-be of the expected priestly forerunner, so setting the whole messianic initiative in motion. Possibly it did not come earlier because it was not expected. The prophet, after all, did not need to precede by very much the advent of the Messiah. Or possibly it actually occurred much earlier than the available records suggest, but was delayed either in its confirmation or in its fulfilment.

At all events, the lot eventually fell on a revered priest by the name of Zechariah — apparently a secret Essene sympathiser in the Temple at Jerusalem.[37] Despite his wife's childlessness, he seems to have received so vivid a psychic revelation as to convince the elders on Carmel that Yahweh was about to repeat the miracle whereby the patriarch Abraham had been granted a son in his old age. The parallelism was strikingly apt, for Abraham

---

[a] Mt. 2:23

was regarded as the father of the nation, and his son Isaac as its very personification, much as the Messiah himself was expected to be. Zechariah, for his part, was reportedly dumbstruck at the news. Nor is this very surprising, for the idea that the Forerunner could be born to a father still living in degenerate Israel — and serving as a priest in the apostate Jerusalem Temple, at that — seemed to fly in the face of the most deep-seated Essene convictions. The saving factor appears, in the event, to have been the fact that Zechariah kept his wife, a practising Essene by the name of Elizabeth, well away from Jerusalem, somewhere in the northern hill-country — and there is reason to suppose that she was actually among the residents on Carmel.[37]

The news, and its confirmation by the elders, excited a fever of expectation among the Essenes. All was now set for the vision or other psychic experience that would identify the Messiah's mother-to-be from among the chosen temple-virgins. Their dreams were scrutinised, their ecstatic utterances while in trance scanned for features of significance. And, as is generally the case with such expectations, what had been expected duly came to pass. The Fourth Law of Prophecy had once more done its work.

It was to a girl called Miriam, daughter of one Anna, that the revelation eventually came.[a] In the vision which she experienced while serving as 'Yahweh's handmaid' on the steps of the altar itself[37], the Archangel Gabriel appeared to announce to her that she was to be the mother of the expected Davidic King. His name was to be Jehoshua, or Joshua, meaning 'God saves', and he would be a child of what the Essenes termed the 'spirit of Truth'. 'Here am I,' she is reported as replying. 'I am the Lord's servant; as you have spoken, so be it.'[b]

The elders probed the vision, questioned the girl. The name struck home. Possibly it had already been secretly specified by the Teacher. It was, after all, Joshua who had first led the Israelites into their Promised Land at the time of the Exodus. It was entirely fitting, therefore, that the new Messiah should also bear the name, in token of his task of leading Israel into the new 'promised land' that was to be the Kingdom of God on earth. Moreover, it also meant that he would almost literally fulfil the prophecy of Micah 5:4 by appearing 'in the majesty of the name of the LORD his God', since that name would actually form part of his own.

Meanwhile, it went without saying that he must also be totally a child of the spirit of Truth — unlike the majority of human beings, who owed allegiance in varying degrees to an often unpromising mixture of the spirits of Truth and Falsehood. It was one of the chief functions of the mebaqqer, or Guardian of the community — as we saw earlier — regularly to assess this

[a] Compare the Book of James, or Protevangelium, and the Gospel of Pseudo-Matthew.[20]
[b] Lk. 1:38

mixture in all those who came under his charge. Until the dawn of the coming Golden Age, it was held, the two spirits would continue to be present in the whole of creation in equal measure, and only then would the spirit of Falsehood finally be defeated. But the Messiah himself, clearly, must be a full-blooded manifestation of the spirit of Truth. Uniquely, perhaps, he must be all Light and no Darkness. It took much later biblical interpreters — themselves largely ignorant of the Essenes' lore — to suppose that Miriam's vision (now known as the Annunciation to Mary) meant that the child would somehow be physically conceived by some exalted heavenly personage, as several archetypal Old Testament figures were also reputed to have been, rather than by Miriam's own husband.

Indeed, it was to this very question that the elders, having finally confirmed Miriam's vision, now had to turn their attention. It may well have been at this time, as a variety of sources suggest[20, 37], that the final selection of a husband was made from among the group of young priests who had been selected and trained from their infancy for the task. The lot, as we have seen, appears to have fallen on one Joseph, and the chosen couple were therefore betrothed forthwith.

At this stage, of course, Miriam was still one of the temple-virgins. It follows, therefore, that she had not yet reached puberty. One psychic source[37] puts her actual age at this juncture as twelve or thirteen. In the short time which still had to elapse before she reached physical maturity, husband and wife-to-be could thus be put through a further course of intensive training in final preparation for their crucial role in history. Tradition has it that Joseph was 36 and Miriam 16 before the marriage was finally celebrated.[37]

Soon afterwards, the news broke that Zechariah's son had been born. Zechariah, still speechless, insisted in writing that he be named Johanan ('Yahweh is gracious'). The elders, respecting his wishes, approved the choice. At this, Zechariah could evidently contain himself no longer. According to Luke 1:68-79, he launched into a paean of thanksgiving in which several favourite Essene themes found their expression. The Davidic succession, the sacred Covenant, the child's task as Forerunner, the forgiveness of Israel and the Zoroastrian sunrise-symbolism of the triumph of Light over Darkness — all are referred to in what is nowadays known and even sung in Church circles as the *Benedictus*, after the first word of its Latin translation.

Still exulting and glorying in Yahweh, Zechariah returned to Jerusalem, where he was evidently now unable to keep his mouth shut. His priestly superiors, convinced that his words — if not entirely the product of a deranged mind — were both religiously heretical and politically dangerous, came to the conclusion that he must be got rid of. If the biblical account is to be believed, a hired assassin eventually murdered him in the very midst of his

Temple devotions.[a]

Meanwhile, the time drew near when the Messiah-to-be must himself be born. That the child might be born a girl never seems to have entered the Essenes' heads. The vision had been a true one and could therefore be trusted — such seems to have been their attitude. And the vision would therefore ensure the birth of the promised boy.

In the event, their expectations were not disappointed. Luck, or the Lord, was on their side. In the very last months of pregnancy the couple — who, after the Essene practice, had refrained from intercourse ever since conception had been confirmed[b] — were duly dispatched on the long and hazardous journey along rough roads to David's home-town of Bethlehem in Judea, in order that Micah's prophecy at 5:2 should be fulfilled and the child be seen to carry on the royal Davidic tradition.

Word has it that they had difficulty in finding accommodation there. In view of the almost universal Essene presence throughout Palestine, this seems an unlikely tale, even allowing for the secrecy which must have surrounded the plan. If the child was later said to have been born in a cave or stable, then it was presumably because the couple, following well-established Carmel practice, simply refused to inhabit any permanent building until the Kingdom should dawn.[c] Alternatively, the whole story may have arisen much later, out of the need that the child should be seen to measure up to the favourite Roman god Mithras, of whom the same tale was told. Even later stories of itinerant shepherds and astrologers likewise seem to have been borrowed from elsewhere — notably (and somewhat astonishingly) from the birth-story of the God-Emperor Nero himself.[42]

But the Essenes themselves had no need to measure up to such divine pretensions. The expected Messiah was to be a man, not a god. And so the young Miriam duly went into labour. The birth took place.

The longed-for boy was born.

---

[a] Mt. 23:35 [b] Mt. 1:24. According to Josephus, the Essene rules stipulated that sexual intercourse should be indulged in by members for procreative purposes only, with a view to producing youngsters to carry on the sect's traditions.[35] [c] Compare Jesus' own later claim, at Lk. 9:58, that he had 'nowhere to lay his head'.

8
The Jesus Initiative

With the birth of Jesus — the Greek form of his name by which, ironically, the latter day Joshua is usually known today — the prophetic blueprint drawn up by the Teacher of Righteousness could at last go into its next phase. No sooner had the news from Bethlehem reached the Essene headquarters on Carmel than a new and much larger force of pioneers — possibly including many of the leading Carmelites — set out southwards once more for the almost deserted monastery at Qumran, only sixteen miles from Bethlehem itself, in fulfilment of the words of Micah's Bethlehem-prophecy: 'Therefore only so long as a woman is in labour shall he give up Israel; and then those that survive of his race shall rejoin their brethren.'[a] There, led by elders who had been young men at the time of the great earthquake, they would (as archaeology reveals[51]) renovate the shattered buildings and restore the former strict monastic life amid the burning wilderness of the Dead Sea. By the same token, they would once again assume the semi-autonomous doctrinal status which had been accorded to the earlier community.

Within a few years, moreover, the young Forerunner Johanan — now known to us as John — would be sent southwards to join them. For it was at their hands that he would receive much of his education and the strict training that he would need for his future role. As Luke's gospel has it: 'As the child grew up he became strong in spirit; he lived out in the wilds until the day when he appeared publicly before Israel.'[b] John's task, after all, would be to personify the prophetic role which the Qumran community had already taken upon itself collectively. He it was who must personally embody Isaiah's 'voice that cries: "Prepare a road for the LORD through the wilderness, clear a highway across the desert for our God."'[c] It is scarcely surprising, therefore, that he is later recorded as acknowledging the fact.[d]

The details of his mission had, we may be sure, already been spelt out by the Teacher. At the appropriate time he must identify himself as Elijah by

[a] Mic. 5:3   [b] Lk. 1:80   [c] Isa. 40:3   [d] Jn. 1:23

adopting Elijah's outlandish garb of camel-hair tunic and leather belt. Long-haired and unshaven, he must proceed to Bethany (now Bethabara — 'fording place'), a spot on the east bank of the nearby Jordan opposite Jericho, and just above where the river finally emptied into the Dead Sea. This, after all, had been the site of Elijah's dramatic and legendary disappearance in a 'chariot of fire' some eight centuries before.[a] Thus doubly identified as 'Elijah returned', he must then proclaim the imminent appearance of the Messiah himself, at the same time offering the Essene sacrament of ritual ablution to the public at large, in symbol of the national repentance and regeneration that was to be an essential prerequisite for the subsequent dawning of the promised Kingdom. This sacrament of 'baptism', indeed, was a familiar ritual for foreigners wishing to become Jews, and was therefore (as the Essenes saw it) totally apt for a nation which had forsaken the very basis of its Jewishness — i.e. its special relationship with Yahweh, as enshrined in the Mosaic Covenant.

But there was to be even greater significance in John's mission of baptism. For the baptised converts must now, it seems, go on to ford the Jordan after the manner of the original entry into the Promised Land at the time of the Exodus. Passing over at what was in all probability the very same spot, the people, guided by John, would thus bring to its conclusion the great symbolic Exodus initiated by the original Essenes some two hundred years earlier. As they emerged dripping on the west bank, they would be acting out in symbol Israel's own final entry into the new Promised Land of the messianic Golden Age. And who could tell how far reality might not come to mirror that potent symbolism?

The people having passed over, the Messiah himself would follow in their footsteps and enter the new-found Kingdom whose foundations they had thus laid. As previously, however, there would be wars to be waged, campaigns to be fought, before the whole Kingdom was finally won. Yet after forty years of turmoil (the expectation of a culminating time of Divine wrath, originally dating from the earthquake of 31 BC, had clearly not yet been fulfilled in all its fury) the new leader's forces would be victorious over the powers of Darkness.

And so it was particularly apt that the infant leader's name, like that of his illustrious predecessor, had turned out to be Joshua.

It is possible that this 'coincidence', too, had been predetermined by the Teacher, as we suggested earlier. Consequently the fact that the name had also appeared in Miriam's vision may have been the very detail which had originally convinced the Essene elders of its Divine origin. The Teacher's detailed predictions were not, after all, noised abroad to all and sundry, least of all to mere temple-virgins scarcely into their teens. 'I will impart

a 2 Ki. 2:1-12

knowledge with discretion,' the Qumran scribe had written[a] — altering the earlier verb 'conceal' in token of what seems to have been a change of policy away from the earlier total secretiveness. But 'discretion' did not include 'casting pearls before swine', nor even giving dangerous, undiluted knowledge to the Essene uninitiated. And if the Essenes' children were to be schooled from their youth in the *Book of Meditation*, as the *Messianic Rule* required[51], then we may be sure that it was in carefully-rationed doses, as indeed the same Rule suggests.

The policy, moreover, seemed to have paid off. It had enabled the mother of the Messiah to be identified and matched. The child, in consequence, had duly been born according to the prophecies.

But the prophecies had not finished with him yet. Indeed, they had barely started. As he grew up, he was quickly to discover that he had, quite literally, a pre-ordained Messianic script to follow. His life, from womb to tomb, was already largely mapped out for him in all its daunting detail. The fact was constantly borne in on him, until he himself could not help but be totally convinced of it too. Indeed, he never tired in later life of reminding his followers that 'everything written about me in the Law of Moses and in the prophets and psalms must be fulfilled.'[b] 'My task is to bear witness to the truth,' he was eventually to tell the Roman Procurator on the day of his execution. 'For this was I born; for this I came into the world.'[c]

So clear, in fact, was the plan which now lay before him that it is still possible for us, some two thousand years later, to piece together the original blueprint arrived at by the Teacher, and updated by his successors, on the basis of the scriptures. Informed conjecture will, of course, have a role to play in eking out the surviving evidence, but not substantially more than is permissible in any court of law. With the model of the Dead Sea Scrolls before us, it will even be possible to set out the result in much the same way as it is likely to have appeared in the original *Hagu* document, the Essenes' much-revered *Book of Meditation* . . .

I will be his father, and he shall be my son.[d]

I will repeat the LORD*'s decree: 'You are my son,' he said; 'this day I become your father. Ask of me what you will: I will give you nations as your inheritance, the ends of the earth as your possession.'*[e]

And I will name him my first-born, highest among the kings of the earth.[f]

In such words King David, the original 'Anointed One' or Jewish King-Messiah, had been proclaimed by the scriptures 'son of God'. It followed,

---

[a] *Community Rule*, X[51] [b] Lk. 24:44[41] [c] Jn. 18:37 and compare Heb. 10:7 [d] 2 Sam. 7:14
[e] Ps. 2:7-8 [f] Ps. 89:27

therefore, that he would continue to fulfil that role when he returned to resume his messianic functions. The title 'the Messiah the son of God', consequently, seems already to have been current even before Jesus' time. Hence, he himself could legitimately refer to Yahweh by the familiar Aramaic term *Abba* (Papa)— just as the more pietistic of the northern Hasidim had long been prone to do — on the grounds that the scriptures meant exactly what they said.[53]

While the title 'son of God' was likewise applicable to Israel as a whole[a], it nevertheless implied (as Jesus himself was later to point out[b]) that its bearer or bearers had dedicated themselves totally to fulfilling the Divine will. To the extent that this was the case, Divine support would be forthcoming for everything undertaken in that role.

I called my son out of Egypt.[c]

The next text, originally applicable to the nation as a whole, could be seen as indicating that the Messiah-to-be must himself visit Egypt at an early stage. An obvious reason for the journey would be to acquire as much as possible of the wisdom of the Egyptian mystery-schools — much as Moses had apparently done before him[d] — which the Carmel Essenes seem to have held in great respect.[37] Numerous traditions and sources, indeed, insist that he was subsequently to visit Persia and India for the same reasons, and even China and Tibet.[37, 29] To this day his alleged 'tomb' is locally revered in Srinagar, Kashmir, and persistent legends also tell of a youthful visit to Glastonbury, in southwest England.

While such journeys were by no means impossible in Jesus' day (centuries-old trade-routes, for example, already connected Palestine with the orient) it is the possible underlying reasons for foreign travel by the Messiah-to-be that most closely concern us here. And the Dead Sea Scrolls confirm that, even at the Essenes' annual general meeting on the Feast of the Renewal of the Covenant (i.e. Pentecost), the Guardian in charge of the whole assembly was to be 'from thirty to fifty years old' and to be one who had 'mastered all the secrets of men and the languages of all their clans.'[e] If, then, such conditions applied to the mere temporary president of the Essenes' general assembly, how much more should they apply to the future Messiah, whose eventual role was to be a truly international one — namely that of everlasting World-King?

At the very least, then, a period in Egypt was called for as part of the Messiah's early training, since this would fully accord with the Mosaic precedent and the scriptural requirement that he should eventually return from there. The journey must therefore be duly arranged with the aid of the

---

[a] *Israel is my first-born son.* Ex. 4:23 [b] Jn. 8:37-47 [c] Hos. 11:1 [d] Compare the extra-biblical tradition quoted at Acts 7:22 [e] *Damascus Rule,* XIV[51]

various Essene communities that were already to be found en route and even within Egypt itself (cf. the celebrated Egyptian Contemplative Healers or *Theraputae*). Psychic sources maintain, meanwhile, that the youthful John the Baptist, too, was in due course to be sent on a similar course of instruction at the great Egyptian cult-centre of Heliopolis.[37]

In such activities, as the Essenes themselves must have realised, there were obvious dangers of doctrinal contamination. Yet such was their confidence in their early training of the two infant prodigies that they seem to have harboured few real fears in this regard. If what the Egyptians told them turned out to be true, then both youngsters would be sufficiently full of the spirit of Truth to recognise it as such; if false, then the fact would immediately become obvious to them. And in any case it seems clear that both would have been accompanied and advised by Essene guardians already skilled in the Hebrew esoteric teachings. The pre-eminent position of Yahweh, his special relationship with Israel and his revelation in scripture were thus in no sense threatened by the exercise.

Probably the least likely reason for the visit, however, was Herod's alleged 'massacre of the innocents' at Bethlehem. Herod, as we saw earlier, had already long been firmly associated in the public mind with the Pharaoh of the Oppression at the time of the original Exodus. It was natural, therefore, that a 'massacre of the firstborn' should be likewise attributed to him by later writers, with only the latter-day counterpart of Moses escaping as though by a miracle. But secular history knows of no such massacre, lovingly though it details Herod's other monstrous crimes.

In this case, then, we seem to have a case of 'wishful hindsight', where alleged facts have been invented purely in order to 'prove' an assumed prophetic antecedent. We shall in due course be going on to a separate consideration of such cases as they have come to affect the Jesus-story.

The LORD your God will raise up a prophet from among you like myself, and you shall listen to him.[a]

Look, I will send you the prophet Elijah before the great and terrible day of the LORD comes.[b]

There is a voice that cries: Prepare a road for the LORD through the wilderness, clear a highway across the desert for our God.[c]

All these predictions, starting with that of Moses, had been taken by the Teacher to refer to the Forerunner, to whose preparation for the role we have already referred. Following the intensive training of both young men, both at home and abroad, the Forerunner must be the first to put in an appearance. Identifying himself as Elijah both by his dress and by the site chosen for his

[a] Deut. 18:15   [b] Mal. 4:5   [c] Isa. 40:3

appearance, he must also take pains to be 'like Moses'. In other words, he must once again lay down the conditions of the ancient Mosaic Law, recall Israel to its long-forsaken Covenant and reinvoke the Divine promise to inaugurate a Golden Age provided it was observed. Moreover, in token of that national rededication, he must ritually purify as many of Israel as would follow him by immersing them in the Jordan, subsequently sending them ahead to establish a regenerate Israel in its ancient Promised Land — just as Moses, too, had sent his own people on ahead under Joshua while himself failing to make the final crossing.

At the appropriate moment, therefore, the Qumran community duly dispatched John to the nearby Jordan, dressed in the outlandish clothes of Elijah, and eating wild locusts and honey — both of them permissible items of Essene diet and mentioned either directly or by implication in their *Damascus Rule*.[a] His message, as recorded at Matthew 3:2, was indeed, 'Repent; for the kingdom of Heaven is upon you!' ('Heaven', 'Power' and 'the Blessed', it needs to be stressed, were among the contemporary euphemisms for 'Yahweh' — the Divine Name which the book of Leviticus forbade to be pronounced at all, on pain of death[b], and which the New English Bible regularly replaces by the expression 'the LORD' (sic)). And the devout of Judea, shocked out of their senses by the sudden apparition of this semi-legendary figure, whom they had long been taught to expect as the final sign that the Messiah himself was at hand, duly flocked to the Jordan for baptism.

Thus shall the glory of the LORD *be revealed, and all mankind together shall see it.*[c]

My servant Moses is dead; now it is for you to cross the Jordan, you and this whole people of Israel, to the land which I am giving them . . . as I was with Moses, so will I be with you; I will not fail you or forsake you. Be strong, be resolute . . . observe diligently all the law which my servant Moses has given you. . . This book of the law must ever be on your lips; you must keep it in mind day and night so that you may diligently observe all that is written in it. Then you will prosper and be successful in all that you do.[d]

The Divine commission originally given to Joshua, here preceded by the verse directly following the 'voice in the wilderness' prophecy, presumably indicated to the Teacher that the appearance of the Messiah-to-be must follow directly on the mission of the Forerunner, the 'prophet like Moses' with his call to repentance and his sacrament of ritual purification. The initial symbol of the Messiah's accession as King of Israel was to be his own crossing of the Jordan in the wake of the people who had gone on before. It followed, therefore, that he, too, must in the process undergo the Forerunner's sacrament of baptism, in token of the fact that, shaking off the alien influences

[a] *Damascus Rule*, XII[51]   [b] Lev. 24:16   [c] Isa. 40:5   [d] Josh. 1:2, 5-6, 7, 8

of his foreign travels, he had at last resumed the pure and uncontaminated Jewishness which was inseparable from the messianic role. Observing the Divine Law in its totality, he could thenceforth not fail to carry through his world-shaking mission to its triumphant conclusion.

David came to the throne at the age of thirty and reigned for forty years.[a]

Like David, then, the Messiah-to-be must take over his Kingdom at the age of thirty. And so, at the predicted time, he duly appeared.

Returning, perhaps, from his rumoured eastern travels[37] via the trade-route to Damascus, Jesus may first have called at Carmel, whose messengers to Qumran may subsequently have provided the original cue for the dispatching of John to the Jordan. Certainly a tradition persists to this day at Carmel that the returning Messiah and his family sheltered in Elijah's cave there on their way back from Egypt.[11] Alternatively, he may have taken the more direct eastern route via Gerasa and Philadelphia, whose Essene communities would likewise have eagerly sent ahead the news of his coming.

In the event, however, John was still overawed at the prospect of his final task. 'Do you come to me?' he said. 'I need rather to be baptised by you.'[b] The contradiction was obvious, for how was he to act as purifier to one who, by his own admission, was 'mightier than I' and whose shoes he was 'not fit to take off'?[c] Yet, once again, it was of overriding importance that the Teacher's blueprint be strictly observed. 'Let it be so for the present,' replied Jesus; 'we do well to conform in this way with all the God requires.'[d]

He shall appear and be their shepherd in the strength of the LORD, *in the majesty of the name of the* LORD *his God. And they shall continue, for now his greatness shall reach to the ends of the earth; and he shall be a man of peace.*[e]

This direct sequel to the Bethlehem-prophecy, with its close associations with the Qumran initiative, indicated to the Teacher that the newly-proclaimed Messiah must next proceed directly to the nearby desert-community by the Dead Sea, which would go on to flourish as never before under his leadership. And at a later date he would take the sectaries with him when, resuming his symbolic inaugural journey at Jericho, he undertook his final, triumphal progress to Jerusalem to take over the promised Kingdom and assume the regal responsibilities of world power.

But at this point there seems to have been a hitch in the arrangements. As we saw earlier, the Teacher's view of the role of the Messiah-to-be, as reflected in the original *Damascus Rule*, was that it would be an essentially dual one. He must embody the functions both of Priest-Messiah (the Messiah ben Aaron)

---

[a] 2 Sam. 5:4   [b] Mt. 3:14   [c] Mt. 3:11   [d] Mt. 3:15   [e] Mic. 5:4-5

and of King-Messiah (the Messiah ben Israel). Hence the text's repeated reference to the 'Messiah of Aaron and Israel' *in the singular*.[51]

Thanks to the doctrinal autonomy granted to the Qumran community, however, a new doctrine seems belatedly to have sprung up by the shores of the Dead Sea, possibly under Pharisaic influence. Indeed, it may even have spread back as far as Carmel during Jesus' long absence abroad, so that Jesus was now doctrinally in a minority — and possibly one of the few Essenes totally faithful to the Teacher's original blueprint.

This new doctrine, reflected in the Qumran *Community Rule*[a], took the view that there would in fact be two separate Messiahs — the priestly Messiah ben Aaron and the kingly Messiah ben Israel. The question therefore arose as to which was to be the superior. Among the priest-dominated Qumran Essenes, there was never much room for doubt. But, just in case, there was always their own autonomous scriptural exegesis to fall back on.

So the people set out from their tents to cross the Jordan, with the [priests] in front of them carrying the Ark of the Covenant.[b]

Here it was clear from the original Exodus-account that the priests had taken precedence over all the people — including Joshua himself — during the final crossing into the Promised Land. It was their symbolic acceptance of the burden of the Covenant — i.e. their shouldering of the sacred coffer containing its terms laboriously engraved in stone — that had held back the waters of destruction and made the whole operation possible in the first place.

Yet, a further fact seems to have escaped the Essene interpreters.

The priests carrying the Ark of the Covenant of the LORD *stood firm on the dry bed in the middle of the Jordan; and all Israel passed over on dry ground until the whole nation had crossed the river.*[c]

The priests, in other words, may have initiated the crossing, but thereafter their role had been merely to act as a catalyst. The people had actually entered the Kingdom before them. This fact, accordingly, could be taken to mean that, initially, the role of the Priest-Messiah must precede that of King-Messiah; but that that precedence was to be a matter of time rather than degree.

However, the Qumran elders had a further scriptural proof-text up their sleeves.

He shall not judge by what he sees nor decide by what he hears.[d]

---

[a] The surviving copies of the *Community Rule* are, in fact, as old as those of the *Damascus Rule*.[52] Sheer geographical logic would suggest, however, that the latter was composed first, and that the original copies of it taken to Qumran were eventually replaced somewhat late in the day because they had simply worn out after decades of use.   [b] Josh. 3:14   [c] Josh. 3:17   [d] Isa. 11:3

So Isaiah had foretold, and in this case we have, recorded in the Qumran Isaiah commentary, the actual words in which the Essenes explained this prediction. 'Interpreted, this means that . . . [the priests] . . . As they teach him, so will he judge; and as they order, [so will he pass sentence].'[51]

The Essene priesthood, then, was to exercise a collective supervision over the King-Messiah, and so it went almost without saying that the Priest-Messiah must be the senior of the two. Nevertheless, it *was* said, just in case there should be any doubt about it. In the *Messianic Rule*—an appendix to the Qumran *Community Rule* — we find an account of the sect's sacred meal (evidently a symbolic anticipation of the eventual Messianic Banquet in the promised New Kingdom) which includes the passage: 'And when they shall gather for the common [tab]le, to eat and [to drink] new wine[a], when the common table shall be set for eating and the new wine [poured] for drinking, let no man extend his hand over the first-fruits of bread and wine before the Priest; for [it is he] who shall bless the first-fruits of bread and wine, and shall be the first to extend his hand over the bread. Thereafter, the Messiah of Israel shall extend his hand over the bread, [and] all the Congregation of the Community [shall utter a] blessing, [each man in the order] of his dignity.'[51]

The precedence, then, was clearly established. The Davidic Messiah might be Israel's mighty secular ruler, but in all things ritual and doctrinal — which meant, of course, in all the principles which were to guide his every action — he must defer to the judgement of the Priest-Messiah.

But in this case there were two messianic roles to fill, and only two suitably-trained men to fill them. Moreover, if Jesus was truly David returned, then his role clearly had to be the kingly one. The priestly role must therefore be filled by John who, as the reborn Elijah, could at least claim totally priestly antecedents. For not only was John physically of priestly stock; Elijah, his spiritual *alter ego*, was widely held to have been a priest, too.

The Essenes' own nomenclature backed up the conclusion with singular aptness. The *Community Rule*, founding charter of the priestly Qumran establishment, had, after all, dubbed the monastery itself 'a Most Holy Dwelling for Aaron'[b], and it followed that John, or any other messianic figure produced by it would, almost by definition, be the 'Messiah ben Aaron' anticipated by the same scroll.

But who, in that case, was to fulfil the role of the Prophet? Here, the sectaries' excessive reverence for their former Teacher of Righteousness seems to have played a vital part. For there is evidence in the scrolls that the Teacher himself was latterly regarded by the Qumran Essenes as the prophet foretold by Moses. He, after all, had clearly initiated a new Exodus, reiterated and reinforced the Mosaic Law and re-established the Divine Covenant on

---

[a] Among the abstemious Qumran Essenes, this was probably grape-juice. [b] *Community Rule*, VIII[51]

Carmel. In all these respects, he had certainly acted as 'a second Moses'.

He shall convey all my commands to them, and if anyone does not listen to the words which he will speak in my name I will require satisfaction from him.[a]

This further verse from the Deuteronomy 'prophet'-prediction, actually quoted in the Qumran *Messianic Anthology*, merely added fuel to the Essenes' conviction that the Teacher — who had clearly fulfilled the role here described — had indeed been the expected prophet. John, as Elijah returned, was therefore the fore-ordained Priest-Messiah, with Jesus his spiritual subordinate, the Messiah ben Israel.

We do not know at exactly what stage this doctrinal change of mind occurred. To judge by John's own evident confusion on the topic, it may, in the event, have been very much a last-minute decision. Questioned by representatives from Jerusalem on the matter, his answers seem to have been somewhat unclear. No, he was not the Prophet; yes, he was Elijah; no, he was not the expected messianic King. Pardonably, perhaps, his Pharisaic investigators, themselves profoundly convinced that Elijah and the Prophet were meant to be one and the same, seem to have finished up unsure as to quite what he *had* said. Not the Prophet, certainly; therefore, presumably, not Elijah, despite his ridiculous attire and the site of his ministry; yet not the King-Messiah either.[b] No wonder that they subsequently left him alone as some sort of deluded maniac.

To Jesus, however, unfamiliar with the evident doctrinal U-turn, there was no cause whatever for confusion. He himself was the predicted Messiah of Aaron *and* Israel, the ultimate Priest-King. John was merely the predicted Prophet, the reborn Elijah, whose effective role was now over. And now the Messiah must join his brethren at Qumran in accordance with the Teacher's blueprint, there to rest and meditate and plan the last-minute details of his long-predicted mission.

To start with, then, he must go into the wilderness.

Whether his stay at Qumran lasted a full forty days, or whether the idea was merely a later borrowing from the forty days spent by Moses on Mount Sinai, we shall probably never know. But what seems to have broken out next was an almighty row with the Essene camp. So bitter was the argument that the Qumran sectaries, it seems, were subsequently cast by the gospel-writers in the role of Satan himself. 'You are the King-Messiah,' they seem to have said. 'Now demonstrate your miraculous powers before the people, either here or in Jerusalem, and they will flock to your banner.'[c]

Jesus violently demurred. It was not a matter of performing miracles, he insisted, but of fulfilling all the words of the scriptures. And, in particular,

---

[a] Deut. 18:19   [b] Compare the account at Jn. 1:19-28   [c] Compare the account of the semi-legendary 'temptations in the wilderness' at Mt. 4:1-10.

there was the prophesied role of the Priest-Messiah to fulfil, with all the suffering and self-sacrifice which that must entail, before he could finally take over the reins of the Kingdom.

'You have no need to worry,' they seem to have replied. 'Our pupil John has taken over that role. All you have to do is set in motion your armed revolt, and then, once the Romans have been expelled, take over the reins of government. Do as we say and in no time the whole world will be yours.'

But behind all the argument and persuasion, Jesus could detect a more sinister development. Passionately though they might quote at him the familiar words *He shall not judge by what he sees nor decide by what he hears*[a] in support of their new thesis of priestly supremacy, an ulterior motive, no doubt unsuspected by the sectaries themselves, had started to show glaringly through the rhetoric. For if the King-Messiah were to be governed by the Essene priesthood through the medium of the Priest-Messiah, then the Qumran elders would effectively be governing the Kingdom themselves. What underlay the argument, in other words, was a scarcely-concealed bid for personal power. Echoes of it still come down to us in the later squabbles among his followers about which of them was to have precedence under the new messianic regime.[b]

No doubt the pious sectaries were unaware of what was really motivating them. They would probably have been shocked and affronted had anybody pointed it out to them. Possibly Jesus did, and if so it would have taken a long time for tempers to cool and ruffled pietistic feathers to be smoothed down. Yet there was no possibility of compromise. Jesus pointed out in no uncertain terms that he had, with clear, Divine approval, been given a dual role to fulfil — first as Priest, then as King — and that, by hook or by crook, he was going to fulfil it. There was no way in which he was prepared to fit in with the sectaries' plans and become a half-Messiah working in tandem with John. And no doubt he used the words then which he was later to repeat, in the light of bitter experience, on another occasion: 'No servant can be the slave of two masters.'[c]

The sectaries were thrown into confusion by his reaction. If Jesus refused to co-operate, then their plan would clearly come to nought. Yet they passionately believed that it had been sanctioned by their own Divine intuition. It could not be wrong. And consequently there could be only one possible conclusion. Jesus was, after all, a renegade, a false Messiah. Until they decided what should be done with him, he must be separated from the sacred community — even, perhaps, confined to a separate outbuilding or remote cave.

Possibly, in the event, it was the best thing for both parties. Among the leading sectaries, passions could be given a chance to cool. For Jesus, it

---

[a] Isa. 11:3   [b] Mt. 20:20-28, Lk. 22:24-30   [c] Mt. 6:24

offered an opportunity to rest after his travels, to recover from the shock of having his very *raison d'être* questioned and undermined by those who should have been his chief friends and supporters. There in his temporary quarters he had time to think, to meditate and to pray.

And if 'angels appeared and waited on him', as Matthew 4:11 suggests, then we may be sure that they were clothed in the white robes of the Essenic lower orders.[a]

In due course, the time came for Jesus to leave. His mission was calling him. And that, as ever, was clearly spelt out in the blueprint drawn up by the Teacher of Righteousness nearly two centuries before.

Then a shoot shall grow from the stock of Jesse, and a branch shall spring from his roots. The spirit of the LORD *shall rest upon him, a spirit of wisdom and understanding, a spirit of counsel and power, a spirit of knowledge and the fear of the* LORD.[b]

That spirit he had already been called upon to display in abundance. As for the next verse, by now something of a sore point with him:

He shall not judge by what he sees, nor decide by what he hears.[c]

this merely indicated that, as Priest-Messiah, it would not be for him to set the world to rights. Only in his later role as King would such matters come into consideration. The Hebrew poetic habit of saying everything twice, in different words, did not necessarily mean that the 'shoot' and the 'branch' were to be regarded as separate figures entirely. And so when the kingly role was next foreshadowed:

He shall judge the poor with justice and defend the humble in the land with equity; his mouth shall be a rod to strike down the ruthless, and with a word he shall slay the wicked . . . Then the wolf shall live with the sheep, and the leopard lie down with the kid . . .[d]

the familiar pairs of poetic statements were likewise to be seen as direct references to himself, but in his later, Davidic capacity, as ruler of the new, ideal World Order. The contradiction, in short, was more apparent than real.

First, then, the priestly role had to be fulfilled. And the specification for it was already clear.

The spirit of the LORD *God is upon me because the* LORD *has anointed me; he has sent me to bring good news to the humble, to bind up the broken-hearted, to proclaim liberty to captives and release to those in prison; to proclaim a year of the*

---

[a] Gk. *aggelos* = 'messenger' [b] Isa. 11:1-2 [c] Isa. 11:3 [b] Isa. 11:4, 6

LORD's *favour and a day of the vengeance of our God . . .*[a]

Shout aloud without restraint; lift up your voice like a trumpet. Call my people to account for their transgression and the house of Jacob for their sins.[b]

Proclaiming the coming Kingdom was clearly the first priority. It was a message of shining hope. Israel would soon be released from its foreign domination, as well as from the misrule of its priestly aristocracy. But all this would be dependent, not just on crude violence and rebellion, but on a total reform of the nation. The Law must be obeyed, the Covenant re-invoked.

This, then, was to be the message. No longer, as under the strict Essene dispensation, was it to be a case of keeping the truth quiet, as if it were a kind of privilege reserved for the Elect Few. True, as the first text suggested, the good news must first be proclaimed to 'the humble' — a term which was habitually interpreted by the Essenes as referring to themselves. But then the good tidings must be proclaimed to all and sundry — the 'captives' and 'those in prison' — in token of the fact that the last chance had come for those who had gone astray to see the light. As many as possible of the populace had to be drawn within the fold of righteousness before the night of terror and darkness descended which must precede the miraculous new dawn.

Many have seen this realisation — enthusiastically espoused by Jesus — as if it were in some way contrary to Essene doctrine. But the evidence shows clearly that even the strict Qumran sectaries had started to move slowly in this direction. Thus, the *Community Rule*'s original insistence that the sect's leader 'shall conceal the teaching of the Law from men of falsehood, but shall impart true knowledge and righteous judgement to those who have chosen the Way'[c] was softened by later copyists within the community, who substituted for the next column's 'I will conceal knowledge with discretion' the phrase 'I will *impart* knowledge with discretion.' 'And (I) will prudently hedge it within a firm bound,' the text goes on; 'I will distribute the Precept by the measuring-cord of the times, and . . . righteousness and lovingkindness towards the oppressed, encouragement to the troubled heart and discernment to the erring spirit . . .'[d]

That was precisely what Jesus set out to do by clothing his teachings on the coming Kingdom in parables and allegories so that only those with ears for his message might hear it. In this way, all who were ready for the necessary transformation could finally be gathered into the fold.

I will search for the lost, recover the straggler, bandage the hurt, strengthen the sick, leave the healthy and strong to play, and give them their proper food . . . I will save my flock, and they shall be ravaged no more; I will judge between one sheep and another. Then I will set over them one shepherd to take care of them, my servant David; he shall care for them and become their shepherd. I, the LORD, will become their

---

a Isa. 61:1-2 *b* Isa. 58:1 *c Community Rule*, IX[51] *d Community Rule*, X-XI[51]

God, and my servant David shall be a prince among them. . . . I will make a covenant with them to ensure prosperity.[a]

Pursuing the farming analogy, then, Jesus must become a shepherd to his flock. He must search for the stragglers, play a healing role, promote and assess their spiritual progress. And only then would he become 'a prince among them', the Davidic King-Messiah, and the age of the New Covenant be finally ushered in.

First, then, find your sheep.

Among the Qumran Essenes, it was evident, supporters were unlikely to be immediately forthcoming. He was going to have to find most of his friends among the less opinionated Essenes of the towns and villages. New 'fishers of men' would have to be found to fulfil Ezekiel's Dead Sea vision at 47:10, and this might take some time. Some of them actually turned out, in the end, to be fishermen by trade. There were also a handful of John's original followers, the odd Zealot or religious freedom-fighter, even a reformed tax-collector. The group itself, after all, must reflect the broad, redemptive character of the mission as a whole. Eventually Jesus was to weld it into a close-knit community whose members, like the Qumran sectaries, sold all their possessions and donated the proceeds to the group's treasurer for the communal benefit. In effect, they had made themselves 'poor' for the sake of the coming Kingdom, and consequently were prone, like later groups of the same type, to refer to themselves as 'the poor' (*ebionim*). 'If you wish to go the whole way,' said Jesus to a would-be follower, 'go, sell your possessions, and give to the Poor, and then you will have riches in heaven; and come, follow me.'[b] But it was a big, almost total commitment, and not everybody was prepared to take it up, despite the Psalmist's promise that the Humble — i.e. as latterly interpreted, the Essenes — would eventually inherit the earth.[c]

Choose twelve men from the tribes of Israel, one man from each tribe.[d]

Such had been the command of the original Joshua, and on this basis his latter-day counterpart and namesake was finally to assemble his support-group. The same tradition underlay the provision of the Qumran *Community Rule* that the sect's governing council should contain twelve lay members.[e] Yet, following the same source, the group should have been headed by three priests. Of these, Jesus, as Priest-Messiah, would clearly have been one. And indeed, as we shall see, there are hints in the surviving literature of two other shadowy priest-figures hovering in the background — Jacob (James), the widely-revered Nazirite and younger brother of Jesus, surnamed The Just; and John the Priest, the influential host of the Last

---

[a] Ez. 34:16, 22-25   [b] Mt. 19:21-22   [c] Ps. 37:11   [d] Josh. 3:12   [e] *Community Rule*, VIII[51]

Supper, whom the fourth gospel calls the Beloved Disciple.[42]

Yet all this still lay in the future. Before Jesus could embark on the formation of his inner cell of supporters, he needed some clear indication of where his mission was to begin. And this, too, had almost certainly been deduced by the Teacher from the biblical prophecies.

For, while the first invader has dealt lightly with the land of Zebulun and the land of Naphtali, the second has dealt heavily with Galilee of the Nations on the road beyond Jordan to the sea.

The people who walked in darkness have seen a great light: light has dawned upon them, dwellers in a land as dark as death. Thou hast increased their joy and given them great gladness; they rejoice in thy presence as men rejoice at harvest . . .[a]

The messianic presence, then, must first be felt amid the 'darkness' of the far north, where there was already much sympathy for the cause and a strong Essenic movement to back it up. For Zebulun took in most of northern Galilee, and Naphtali embraced part of Syria beyond. The territories mentioned thus bordered the very centre of the movement itself, namely Mount Carmel. Here was where he would find most of his potential followers.

It was northwards, then, that Jesus must now direct his steps in order to assemble his 'inner cabinet'. There they must help him proclaim his vital message — his 'gospel' or Good News — and so prepare the ground for Jesus the Priest-Messiah to bring his mission to its long-predicted culmination. Then, and only then, could the rest of Isaiah's just-quoted prophecy at last be fulfilled:

For a boy has been born for us, a son given to us to bear the symbol of dominion on his shoulder; and he shall be called in purpose wonderful, in battle God-like, Father for all time, Prince of Peace. Great shall the dominion be, and boundless the peace bestowed on David's throne and on his kingdom, to establish it and sustain it with justice and righteousness from now and for evermore. The zeal of the LORD *of Hosts shall do this.[b]*

[a] Isa. 9:1-3   [b] Isa. 9:6-7

9
Conflicting Testimonies

The accounts that have come down to us reveal in a myriad incidental details the basically Essenic nature of Jesus' life and teaching during the three years or so which now remained to him. Even ignoring the clear indications of his northern sectarian origins, and his manifest determination to fulfil all the Law and the Prophets after the familiar manner of the Essenes, the picture is unmistakable. It is of a particularly charismatic Hasid, an itinerant Galilean preacher ('Galilean' and 'itinerant preacher' were virtual synonyms in contemporary Judean parlance) moving easily with his cell of supporters from town to town, taking with him nothing but the clothes he stood up in, and refusing point blank to touch, handle or have anything to do with money. When asked to adjudicate on the payment of Roman taxes, for example, he actually has to ask someone else to produce a humble *denarius*.[a] These facts alone are enough to point a strong finger of probability towards an Essenic identity. For only among the Essenes, with their widespread town-communities, each with its guest-master appointed specifically to minister to the needs of the sect's itinerants, was such an existence even remotely possible.

Then there is the question of Jesus' apparent celibacy. For a man to be still unmarried at the age of thirty was regarded as highly abnormal in contemporary Jewish society. Refusal to obey Yahweh's primordial command to 'be fruitful and increase'[b] was, in the eyes of the influential Pharisees, tantamount to murder. In the light of this fact, and Jesus' frequent castigation of Pharisaic smugness and sanctimoniousness, the view some-time advanced that he might himself have been a Pharisee[7] just refuses to stand up to serious examination.

Among the Essene monastics, however, celibacy had long since become a respected, even revered way of life. Not only did the resultant ritual purity assure instant priestly readiness for any eventuality, however apocalyptic: it

a Mk. 12:15   b Gen. 9:1

also constituted, as the Essenes saw it, a perpetual sacrifice on behalf of Israel, a constant invocation of the terms of the Covenant with Yahweh, a guarantee, as it were, to deliver the messianic goods. As Jesus himself was to put it, 'There are others who have themselves renounced marriage for the sake of the kingdom of Heaven. Let those accept it who can.'[a]

In Jesus' case, moreover, celibacy had a particular aptness. He was, after all, the Priest-Messiah. His sole and overriding function at this stage was active priesthood. It behoved him, therefore, to maintain the ritual purity demanded of any duty-priest. But in addition, the Essene Teacher of Righteousness's original blueprint had revealed that the Priest-Messiah's *raison d'être* was to be not a whole lifetime of leadership, but a short period of teaching and proclamation of the Kingdom, followed by a dramatic act of national atonement. His life, as we shall see, would have no other purpose than to permit him to preach, to be rejected, to suffer and to be condemned to death. The Priest-Messiah would have no future. His mission must last no longer than was absolutely necessary to fulfil the relevant prophecies. Hence, in the event, its extraordinary briefness.

It was as King-Messiah that he was expected, after his survival of death, to live for evermore. That, in consequence, would be the time to take a wife, as David had done before him.[b] But until that time, celibacy must be the order of the day. His Kingdom, as Jesus himself was to point out, was 'not of this world'; it did not belong, in other words, to the pre-millennial dispensation at all.[c]

Other details, meanwhile, less specifically Essenic, nevertheless help to fill in our picture of Jesus the Essene. His evident addiction to praying and meditating on hilltops finds strong echoes in the story of the Mosaic Exodus, whose symbolism was to figure so strongly in Essenic thinking. His conviction that he was not strictly liable to the annual half-shekel Temple tax[d] accords with the Essenes' own view that the tax as originally instituted[e] envisaged a single down-payment for life. His insistence that social precedence in the coming Kingdom had 'already been assigned'[f] squares totally with the Essenes' strict hierarchical outlook. And by his constant use of parable to mask his teachings on the coming Kingdom he not only avoided incriminating himself with the suspicious Roman authorities; he also neatly satisfied the prophetic requirement that the good news be preached to the humble, and succour brought to the broken-hearted, the captive and the prisoner,[g] while deferring to the still-developing Essene conviction that knowledge might be imparted 'with discretion'.[h] He could even justify the

---

[a] Mt. 19:12   [b] Compare Ps. 45:9   [c] Compare Schonfield's footnote to Jn. 18:36.[41] The other-worldly spirituality commonly read into this statement is, of course, purely the result of seeing it through the stained glass of much later Christian theology.   [d] Mt. 17:26   [e] Ex. 30:13   [f] Mk. 10:40: the words 'by my Father', found at Mt. 20:23, are an obvious later addition.   [g] Isa. 61:1-2   [h] *Community Rule*, X[51]

process in scripture: 'I will open my mouth in a parable,' the Psalmist had declared, no doubt prefiguring the coming Messiah: 'I will utter dark sayings of old.'[a] As a result, the truth would still be hidden from 'men of falsehood', as the Essenes' *Community Rule* required, while 'true knowledge and righteous judgement' would be imparted to 'those who have chosen the Way.'[b]

And so Jesus, explaining to his disciples why he teaches in parables or riddles, declares that it is because 'It has been granted to you to know the secrets of the kingdom of Heaven; but to those others it has not been granted.'[c] Knowledge, in other words, would come only to those who already knew subconsciously, salvation only to those for whom Yahweh had already pre-ordained it from even before time began — and this doctrine of pre-election and Divine grace is likewise prominent in the Qumran literature, and especially the thanksgiving *Hymns*.[d]

But these are not the only doctrinal similarities. Jesus, like the Essenes, imposes a strict ban on the swearing of oaths by anything holy.[e] Indeed, he goes further: 'Plain "Yes" or "No" is all you need to say',[f] he declares. Quoting the commandment 'Love your neighbour, hate your enemy', he substitutes, 'Love your enemies and pray for your persecutors,'[g] yet omits to point out that the supposed commandment is not part of scripture, but apparently derives from the Qumran *Community Rule*, which lays down that members shall 'love all the sons of light, and hate all the sons of darkness.'[h] Again, his exhortation to 'Do good to those who hate you'[i] mirrors exactly the *Community Rule*'s 'I will pay to no man the reward of evil; I will pursue him with goodness.'[j]

On the question of personal disputes, Jesus lays down that the plaintiff should first take up the point at issue with the person concerned, then in front of witnesses, and only then before the local community.[k] The self-same procedure is advocated by the *Community Rule*.[l] Meanwhile Jesus' quotation of the Divine promise 'Where two or three have met together in my name, I am there among them,'[m] appears to derive from an already long-established Jewish tradition — particularly relevant to the Essene communities — that, in doctrinal matters, a democratic decision automatically reflects the will of God.

There are further similarities. Jesus counsels his followers to sell their possessions and donate the proceeds to 'the Poor' (i.e. the sect itself)[n] — a practice known to have been continued by the Nazarenes after his death:[o] the monastic Essenes followed the same procedure.[l] He likens those who put the coming Kingdom before all other considerations to a man who builds his

[a] Ps. 78:2 (A.V.)   [b] *Community Rule*, IX[51]   [c] Mt. 13:11   [d] Compare, for example, *Hymn* 22.[51]   [e] Mt. 5:33-37; *Damascus Rule*, XV[51]   [f] Mt. 5:37   [g] Mt. 5:43   [h] *Community Rule*, I[51]   [i] Lk. 6:27   [j] *Community Rule*, X[51]   [k] Mt. 18:15-17   [l] *Community Rule*, V-VI[51]   [m] Mt. 18:19-20   [n] Mt. 19:21   [o] Acts 2:44-45, 4:32

house on solid rock:[a] the author of the Qumran Hymn-scroll uses the same imagery.[b] Just as Jesus sees it as his function to atone for Israel's apostasy through his own suffering[c], so the Qumran scribes saw their own purpose in the same light.[d] And Jesus expects his followers to be able eventually to combine the received scriptural wisdom with new, intuitively-inspired interpretation[e] — a practice which we have already seen to be typical of the Essenes' Teacher of Righteousness and his successors.

Then again, Jesus' attitude towards John the Baptist gives clear indications of where his true sympathies lay. John, he insisted, was 'the destined Elijah, if you will but accept it.'[f] The Law and the Prophets had foretold events right up until his coming — the two collections of scripture actually ended, as we have seen, with Malachi's 'Elijah' prophecy — and now 'violent men' were taking the Kingdom of Heaven by storm.[g] The phrase suggests inside knowledge of a deliberate plan to 'force' the coming of the Kingdom — which is likely only if Jesus himself were, like John, secretly party to it. Indeed, the ensuing phrase, 'If you have ears, then hear,'[h] gives precisely the impression of a withheld secret. And such a plan, as we have seen, bore clear Essenic trademarks — not least in the attitude to prophecy which it revealed.

Meanwhile, John himself seemed less sure of Jesus' credentials. Evidently bewildered by Jesus' refusal to launch directly into the kingly role assigned to him by the Qumran leadership, the now-imprisoned Baptist — presumably convinced that he himself was in the process of undergoing the self-instigated suffering and condemnation prophesied for the Priest-Messiah[i] — sent to him with the question 'Are you the one who is to come, or are we to expect some other?'[j] Inviting the messengers to use their own eyes and ears, Jesus apparently commented that John, for all the undoubted importance of the role he had played, had nevertheless fallen short of the minimum qualifications for entry into the expected Kingdom.[k] And in his reply we may sense the internal friction which was still, it seems, renting asunder the Essene cause.

Perhaps the strongest evidence of Jesus' Essene way of life, however, derives from the calendar which he evidently followed. For one of the curiosities which have long puzzled biblical commentators has been the problem of how Jesus managed to celebrate his final Passover with his disciples *some days before* the official festival — by which time Jesus himself was, by most accounts, already dead and buried. The fact that the Essenes' Passover, as we have already noted, always fell on a Tuesday/Wednesday, neatly resolves the whole issue. In the year in question, in fact, the Essene

---

[a] Mt. 7:24-27 [b] Hymn 10[51] [c] Mt. 20:28 [d] Community Rule, V, VIII, IX, Hymn 9[51]
[e] Mt. 13:52 [f] Mt. 11:13-14 [g] Mt. 11:12 [h] Mt. 11:15 [i] John had already virtually ensured his own martyrdom by condemning, as contrary to the Law, the remarriage of the Tetrarch Herod Antipas to his brother's wife — a view totally in accord with Essene teaching (compare Mt. 5:31-32). [j] Mt. 11:3 [k] Mt. 11:11

festival celebrated by Jesus and his followers preceded the official one by three days — ample time for the dramatic events of what is nowadays known as the Passion to supervene.

It would follow, incidentally, that the household in which that final communal meal took place — with all its obvious similarities to the sacred meal celebrated at Qumran[a] — must, similarly, have been an Essene household, and thus one of the Essenes' own town-communities (presumably the all-male one at Jerusalem already referred to).

In the light of all the circumstantial evidence, it at last starts to become clear whom Jesus was addressing in the collection of sayings now known as the 'Sermon on the Mount'. Paradoxically placed by Luke at the bottom of a hill,[b] but more probably assembled over a number of months, in any case, by fellow-members of Jesus' group, it recounts the blessings that awaited the poor in spirit, the sorrowful, the gentle, those who hungered and thirsted for righteousness, the merciful, the pure in heart, the peacemakers, the persecuted, the scorned, the salt of the earth and the light of the world. Consoled, satisfied, pardoned and 'numbered among the sons of God', they would finally inherit the earth and see the Kingdom of Heaven.[c]

The conclusion is virtually inevitable. For such were the terms in which the Essenes, on the evidence of the Scrolls, habitually saw *themselves*.[d]

As against all these considerations there are some strange anomalies. As those who remain unconvinced of Jesus' Essenism are quick to point out, his conduct was often far from typical of what we should expect of a Qumran sectary. Not only did he apparently mingle with all and sundry; the records suggest that he associated with immoral women, actually ate and drank with tax-gatherers and others who were regarded as betrayers of the Law — without even washing his hands before eating, at that — allegedly plucked corn and healed the sick on the Sabbath and, worst of all, revealed the secrets of the coming Kingdom to beggars, outcasts and the ordinary man in the street.

Regarding the last charge, we have already seen how Jesus, by clothing his teaching in riddles and parables, actually managed to combine observance of the Essene rules on secrecy with the prophetic requirement that the news of the Kingdom be preached to Israel at large. Just such a mission had been proclaimed by Yahweh at Isaiah 40:9-11, and again at Ezekiel 34:15-16 and elsewhere, and had thus, in all probability, found its way into the Teacher's blueprint. *I myself will tend my flock, I myself pen them in my fold*, the latter text had announced: *I will search for the lost, recover the straggler, bandage the hurt,*

---

[a] Compare Mt. 26:26-29 with *Community Rule*, VI and *Messianic Rule*, II.[51]   [b] Luke 6:17
[c] Mt. 5:3-16   [d] Compare, for example, *Hymn* 9.[51]

strengthen the sick, leave the healthy and strong to play, and give them their proper food. Jesus, as Yahweh's earthly representative, must clearly do his utmost to see to it that these conditions were fulfilled — and his words testify repeatedly to his awareness of Ezekiel's imagery at this point, as itself prefigured in the passage from Isaiah.

Not that Jesus always taught in parables, however. Indeed, he often taught his own followers in plain speech, and also felt free to decipher his parables for them. But it seems reasonable to take with a pinch of salt the gospel-suggestions that he habitually offered 'sacred' teachings to the public at large. The existing gospel-accounts, it should be remembered, were not written down until many years after Jesus' death. Apparently based, in part, upon simple collections of Jesus' sayings taken largely out of context[a], and demonstrably subject to free interpolation and editing, we should therefore not expect them to reflect accurately the exact circumstances under which every statement was made. A more reliable index of Jesus' view on the dissemination of 'sacred doctrines' might be his own reported words on the matter: 'Do not give dogs what is holy: do not throw your pearls to the pigs: they will only trample on them, and turn and tear you to pieces.'[b] And be it noted that this admonition is part of the celebrated 'Sermon on the Mount', which we have already identified as for specifically Essene consumption, and which the gospel-reports themselves describe as having been delivered by Jesus to his own coterie of disciples.

One important result of Jesus' public use of allegory and generalised language, interestingly enough, was that many of his teachings in due course took on an aura of universality which was to add immeasurably to his stature as a world religious teacher. Cryptic statements and admonitions originally intended to apply to the specific circumstances of first-century Roman-occupied Palestine could be taken out of context to refer to situations and levels of experience which were, in all probability, far from Jesus' conscious mind when he first uttered them, as certain features of his terminology suggest.[42] Such appeals to avoid violent confrontation with the occupation-troops as 'If someone slaps you on your right cheek, turn and offer him your left'[c] have come to be taken as general ideals of conduct rather than instructions for passive resistance. The exhortation to abandon personal involvement in the contemporary money-economy and to join a sharing Essene community[d] has become transmuted into a piece of homely wisdom about relinquishing possessions and trusting to the universe to provide. And his attempt to point out that the promised Kingdom was within his contemporaries' very grasp, if only they cared to take it,[e] has come to be interpreted as a sublime affirmation of inner divinity within the heart of everyman.

---

[a] Compare, for example, the conflicting settings of the 'Sermon on the Mount' referred to above.   [b] Mt. 7:6   [c] Mt. 5:39   [d] Mt. 6:19-34   [e] Lk. 17:21

Against the charge of 'spilling the Essene beans', however, we can probably absolve both Jesus and his immediate followers. True, there does seem to have been something of a shift of emphasis during the course of his ministry. Possibly we can trace this to the return-visit by Jesus to his home-community of 'Nazarenes' on Carmel recounted by Luke at 4:14-30. Conceivably the movement's mountain-headquarters was his first port of call on reaching northern Palestine after his contretemps with the Qumran Essenes. At the Sabbath assembly (for the Essenes, like the Pharisees, had their synagogues, or assemblies) the assembled sectaries, it seems, handed him the Isaiah scroll and invited him to read aloud from it. By his choice of text, and his reaction to it, they evidently hoped that the returned prodigal would assure them that he had at last come to his senses and accepted the new, exclusive, kingly role that had been mapped out for him. But in the event he chose the messianic text already cited from the beginning of chapter 61 (here badly misquoted by Luke): 'The spirit of the LORD God is upon me because the LORD has anointed me; he has sent me to bring good news to the humble, to bind up the broken-hearted, to proclaim liberty to captives and release to those in prison; to proclaim a year of the LORD's favour and a day for the vengeance of our God.'[a] As he sat down, all eyes were on him. Would he indicate that he had at last delegated to John the prophetic and priestly role referred to by the text? Their hopes were quickly dashed. 'Today,' commented Jesus, 'in your very hearing this text has come true.'[b]

Instantly there was uproar. Despite everything, Jesus was clearly still insisting on arrogating to himself the combined role of Priest and King. He was an upstart. More, he was the Devil himself.[c] Sourly observing that 'no prophet is recognised in his own country', he was roughly hustled out and narrowly avoided being thrown down the steep slope of the mountain.[d]

As the news spread throughout northern Galilee, the other Essene communities seem to have turned against him one by one. At Chorazin, Bethsaida and Capernaum he was successively disowned, or possibly it was he who disowned them.[e] Meanwhile Jesus found the realisation rapidly forced in upon him that he could no longer take orders from the Essene hierarchy, and that he would henceforth have to take the whole messianic initiative upon his own shoulders. Moreover, since the Essene communities were clearly in the process of rapidly ruling themselves out as the repositories of Divine Knowledge and Truth, new converts would have to be found and new groups established on his own initiative.

---

[a] Isa. 61:1-2   [b] Lk. 4:21   [c] Mt. 10:25   [d] Lk. 4:24-30. Such a steep slope, it has been pointed out by numerous observers, is conspicuously lacking at the town of Nazareth, where the gospel account actually sites the incident.   [e] Compare Mt. 11:20-24.

And this in turn would mean revealing the long-hidden Essene secrets to his new would-be followers.

Jesus, after all, believed himself to be David returned. Thus, by definition, he was God's son. It followed, therefore, that only he could legitimately interpret God's will for Israel. Alternatively, as Priest-Messiah, it was for him to act, in Essene terms, as the sole 'Interpreter of the Law'. Either way, final authority lay with him, and not with the Essene leadership. 'I thank thee, Father,' he is reported as having said, '. . . for hiding these things from the learned and wise, and revealing them to the simple. Yes, Father, such was thy choice. Everything is entrusted to me by my Father; and no one knows the Son but the Father, and no one knows the Father but the Son and those to whom the Son may choose to reveal him.'[a]

The sense of relief still breathes through the words to us across the centuries. The crisis of confidence had, it seems, led to sudden realisation. The Essenes had wanted a Messiah. Now, much to their apparent chagrin, they had actually got one.

And so that Messiah must next set about choosing his own inner cell of followers, as well as his wider circle of supporters. Possibly it was from this date that he actually started to assemble his familiar group of twelve close disciples. Possibly that was the real reason why they apparently came from such diverse backgrounds. Not that there was a total lack of supporters among the Essenes. But now the gates must be thrown open, the teachings imparted to anybody who would join him. In the familiar words of the Authorised Version: 'He that is not against us is for us.'[b]

And that, no doubt, is why Jesus now went on to quote the last few verses of the book of Ecclesiasticus, whose words appear much mangled in Matthew's version: 'Come to me, you who need instruction, and lodge in my house of learning . . . I have made my proclamation: "Buy for yourselves without money, bend your neck to the yoke, be ready to accept discipline; you need not go far to find it." See for yourself how little were my labours compared with the great peace I have found.'[c]

Starting from a typical Essene position of reserve and secretiveness Jesus thus seems to have sensed the need progressively to broaden the audience for his 'plain-speech' teachings to include all who would follow him, whether of Essenic origin or not. On the other hand, if he later felt justified in sending out his disciples with the words: 'What I say to you in the dark you must repeat in broad daylight; what you hear whispered you must shout from the housetops,'[d] it was more likely because he was dispatching them to the various Essene communities throughout the land with clear instructions to

---

[a] Mt. 11:25-27   [b] Lk. 9:50   [c] Ecclesiasticus 51:23-27: compare Mt. 11:28-30.   [d] Mt. 10:27

lay bare all that had been going on behind closed doors. The attempt must still be made, in other words, to regain full Essene support, even though Jesus clearly anticipated widespread rejection of his embassies. His disciples, he warned, would be like sheep among wolves; they would be expelled, beaten, tried on trumped-up charges, handed over to the authorities, perhaps even killed. 'If the master has been called Beelzebub,' he observed wrily, 'how much more his household.'[a]

It is verses such as this, together with the very extent of the expected opposition, that suggest an intended Essene audience. The northern populace, for its part, was, on the whole, highly enthusiastic about the messianic cause. At any moment they expected the Messiah to appear, and they were hardly likely to reject messengers who proclaimed that he actually had. Only from the Sadducees and the rest of the Jerusalem hierarchy was violent opposition likely to come; but they were few in number and mostly far away to the south.

From charges of indiscriminate propaganda, then, we can safely absolve Jesus. Outside the restricted Essene circle, his choice of hearers seems likely to have been quite circumspect — despite some scriptural suggestions to the contrary — and his words even more so. Admittedly, he was often considerably more forthcoming than the typical Qumran Essene, but then it should be remembered that he was not a Qumran Essene. Not only was he a Carmelite or 'Nazarene', a product of the Essene movement's necessarily 'ecumenical' headquarters-group, but he was — or at least believed himself to be — the intended messianic Priest-King, the ultimate 'Interpreter of the Law', the re-embodiment of King David himself. As such, his rank was superior by far to that of the Essene leadership, and even to the original Teacher of Righteousness himself. Consequently he was free to interpret the Law and the Prophets in his own way and to whom he pleased, as the spirit guided him. And if, as a result, the Sabbath laws came to be seen in less dogmatic perspective, or ritual separation from lay society as a less demanding imperative, those facts did not disqualify him either as an Essene or as messianic Priest-King. As he himself was quick to point out, King David had actually put himself above the Law, and the priests broke the Sabbath every time they celebrated it.[b] And as for washing before meals, might there not be a danger, he suggested, of putting the tradition of men before the commandment of God, the letter of the Law before its spirit?[c] Had not Isaiah written: 'This people approach me with their mouths and honour me with their lips while their hearts are far from me, and their religion is but a precept of men, learnt by rote'?[d] Was not this, indeed, one of the prime reasons for the coming cataclysm? 'Therefore,' the prophet had continued, 'I

---

[a] Mt. 10:25   [b] Mt. 12:1-8   [c] Mk. 7:1-8   [d] Isa. 29:13, apparently misquoted at this point either by Jesus or by the evangelist.

will yet again shock this people, adding shock to shock.'[a]

Curiously enough, however, while the evidence for Jesus' Essenism is clearly overwhelming, it is a moot point, in the light of our reconstruction of their internal quarrel, whether the Essenes themselves now regarded him as one of their number. Jesus' obvious awareness of widespread opposition to his cause suggests that they may not have done. As a result, he seems to have felt impelled to devote a great deal of time and energy to convincing his critics of that cause's rightness. The fact that his ministry was (according to some accounts) to last some three years, rather than much less, may derive directly from the necessity for doing so. But it was the eventual beheading of John the Baptist by Herod Antipas that seems finally to have clinched the issue. For, contrary to prophetic expectations, the supposed Priest-Messiah failed either to survive the experience or to rise from the dead. Moreover, such popular rumours as suggested the contrary tended to see him as actually reincarnated in Jesus himself.[b]

With no separate Priest-Messiah left to share the reins of power in the millennial Kingdom, therefore, there was nothing for it but to accept that Jesus had, after all, been right all along. No doubt reluctantly and painfully at first, the various Essene camps started to re-align themselves with the new, or rather the original, view. Heads — metaphorically, this time — may well have rolled at the top, and especially at Qumran. And eventually, with the necessary Essenic power-base and logistical support-system finally secured at his back, Jesus could go quickly forward towards the ritual culmination of his role as Priest-Messiah.[c]

At this point, then, his attention was once more turned towards the blueprint originally drawn up by the sect's Teacher of Righteousness. And this stipulated that the final act of national atonement by the Priest-Messiah must, as we should expect, directly reflect the atonement-symbolism of the original Exodus under Moses, which had already figured so largely in the Teacher's thinking. How else, after all, could the Covenant with Yahweh be reinvoked, other than through a repetition of the act which had set its ancient original in motion? That first atonement had been effected through the sacrifice of a lamb or kid 'without blemish, a yearling male'.[d] Its latter-day counterpart ought therefore to take the same form. Yet, in the Essene view, the official animal-sacrifices in the Jerusalem Temple were now invalid, being celebrated on the wrong days of the month and by a corrupt and unclean priesthood. As we have seen, the Essene reaction, especially at Qumran, had been to regard *themselves* as 'a living sacrifice, dedicated and fit for his acceptance, the worship offered by mind and heart.'[e] To use their own

---

[a] Isa. 29:14   [b] Mt. 14:1-2, 16:14   [c] As Heb. 3 suggests, the later Paul, too, was to accept the identification, naming Jesus 'Apostle and High Priest'. Meanwhile, compare the detailed timetable suggested by Schonfield.[43]   [d] Ex. 12:5   [e] Rom. 12:1. The words are those of Paul, who shows considerable familiarity with Essene ideas.

words, 'They shall atone for guilty rebellion and for sins of unfaithfulness that they may obtain lovingkindness for the Land without the flesh of holocausts and the fat of sacrifice. And prayer rightly offered shall be as an acceptable fragrance of righteousness, and perfection of way as a delectable free-will offering.'[a] Such an approach, after all, was totally compatible with the revelations of the later prophets.

But now the time had come for the Priest-Messiah to merge the two symbolisms into one. The old and the new dispensations must be finally reconciled. As Priest, Jesus must perform the ultimate sacrifice that was to reconcile Yahweh to Israel; but as the Essenes' Messiah he must himself personify that sacrifice. In the words of Psalm 40 specifically applied to Jesus by the later Paul, 'Sacrifice and offering thou didst not desire, but thou hast prepared a body for me. Whole-offerings and sin-offerings thou didst not delight in. Then I said, "Here am I: as it is written of me in the scroll, I have come, O God, to do thy will."'[b] A similar idea had long been familiar to devotees of a far different religion: 'I am the sacrifice and the offering, the sacred gift and the sacred plant. I am the holy words, the holy food, the holy fire, and the offering that is made in the fire.'[c]

In short, the body of the traditional sacrificial lamb must be replaced by his own body, its blood by his blood. And so there was only one possible place where this culminating scene could finally be played out: at the annual Passover-festival in Jerusalem.

Ideally, as we have seen, the sacrificial animal should have been a 'yearling male': the ritual act, in other words, should have taken place only a year after the official start of Jesus' mission beside the Jordan. How far this presumed departure from plan — necessitated by the protracted internal dispute among the Essenes — had fatally flawed the eventual outcome, nobody could be quite sure. The best that could be done was to carry on as soon as possible and hope for the best.

In the event, 'as soon as possible' may well have been as little as six months.[43] Before the full moon following the next spring equinox Jesus had to make all his preparations, brief all his agents and collaborators — for security reasons, independently of each other[42] — and complete any aspects of his appointed life's work that were still outstanding. Prime among these was, of course, the continuing proclamation of the Kingdom's imminence and the exhorting of the nation to repent and reform in preparation for it. To this dual theme he must devote the whole of the remainder of his time until that final Passover-act — and the evidence suggests that that is precisely what he did. Traditional it may be to assert, on the basis of the texts, that he went on to invent some new and totally un-Jewish 'religion of love' which (despite his own vehement protestations[d]) rendered the ancient Law obsolete; that he

[a] *Community Rule*, IX[51]   [b] Heb. 10:5-7   [c] *Bhagavad Gita* 9:16[32]   [d] Mt. 5:17-20

regarded his approaching self-sacrifice as a kind of *carte-blanche* and prior atonement for all kinds of backsliding thereafter; that he went about performing magical acts of the most flamboyant extravagance; or that he intended deep meanings of universal import to be read into his words and subsequently applied indiscriminately outside the context of first-century Judaism. But nothing, as it happens, could be more misleading.

Jesus' much-quoted summary of the Law and the Prophets at Matthew 22:34-40, for example, is far from the revolutionary doctrinal departure that it is often supposed to be. Adept as he clearly was at distilling from the scriptures their inner meaning and deeper significance, Jesus' dual exhortation to 'love the Lord your God with all your heart, with all your soul, with all your mind' and to 'love your neighbour as yourself' was in fact far from original. Already familiar on the lips of the eminent Pharisaic rabbi Hillel, it was, as quoted by Luke[a], merely a stitching-together (in reverse order) of two Old Testament texts[b] — a characteristic technique long familiar to Essenes and Pharisees alike, used both in the New Testament and in the Dead Sea Scrolls themselves. Indeed, neither the idea of love nor that of Divine forgiveness is peculiar to the New Testament, as even the most superficial glance at the Psalms and the Qumran Hymn-scroll will reveal.

On the other hand, there is no suggestion in the Dead Sea literature or in the recorded words of Jesus that the ritual atonement performed either by the Qumran community as a whole or by the expected Priest-Messiah in person was ever intended to be the 'once-and-for-all sacrifice' proposed by later Christian theology. Admittedly it was conceived of as a symbolic payment for accumulated sin. But that sin was the past sin of Israel itself, its abandonment of the Divine ordinances, its reneging on the ancient Covenant. Such aberrations, certainly, had to be paid for, and rather by one man than by the nation as a whole.[c] But the sacrifice could be effective only in respect of sins committed up to the time of its performance: if Israel were to stay reconciled to its God it must simultaneously undergo a change of heart. It must repent and mend its ways. That was why Jesus spent so much time saying precisely that. The need for repentance was as urgent as the Kingdom was imminent. The latter could not begin without the former.

Jesus' function as a healer, meanwhile, was directly related to his atoning role. Yet not exclusively so. Jesus, after all, was also a typical Hasid, and the Hasidim, by virtue of their very sanctity and eccentricity, were traditionally regarded as miracle-workers, just as their prototypes, Elijah and Elisha, had been before them. Especially were they credited with curative powers, and it was traditional for the sick to seek to touch the hem of the garment of any passing Hasid by way of a healing talisman. Moreover Jesus, as a trained Essene, had in all probability some specific familiarity with herbal medicine,

---

[a] Lk. 10:25-28   [b] Deut. 6:5 and Lev. 19:18   [c] Compare Jn. 11:50

for their skill in which the Essenes were justly renowned. In the overwrought and neurotic psychological environment of first-century Palestine, rife with psychoses ('devils') and psychosomatic disorders of every kind, the appearance of Jesus was therefore a double godsend, and it seems reasonable to assume that many sought and obtained healing at his hands. The process was even justified by certain of the scriptural texts relating to the Priest-Messiah — and, in particular, by the passage from Ezekiel quoted on page 115 above.

On the other hand, Jesus was frequently at pains to point out that it was the sufferers' own faith, rather than any presumed healing-powers of his own, which had brought about their cure.[a] He himself seems to have been much more inclined to see health in terms of inner wholeness than in terms of mere freedom from the outer symptoms of disease, and the texts make it clear that Jesus, acute psychologist that he was, saw inner guilt as one of the main obstacles to that wholeness. 'Your sins are forgiven,' he told a would-be patient on at least one occasion, and instantly the symptoms disappeared.[b] That he was qualified to make such assertions derived, once again, from his imminent atoning mission, of whose effectiveness as payment for the nation's past sins he was clearly so sure as to convince many of those around him as well. Nowhere in it, however, was there any sanction for the more flamboyant acts of magic attributed to him by the gospels, and it therefore seems probable, as we shall be seeing later, that these owe more to prophetic expectation than to factual reporting.

As for the universal impact of Jesus' teachings, this derives from a variety of contributory factors, all of which, for a variety of reasons, tended to converge at this point in time and space. One of them, as we have already seen, was the Essenic necessity for Jesus to mask his teachings in riddles and parables. The result was a cryptic series of public pronouncements well-suited to re-application in fields other than those for which they were originally intended, and capable of being interpreted in any one of a number of often contradictory ways. Prominent among them were, of course, his celebrated paradoxes — his description of the living as the dead[c], his promise that the last would be first and the first last[d], his warning that the spiritually rich would get richer and the poor poorer.[e] All of them bear the unmistakable stamp of a deep wisdom that transcended the bounds of mere national creeds and plumbed the unfathomable wells of human experience that lie at the heart of every major religion. There may, as we have seen, have been good reason for this: Jesus may actually have studied certain of the other major religions of his day. Yet the gospel-teachings contain little or no specific evidence of this. Their wisdom is all-embracing. And it is this very fact that has endeared his teachings to followers of every religion and helped

---

[a] Compare Mt. 9:22, 29, 15:28   [b] Compare Mt. 9:2-8   [c] Mt. 8:22   [d] Mt. 19:30   [e] Mt. 13:12

to elevate him to the rank of major world-teacher.

Yet, just as his teachings as originally expressed were compatible — for largely accidental reasons — with those of other religions, they were also totally and supremely compatible with those of first-century Judaism itself. Not for one moment did Jesus ever contemplate altering or replacing the religion of his forefathers. Not one iota of the Law could be altered, he insisted, until the Kingdom had been safely ushered in.[a] And, in case there should be any doubt about it, he left us a summary of what he did believe in the form of the familiar Lord's Prayer.[b]

This succinct doctrinal manifesto, so often recited today as if it were a kind of magical talisman, and with total disregard for what it actually says, is not untypical of Jewish prayers of the period. It starts with a collective affirmation by the faithful of the fatherhood of Yahweh, and thus implies that all those who conform to the Divine will are, *ipso facto*, 'sons of God'. It goes on to stress the intangible, non-physical nature of the Godhead and the awful sacredness of the Divine name. Next comes a total commitment to the ushering-in of the Kingdom — the ultimate fulfilment of God's will — that is already there in essence and merely needs to be brought into physical manifestation. The actual words 'on earth as it is in heaven' reflect the ancient Hermetic motto 'As above, so below'. There follows, in the Greek original of the text, a request for 'supersubstantial bread' — the daily spiritual sustenance and guidance needed during the sect's current 'wilderness journey', reflecting the physical *manna* of the original Exodus. After this, the forgiveness on which the appearance of the Kingdom is dependent is craved, and the willingness to forgive affirmed, in terms strangely reminiscent of the oriental doctrine of karmic debts. And the prayer concludes by beseeching Yahweh to spare the sect during the impending period of Divine wrath and so to deliver them finally from the powers of Darkness.

The prayer, in short, is thoroughly Jewish, and thoroughly typical of the first-century cast of religious thought subscribed to by the Essenes. If it contains possible references to non-Jewish ideas, they are used not to modify but to cast light on the essentially Jewish core of this powerful statement of belief. For that, indubitably, is what Jesus intended it to be. If he cast it as a prayer, it was not because he believed that endless recitation of it would prove materially effective — indeed, he suggested that the mere recitation of words was actually counterproductive as a means of communicating with the Deity[c] — but because he knew that, despite his reservations on the matter, it *would* be recited virtually *ad infinitum*, and so would continually bring before the minds of the faithful the central tenets of their belief.

And so, as we have seen, his words were to spread until today they are widely known, if not observed, across the major part of the globe. And not

___

[a] Mt. 5:18   [b] Mt. 6:9-13   [c] Mt. 6:7-8

merely because they were of necessity expressed in terms that were both generalised and somewhat cryptic. For Jesus' language was Aramaic, which since Persian times had been the *lingua franca* of the entire Middle East. Moreover, Greek had, since the time of Alexander, been a second *lingua franca* among the educated classes from as far west as Rome to as far east as India. Whether in their Aramaic original or in Greek translation, therefore, Jesus' words had every chance of being propagated virtually world-wide.

Geography and international power-politics, too, had a contributory part to play in this. For not only was first-century Palestine situated at almost the exact centre of the known world — connected to the east via the overland trade-routes, to the north via Syria and Greece, to the south via Egypt and to the west via the Mediterranean sea-routes: it had, a mere sixty years or so before Jesus' birth, become a province of the Roman Empire. And so the whole, vast communications-network of Imperial Rome was placed at the disposition of whoever cared to use it.

Among the ranks of Jesus' subsequent followers there were many who were more than eager to do so. For Jesus, they believed, had not only proved himself to be the Messiah, but by conquering death had actually achieved godlike status in opposition to Caesar. To the subject-peoples of the Empire, already deeply-imbued with Greek religious ideas, and not least the concept of the immortal, heroic god-man, the news that a deliverer had at last arisen to free them from the yoke of Rome came as a psychological bombshell. For this saviour had arisen at the very moment when people were most ready for him. To the extent that he would free all the nations subject to Rome he was a potential saviour of the world. His words and teachings, apparently compatible with the earlier sacred sayings of Mithraism and the ancient lore of even earlier gods, were eagerly passed from mouth to mouth as secret talismans of deliverance. They represented knowledge, power, reassurance. They gave heart to the subversives, justification to the waverers, an ideology to the planners of revolt.

Everything conspired, then, to turn Jesus into a world-teacher, his words into teachings of universal import. It was a matter — whether accidental or deliberate — of right timing and right siting. Perhaps Jesus himself was aware of this. But whether his teachings were subsequently accepted as significant would depend very largely, as he well knew, on his own success in bringing his allotted mission to its predicted, triumphant conclusion. So, too, would the inception of the Kingdom.

It was to this pre-eminent task, therefore, that Jesus must now address himself.

According to the Scriptures

As the crucial Passover-festival approached, Jesus finally and resolutely set his face towards Jerusalem, fully conscious of a whole series of predictions that he must now strain every muscle to fulfil. Yet up to this point his disciples seem to have been largely ignorant of this penultimate chapter in the Essene Teacher's book of prophetic testimonies. Hitherto they had apparently assumed — perhaps a trifle naïvely — that, since Jesus was clearly the promised all-in-one Messiah, the Kingdom would shortly follow of itself, as summer follows spring. The prophetic niceties of the messianic task, and in particular the dichotomy between the role of the teaching and suffering Priest-Messiah and that of the final, triumphant King-Messiah, had evidently not been explained to them. Still less had it been made clear to them that the essential link between the two must, according to the scriptures, be a narrow brush with death itself.

It was precisely this fact, therefore, that Jesus now started to explain to his closest followers.[a] On the basis of the available texts, it would seem that he first took them back through the scriptures to his prophetic antecedents in Moses and Elijah, explaining to them the Essene symbolism of the New Exodus — wilderness-journey, temporary shelters and all. And as he went on to expound the messianic prophecies and the need for their deliberate fulfilment, it suddenly began to dawn on them what his whole mission thus far had really been about. In a flash of illumination, they at last saw Jesus in his true light.[b]

And now, evidently for the first time, he started to initiate them into those mysteries of the Essene Teacher of Righteousness's *Book of Meditation* which still remained to be fulfilled.[c] His followers were tense, incredulous. Probably he had known in advance that they would be shocked, even affronted, by the apparently brutal requirements of the plan. Yet now he had

---

[a] Compare Mt. 16:13-28   [b] Compare Mt. 17:1-13 — the story of the 'Transfiguration'.
[c] Compare Lk. 18:31-34

no choice but to share with them all its secrets, for it was they who must now help him put it into effect and act as his interpreters to the world at large.

And so the task of exposition commenced, much after the manner, it may be, of the original Teacher himself . . .

O people of Zion who dwell in Jerusalem, you shall weep no more. The LORD *will show you favour and answer you when he hears your cry for help. The* LORD *may give you bread of adversity and water of affliction, but he who teaches you shall no longer be hidden out of sight, but with your own eyes you shall see him always. If you stray from the road to right or left you shall hear with your own ears a voice behind you saying, This is the way; follow it.*[a]

The 'hidden Messiah' of the north, it was clear, must now come out into the open in order to stage his final manifestation in Jerusalem itself. More specifically, he must appear on Zion, the hilltop site of David's original city, which now supported the Temple and the priests' quarter known as the Ophel. The manner of his appearance was to be closely akin to that of Moses before him, who had returned to save his captive people in Egypt when 'their appeal for rescue from their slavery rose up to God.'[b] At that time, Yahweh had delivered his people under the terms of the earlier Covenant; so, now, he would redeem them under the terms of the new one. It was southward to Jerusalem that the Messiah must now direct his steps, there to exhort all who would hear him to follow the way of the Law as a precondition for the now-imminent dawning of the Kingdom.

Comfort, comfort my people . . . You who bring Zion good news, up with you to the mountain-top; lift up your voice and shout, you who bring good news to Jerusalem, lift it up fearlessly; cry to the cities of Judah, 'Your God is here.' Here is the Lord GOD *coming in might, coming to rule with his right arm. His recompense comes with him, he carries his reward before him. He will tend his flock like a shepherd and gather them together with his arm; he will carry the lambs in his bosom and lead the ewes to water.*[c]

In the name of Yahweh, then, Jesus must go on to announce to Jerusalem its impending liberation from the foreign yoke and the imminent inception of the Kingdom. The good news must be proclaimed on Mount Zion, in the Temple precinct itself. Thanks to the faithfulness of the 'righteous remnant' and the atoning mission of the Priest-Messiah, Yahweh would once again gather up Israel like a shepherd — the theme having been explicitly foreshadowed in the twenty-third Psalm[d], and later taken up again, as we have already seen, by the prophet Ezekiel.[e]

[a] Isa. 30:19-21   [b] Ex. 2:23   [c] Isa. 40:1, 9-11   [d] Compare especially Ps. 23:1-2   [e] Ez. 34: 11-24

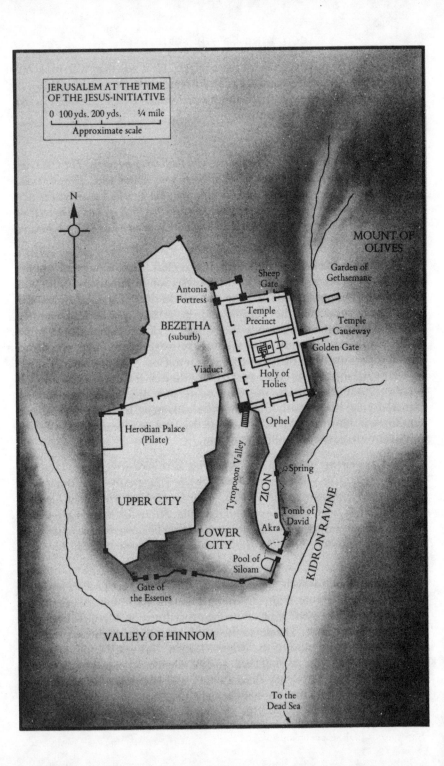

JERUSALEM AT THE TIME
OF THE JESUS-INITIATIVE

0 100 yds. 200 yds.   ¼ mile

Approximate scale

N

MOUNT OF
OLIVES

Garden of
Gethsemane

Sheep
Gate

Antonia
Fortress

BEZETHA
(suburb)

Temple
Precinct

Temple
Causeway

Golden Gate

Holy of
Holies

Viaduct

Ophel

Herodian Palace
(Pilate)

Spring

UPPER CITY

ZION

Tomb of
David

Akra

LOWER
CITY

Pool of
Siloam

KIDRON RAVINE

Gate of
the Essenes

VALLEY OF HINNOM

To the
Dead Sea

Hark, your watchmen raise their voices and shout together in triumph, for with their own eyes they shall see the LORD *returning in pity to Zion. Break forth together in shouts of triumph, you ruins of Jerusalem; for the* LORD *has taken pity on his people and has ransomed Jerusalem.*[a]

Pursuing the theme of the proclamation to Jerusalem of the news of the Kingdom's advent, this text now revealed that Jesus must serve as a visible symbol of Divine atonement, and that the populace must respond positively to his self-revelation — for it was on that response that the new dispensation would ultimately depend. Consequently a mere, inconspicuous arrival would not be enough: his entry into Jerusalem must, despite its obvious dangers, be public, and undertaken in the full glare of publicity.

Look, I am laying a stone in Zion, a block of granite, a precious corner-stone for a firm foundation; he who has faith shall not waver.[b]

Open to me the gates of righteousness;[c] *I will enter by them and praise the* LORD*. This is the gate of the* LORD*; the righteous*[d] *shall make their entry through it. I will praise thee, for thou hast answered me and hast become my deliverer. The stone which the builders rejected has become the chief corner-stone . . .*[e]

Once in Jerusalem, Jesus' mission would be to lay the foundations for the new dispensation. Consequently his presence there was absolutely essential to the plan. There could be no going back. Putting all self-doubts aside, Jesus must openly enter the gates of Jerusalem, supported by the serried ranks of the 'righteous' — i.e. the Essene devout. He should not fear rejection by the official priesthood (the 'builders'[f]): indeed, he should expect it. Yet his fallen star, he could be assured, would eventually be restored in glory. His own later quotation of the second text witnesses to his absolute conviction of the fact.[g]

He shall appear and be their shepherd in the strength of the LORD*, in the majesty of the name of the* LORD *his God. And they shall continue, for now his greatness shall reach to the ends of the earth; and he shall be a man of peace.*[h]

As we suggested on page 102, this passage was almost certainly taken to refer directly to the relationship between the Messiah and the Essene community at Qumran. It was held to allude specifically to his entry into his final Kingdom and his inaugural progress from Jericho to Jerusalem at the head of the Essenes' 'spiritual shock-troops'. At one time, the Qumran covenanters had, it seems, expected that triumphal progress to follow directly on his baptism and original Jordan-crossing. But as Jesus had

[a] Isa. 52:8-9 [b] Isa. 28:16 [c] Variant reading; otherwise 'victory'. [d] Variant reading; otherwise 'victors'. [e] Ps. 118:19-22 [f] Herod the Great's reconstruction of the Temple was in fact in its forty-sixth year of building at the time (Jn. 2:20) [g] Mt. 21:42 [h] Mic. 5:4-5

insisted, and as events had proved, they had been wrong.

Now, however, the time for that initiative had at last arrived. And so Jesus, once more approaching Judea via Transjordan[a], must resume his former journey at Jericho, gathering up his small army of desert-monastics somewhere along the way. An obvious assembly-point would be the village of Bethany, just outside Jerusalem, which the Qumranites themselves could reach both directly and secretly via the Kidron Ravine, passable now after its winter spate. And so Bethany (where, it is clear, he already had Essene contacts[b]), must be his next port of call.

Expiation shall be made by the priest duly anointed . . .[c]

Take the anointing oil, pour it on his head and anoint him.[d]

Even though I walk through a valley as dark as death I fear no evil, for thou art with me, thy staff and thy crook are my comfort . . . thou has richly bathed my head with oil and my cup runs over.[e]

At birth you were endowed with princely gifts and resplendent in holiness. You have shone with the dew of youth since your mother bore you. The LORD has sworn and will not change his purpose: 'You are a priest forever, in the succession of Melchizedek.'[f]

At this point, then, Jesus must arrange for his local supporters to perform a solemn anointing-ceremony, at which oil of spikenard would be poured over his head in token of his official installation as Priest-Messiah. Since this oil was reserved strictly for the coronation-ceremonies of Kings and High Priests, its acquisition and possession would involve considerable risks and difficulties, and much would depend upon the secret co-operation of sympathetic agents in high places — of whom there seems to have been no shortage. The rite once performed, however, Jesus (clad in the typical, white linen clothes of the Essenes) would be finally invested with the Divine authority to atone in person for all Israel's past backslidings, just as Aaron had been before him.[g] He would, in short, have taken on, finally and irrevocably, the role of the priestly 'Messiah ben Aaron', and so, by the same token, would have entered what he already knew from the prophecies to be the 'valley of the shadow of death.'

The account at Matthew 26:6-13, clearly based on the recollection of a ritual of this kind, reveals just such an awareness by Jesus of his approaching fate. As retold at John 12:1-11, his anointer is identified as one Mary, while the author appears to display some confusion as to whether it was hair (Mary's) or feet (those of Jesus) that were anointed. The same passage testifies to the fact that considerable numbers of sympathisers assembled at Bethany

---

a Mt. 19:1   *b* Mt. 21:17, 26:6   *c* Lev. 16:32   *d* Ex. 29:7   *e* Ps. 23:4, 5   *f* Ps. 110:3-4
g Ex. 29:7 (above)

during Jesus' stay there.

*Rejoice, rejoice, daughter of Zion, shout aloud, daughter of Jerusalem; for see, your
king is coming to you, his cause won, his victory gained, humble and mounted on an
ass, on a foal, the young of a she-ass.*[a]

*We pray thee, O LORD, deliver us; we pray thee, O LORD, send us prosperity. Blessed
in the name of the LORD are all who come; we bless you from the house of the LORD.*[b]

The triumphal entry into Jerusalem must then follow. Before reaching
Jerusalem, however, a donkey must be acquired for Jesus to ride, since this, in
Zechariah's prophetic terms, was to be the token of his approaching reign as
Prince of Peace. Since things, therefore, could not be left to chance, arrangements must be made for reliable Essene sympathisers to procure a donkey
and hold it ready at some point en route, to be released on receipt of a predetermined codeword. The nearby village of Bethphage, on the Mount of
Olives, and thus within view of Jerusalem itself, would provide an obvious
venue for this, as well as being sufficiently far removed from Bethany for
Jesus to keep his two groups of agents in ignorance of each other's actions, as
apparently was his wont for security reasons.

Now, bearing the palm-leaves for which the Jericho valley was famous in
token of the return from their long Exodus[c], the growing procession of
Essenes and hangers-on must set out on its final stage down from the Mount
of Olives, and across the Kidron ravine via the eastern causeway which led
directly into the Temple precinct. At this point the Essene monastics must
raise a great chorus of rejoicing and exultation at their long-awaited return to
Zion with the promised Messiah in their midst. Their joy would, of course,
prove contagious. Agog at the army of 'Galileans' and men of the desert, and
convinced by them that Jesus was the promised saviour who would at last
free Jerusalem of its military occupation-forces, the populace, swollen by the
masses who were assembling for the Passover, would stream out via the
Temple Gate to meet the growing army of pilgrims. There they would be
encouraged to join in the popular, if inaccurate, chant of 'Deliver us, Son of
David' and 'Blessed in the name of the LORD are all who come; we bless you
from the house of the LORD' — the latter in fulfilment of the extract from
Psalm 118 quoted above. And at this time of national religious festival, it
would not occur to the bored and uncomprehending Roman occupation-
forces to try and stop them.

And so it proved to be. The donkey was indeed released at the password
'Our Master needs it', though the author of Matthew[d], apparently working
from the faulty Greek Septuagint translation of the extracts quoted, is at pains
to prove that Jesus rode not one donkey but two into Jerusalem — a clear

---

[a] Zech. 9:9   [b] Ps. 118:25-26   [c] Compare Lev. 23:39-43, as well as Isa. 30:29 below.
[d] Mt. 21:1-11

example of what we earlier termed 'wishful hindsight'. The procession duly reached the approaches to the city, where the shout was reportedly raised, 'Hosanna (= 'Save us'), Son of David' and 'Blessings on him who comes in the name of the Lord'. Since it is unlikely that the Essene sectaries would have thus misquoted the scriptures without good reason, it is probable, once again, that either the Greek-speaking evangelist or his source is in error. Indeed, he actually has the crowd shout 'Hosanna *to* the Son of David', which in Hebrew is totally meaningless. 'Save us, Son of David', however — using the verb *yasha*, as in the original text — would have been an entirely apt cry, since Jesus's name (Joshua) actually *meant* 'God saves'.

I rejoiced when they said to me, 'Let us go to the house of the LORD.*' Now we stand within your gates, O Jerusalem . . . For in her are set the thrones of justice, the thrones of the house of David . . .* [a]

See, the name of the LORD *comes from afar, his anger blazing and his doom heavy. . . . But for you there shall be songs, as on a night of sacred pilgrimage, your hearts glad, as the hearts of men who walk to the sound of the pipe on their way to the* LORD*'s hill, to the rock of Israel. Then the* LORD *shall make his voice heard in majesty and show his arm sweeping down in fierce anger . . . for at the voice of the* LORD *Assyria's heart fails her, as she feels the stroke of his rod.* [b]

The priests went inside to purify the house of the LORD. *They removed all the pollution which they found in the temple . . .* [c]

My house shall be called a house of prayer for all nations. [d] *Do you think that this house, which bears my name, is a robbers' cave?* [e]

So when that time comes, no trader shall again be seen in the house of the LORD *of Hosts.* [f]

No sooner had the Messiah entered Jerusalem than he would be confronted with the Temple and its sacrilegious iniquities. Jesus, therefore, who bore in his own name (Joshua) 'the name of the LORD' (Jah, or Yahweh), must vividly represent the Divine wrath towards those who habitually profaned the sacred precinct with buying and selling. His followers, meanwhile, still rejoicing at his presence, must also enter the Temple, but as on one of the great pilgrim-feasts, such as the feast of Tabernacles: this feast, a memorial to the fact that the people had lived in temporary shelters during the original Exodus, was now celebrated, as we saw earlier, by the cutting down of palm fronds and branches. [g] The impending Passover was another such feast.

And so it duly came to pass. According to Mark, [h] Jesus forthwith drove out all the merchants and money-changers in an act which those addicted to the 'gentle Jesus, meek and mild' of Christian tradition often find strangely at

a Ps. 122:1-2, 5   *b* Isa. 30:27, 29-31   *c* 2 Chr. 29:16   *d* Isa. 56:7   *e* Jer. 7:11   *f* Zech. 14:21   *g* Lev. 23:39-43   *h* Mk. 11:15-19

odds with what they assume his character to have been. In the light of the clear prophetic requirements, however, the apparent problem disappears. Meanwhile the evangelist has Jesus say, 'My house shall be called a house of prayer for all the nations. But you have made it a robbers cave'[a] — an 'edited' stitching together of two separate biblical texts[b] typical, as we have seen, of contemporary prophetic testimony-books and, by implication, the Teacher's own *Book of Meditation.*

How can I repay the LORD *for all his gifts to me? I will take the cup of salvation and invoke the* LORD *by name . . . A precious thing in the* LORD*'s sight is the death of those who die faithful to him. I am thy slave, thy slave-girl's son; thou hast undone the bonds that bound me. To thee will I bring a thank-offering and invoke the* LORD *by name. I will pay my vows to the* LORD *in the presence of all his people, in the courts of the* LORD*'s house, in the midst of you, Jerusalem.*[c]

Heartened, no doubt, at his own initial success, the Messiah must now address himself to his central mission. Jesus must take up the cup of sacrifice which would, he knew full well — as his own words later confirm[d] — eventually involve the pouring-out of his own life's blood. He must carry out his Essenic vows to fulfil all the demands of the Law and the Prophets, faithful, if necessary, unto death. He must never forget that he was born specifically to fulfil the purposes of Yahweh, just as his mother had been dedicated to that same service.

Then I heard the LORD *saying, Whom shall I send? Who will go for me? And I answered, Here am I, send me. He said, Go and tell this people: You may listen and listen, but you will not understand. You may look and look again, but you will never know. This people's wits are dulled, their ears are deafened and their eyes blinded, so that they cannot see with their eyes nor listen with their ears nor understand with their wits, so that they may turn and be healed.*[e]

For Zion's sake I will not keep silence, for Jerusalem's sake I will speak out.[f]

The stone which the builders rejected has become the chief corner-stone.[g]

The Messiah's initial act in Jerusalem, however, was bound to arouse official resentment. And though he might go on to expound in parable the true Essene teachings in the Temple itself, the people, too, would remain intoxicated with expectations of liberation from foreign rule and eventual national glory, blind to the personal renewal which must lay at the very basis of it. The Jewish authorities, ('the builders') therefore, would be no less anxious than the Roman occupying power to get rid of him as a potential rabble-rouser. And so his rejection must, in the end, necessarily precede his eventual glorification as King-Messiah.

---

[a] Mk. 11:17 [b] Isa. 56:7 and Jer. 7:11, quoted above. [c] Ps. 116:12-13, 15-19 [d] Mt. 20:22, 26:27-28, 39, 42 [e] Isa. 6:8-10 [f] Isa. 62:1 [g] Ps. 118:22

Thou didst give thy Thummim to Levi, thy Urim to thy loyal servant . . . who said of his parents, I do not know them, who did not acknowledge his brothers . . . [a]

I have become a stranger to my brothers, an alien to my own mother's sons. Bitter enemies of thy temple tear me in pieces. [b]

The Messiah, having taken on the ancient priestly mantle of Levi, must now finally dedicate himself to his self-sacrificial role. His sole loyalty must be to those who had been chosen to assist him in the task. Already, as far as his immediate family was concerned, he must regard himself as one dead.

And so Jesus is recorded as taking precisely this attitude at Matthew 12:48-50, and again at 19:29.

It is the LORD's *Passover. On that night I shall pass through the land of Egypt and kill every first-born of man and beast. Thus will I execute judgement . . . And as for you . . . when I see the blood I will pass over you; the mortal blow shall not touch you, when I strike the land of Egypt.* [c]

Moses then took the blood and flung it over the people, saying, 'This is the blood of the covenant which the LORD *has made with you on the terms of this book.'* [d]

Thou spreadest a table for me in the sight of my enemies. [e]

On this mountain the LORD *of Hosts will prepare a banquet of rich fare for all the peoples, a banquet of wines well matured and richest fare, well-matured wines strained clear. On this mountain the* LORD *will swallow up that veil that shrouds all the peoples, the pall thrown over all the nations; he will swallow up death for ever. Then the Lord* GOD *will wipe away the tears from every face and remove the reproach of his people from the whole earth.* [f]

For the LORD *delights in you and to him your land is wedded. For, as a young man weds a maiden, so you shall wed him who rebuilds you, and your God shall rejoice over you as a bridegroom rejoices over the bride.* [g]

Now, therefore, arrangements must be made to celebrate the coming Passover — the festival which symbolised and commemorated the story of the ancient Exodus and original Mosaic Covenant between Yahweh and Israel. Yet the festival could not be the official one, since this, being celebrated by a corrupt priesthood on the wrong day, was invalid and therefore ineffective. What the Priest-Messiah must celebrate with his close followers in a hideout in the very midst of the priests' quarter ('in the sight of my enemies') was the Essenic Passover, which occurred on the Tuesday/Wednesday before its official counterpart. It would serve as a token and an assurance that his little group of faithful disciples would be spared ('and do not bring us to the test'[g]) when the ultimate Day of Divine wrath —

---

[a] Deut. 33:8-9   [b] Ps. 69:8, 9   [c] Ex. 12:12-13   [d] Ex. 24:8   [e] Ps. 23:5   [f] Isa. 25:6-8   [g] Isa. 62:4-5   [h] Compare the Lord's Prayer at Mt. 6:13.

expected now for at least the last sixty years — finally descended on Israel (= 'Egypt') immediately prior to the coming Kingdom.

But now the celebration would have an added meaning. For, just as the sacrificial Passover lamb had been the original scapegoat, the symbol of the nation's atonement to Yahweh, so now Jesus the Essene, as Priest-Messiah, was about to atone in person, through his own suffering, for the past sins of Israel. Just as the roast meat of the Passover meal represented the body and blood of the sacrificial lamb of the old Covenant, so now the bread and the wine that were also part of the same meal would represent his own body and blood of the new Covenant (= Testament). Both were guarantees of atonement, of Divine forgiveness, of the remission of past sins. Both were linked in terms of a single, ritual celebration. And that celebration, reflected in the Essene sacred meal of the *Community Rule* and *Messianic Rule*[51], in turn looked forward to the final Messianic Banquet which the Essene faithful expected to celebrate in Jerusalem when the expected Kingdom finally dawned.

And, as if that were not enough, the Passover had long been seen by the Jews as a symbol of God's 'marriage' to his chosen people. Echoes of it were found in the contemporary Jewish marriage-ceremony. As part of the latter's ritual, moreover, the bridegroom washed the feet of the bride.

And so Jesus duly arranged for the celebration of this vitally symbolic festival in his own way and at a place of his own choosing. For this he needed trustworthy accomplices. One of his chief secret supporters, it seems, was an influential member of the Jerusalem priesthood by the name of Johanan (John) — the shadowy 'beloved disciple' who seems to have been a major source for the author of the fourth gospel.[42] Together with Jesus' younger brother Jacob (James), he appears to have played an important behind-the-scenes role in the affairs of Jesus and his cell of followers, possibly during the whole of their time together. Indeed, since the normal Essene practice was, as we have seen, to appoint a central executive body consisting of twelve laymen led by three priests, it seems quite likely that Jesus, James and John were the group's controlling triumvirate or, in Essene parlance, the 'Foundations of the Community' — respectively the Master (*maskil* or *mebaqqer*), the Supervising Priest and the more secularly orientated Steward (*mebaqqer 'al melekheth ha-rabbim*) described in the sect's original *Damascus Rule*.[51, 52] And so, to take a theatrical analogy, we could see Jesus, the actor-manager and producer of the Essenes' messianic drama, as having the last word on the script; while James and John, the play's director and production-manager respectively, stayed hidden in the wings. Indeed, they long remained a largely unknown quantity even to the disciples who provided the rest of the professional cast, while the populace — and even the Roman occupation-forces — unwittingly provided not only an audience but also an additional, amateur 'cast of thousands'.

What Jesus had embarked upon, in short, was a theatre of total involvement. And in the next act the production-manager himself must help out by playing a walk-on part. For it was in John's house on the Ophel (formerly the site of David's city atop Mount Zion, and now occupied by the priests' quarter) that the Essenes' version of the ritual Passover meal must be celebrated, possibly for the last time, in the presence of the Messiah whose participation their version of it had long anticipated.[a] He must then go on to bring about the fulfilment of the Covenant which it had always represented.

Yet secrecy was essential, for the authorities were by now hot on Jesus' trail, following his triumphal entry into Jerusalem and his unpardonable conduct in the Temple. True, he had not yet explicitly claimed the Messiahship, yet already his acts symbolically proclaimed that office. The Romans might not be familiar with the symbolism of the prophecies, but the Jewish priesthood, and the Pharisees particularly, certainly were. The fool had to be stopped before he sparked off a popular rising, with all the bloodshed and social chaos which the inevitable, heavy-handed Roman reaction would obviously produce.

Detaining Jesus in the midst of his crowds of adoring followers was out of the question. Clearly it would produce exactly what the authorities most wished to avoid. But corner him in private, and the would-be Messiah could be quietly removed from the scene and, with luck, never heard of again.

The same thoughts, meanwhile, had evidently occurred to Jesus. And so there could be no question of giving his disciples names or street-directions. What they did not know they could not accidentally reveal. It was enough for them to know that Jesus had friends in high places, and that it was at the house of one of them that they were to prepare for the Passover. The rest must depend, as previously, on the giving and receiving of a sign.

In the event, that sign was to be deceptively simple. Jesus, it seems, had up to this point withdrawn from the city each night and retired to the western slopes of the Mount of Olives, just to the east of the city and beyond the Kidron ravine. On the evidence available, it would seem that he had set up his secret temporary headquarters in the upper part of a private olive-orchard or herb-garden whose name has come down to us as the Garden of Gethsemane[b], and which lay almost directly opposite the Temple and within full view of it. The original name, it appears, was probably either *Jessamine* (Jasmine)[21] or *Gethshemen* (olive-oil press). He now dispatched his disciples down the Kidron valley itself, with instructions to enter the city via the south-east gate, which lay directly below the Akra, or citadel. Here they would find the Pool of Siloam, which was ancient Jerusalem's major water-supply, and by it they were to wait until they saw a man come and draw

---

[a] *Community Rule*, VI; *Messianic Rule*, II[51]   [b] In all probability, not the one currently pointed out to tourists.

water. By this sign they would automatically know that he was a member of the city's all-male Essene community, since only in such a community would the fetching of water, normally women's work, be undertaken by a man. Following him, they would arrive at the community's headquarters, and were then to say to the owner of the house, 'The Master says, "Where is the room in which I may eat the Passover with my disciples?"'[a] The titular householder — none other than John the Priest, official Steward of the Jesus-group — who had been primed by its Master, or *maskil*, (Jesus) to expect this very message, would immediately show them the room which had been set aside for this purpose. And so, in due course, the long-awaited Passover supper could commence, some days before its official counterpart in Jerusalem at large.

The events of that meal are recorded at Matthew 26:20-35, and the account is supplemented by John in chapters 13-17. First, it seems, Jesus laid aside his clothes and, wrapping a linen sheet about him, washed his disciples' feet — the nearest thing possible, in comparatively waterless Jerusalem, to the Qumran Essenes' similarly sheet-shrouded sacrament of ritual immersion before meals. Enlarging on the meaning of the act, he explained to his disciples that they were to see it as a symbol of Yahweh's ultimate marriage to his people in the new Golden Age, as foreshadowed by Isaiah.[b]

Next, as required by the Teacher's *Book of Meditation* and the Essenes' various ritual handbooks, the bread and wine were duly blessed by the Priest-Messiah, followed by each participant in turn. Then Jesus duly went on to expound the new, added symbolism of the familiar sacrificial meal. For, just as the roast lamb signified the original atoning sacrifice which had been performed ever since the time of Moses, so the bread and the last of the four obligatory cups of wine (the 'Cup of the Kingdom') that completed the meal were to stand for his own self-sacrifice — the supreme, atoning act which itself would complete Israel's redemption, and so make possible the inception of the final Golden Age of righteousness, peace and prosperity. 'I did not come to abolish, but to complete,' he had said on an earlier occasion.[c] And now that completion, or fulfilment, was at hand.

They say, 'Put up some rascal to denounce him, an accuser to stand at his right side.' But when judgement is given, that rascal will be exposed and his follies accounted a sin. May his days be few; may his charge[d] fall to another! May his children be fatherless, his wife a widow![e]

Even the friend whom I trusted, who ate at my table, exults at my misfortune.[f]

Even while the meal was in progress, Jesus started to put into effect the

---

[a] Lk. 22:11   [b] Isa. 62:4-5 (see above)   [c] Mt. 5:17. A.V. the King James' translation specifically uses the word 'fulfil'.   [d] Alternative reading: otherwise 'hoarded wealth' — see Acts 1:20.   [e] Ps. 109:6-9   [f] Ps. 41:9

next part of the Teacher's plan. This would involve an act of extraordinary self-sacrifice that could be assigned only to the most trustworthy of all the disciples. For, after the Essene Passover, that man was going to have deliberately to betray to the authorities the Messiah's presence at his secret hideout in the Garden of Gethsemane. In the process, he would be consciously taking on the role of stage-villain, and his act was all too likely to be taken subsequently at face-value. On his shoulders would be heaped not only the responsibility for the Messiah's subsequent execution, but also all the expectations of the prophecies regarding the Messiah's betrayer. In choosing him, Jesus would, in effect, be condemning him to death; and in accepting the charge he would, by the same token, be consenting to it.

But the most trustworthy of the disciples was, of course, already well-known to those concerned. In token of his reliability he had already been entrusted with the group's money — its 'hoarded wealth' — and the conduct of its day-to-day financial affairs. He was Judas, the group's treasurer. And now Jesus, having spelt out to the assembled company the awful responsibility of the betrayer's role, indicated that it would fall to the man to whom he offered the next piece of bread that he dipped into the bowl.

'Is it me?' they all wondered, in utmost dread.

But no, it was, as expected, to the trusty Judas that Jesus had assigned the task. 'Do quickly what you have to do,' he said[a], handing him the fateful sop. Heart thumping, head in a whirl, the shattered disciple staggered to his feet and fled in panic from the room.

And, not long afterwards, Jesus himself followed with his disciples, and set out into the darkness for his long-awaited tryst with destiny.

[a] Jn. 13:27

I I

A Matter of Life and Death

With the Essene Passover duly celebrated, events were moving swiftly towards their predicted, symbolic climax. Timing was now crucial. A moment too soon or too late, and the Priest-Messiah's self-sacrifice would not coincide with that of the ritual Paschal lambs. The symbolic association would be lost, the psychological impact lessened, the prophetic requirements imperfectly catered for.

The whole timetable, as Jesus saw it, had thus to be geared to two events. One was his betrayal to the authorities, the other his own final proclamation that he was the Messiah. The latter he himself could control, the former depended totally on Judas.

And so, as the group waited apprehensively in the darkness of the Garden of Gethsemane, the doubts and worries gnawed menacingly at their minds. Would Jesus really go through with the plan? Had he really meant what he said? Could Judas bring himself to carry out his awful mission, or even succeed in it if he did?

The doubts were not confined to the disciples. Jesus, too, if we are to believe our sources, was almost uncontrollably aghast ('My Father, if it is possible, let this cup pass me by . . .') at the chain of events that he had now set irretrievably in motion.[a] However, a period of prayer and meditation restored his self-confidence and determination. Shortly before dawn, still sleepless, he first heard, then saw the armed line of Temple servants bearing down on him through the trees. Awakening his followers, he advanced towards Judas, who was at the head of the file. 'Friend, do what you are here to do,' he said encouragingly[b], and Judas, no doubt in tears, duly gave him the fateful kiss that marked out the man to arrest.

Affronted as Jesus evidently was at being seized like a common bandit, rather than with the dignity appropriate to the nation's Priest-Messiah going his appointed way, he must nevertheless have known that this was merely a

[a] Compare the account at Mt. 26:36-56. [b] Mt. 26:50

sign of things to come. 'Do you suppose that I cannot appeal to my Father, who would at once send to my aid more than twelve legions of angels?' he remonstrated, no doubt endeavouring at the same time to relieve his betrayer's overwhelming sense of personal guilt. 'But how then could the scriptures be fulfilled, which say that this must be?'[a]

O sword, awake against my shepherd and against him who works with me. Strike the shepherd, and the sheep will be scattered.[b]

Let none of those who look to thee be shamed on my account, O Lord GOD *of Hosts . . .*[c]

The prisoner was led away. The remaining disciples fled for their lives, as Jesus had no doubt instructed them to do, in fulfilment of Zechariah's prophecy. Hard on their heels followed an evidently Essene bystander; a young man who, hearing of the imminent arrest, had hurried straight from the Essene ceremony of ritual ablution to the Garden, still dressed only in his ritual veil or sheet — and who, in his panic to escape, left it behind in the hands of his pursuers.[d]

The kings of the earth stand ready, and the rulers conspire together against the LORD *and his anointed king.*[e] *'His case is desperate,' my enemies say; 'when will he die, and his line become extinct?. . .' All who hate me whisper together about me and love to make the worst of everything.*[f]

O God of my promise, be silent no longer, for wicked men heap calumnies upon me . . . They say, 'Put up some rascal to denounce him . . .'[g]

And so the Priest-Messiah, having — as predicted — already made little moral impression on the common people, must now be finally rejected by the priestly establishment as well. Indeed, they must actually be persuaded to collude with the occupying power in plotting his torture, downfall and death. False accusations must be levelled, but in the end the authorities must be given good reason to act.

These prophetic requirements may appear to demand a degree of control over the ruling circles in Jerusalem which Jesus did not have. Yet he did know the ground-rules by which both Jewish and Roman authorities were bound. And, as we shall see, he also had surprisingly influential friends in high places.

Thus, in the present case, he knew that both groups of rulers would be more than anxious to dispose of any would-be King-Messiah — the Romans because of the direct threat which the title posed to the authority of Caesar, and the Jews because of the inevitably catastrophic results of any attempted popular rising against that authority. Until Jesus made the claim explicitly, however, neither authority was empowered to act, and even then there was

---

[a] Mt. 26:53-54   [b] Zech. 13:7   [c] Ps. 69:6   [d] Mk. 14:51-52   [e] Ps. 2:2   [f] Ps. 41:5, 7   [g] Ps. 109:1-2, 6

nothing in the Jewish Law to render the claim illegal. Yet it was specifically to the Jewish authorities that Jesus had dispatched the faithful Judas, and so his condemnation would necessarily entail an act of collusion between the two sets of rulers, as foreshadowed by the scriptures.

First, however, he would have to be formally investigated by the Jewish Sanhedrin. Evidence would be called for — and it was well within the competence of Jesus to infiltrate his own witnesses and so ensure that no consensus was forthcoming. Since he had in any case done little or nothing so far that was strictly illegal, the case would thus be inconclusive, whether under Jewish or Roman law. Only when he indicated specifically in some way that he was claiming the Messiahship would there be occasion to act 'in the interests of public safety' — and even then the matter would have to be referred to the Roman Procurator for judgement, under whose law alone the claim constituted a crime.

He was afflicted, he submitted to be struck down and did not open his mouth; he was led like a sheep to the slaughter, like a ewe that is dumb before the shearers.[a]

The only prophetic requirement relating to Jesus' own conduct during the investigation was that he should not attempt to defend himself against his accusers. The reports suggest that this requirement was duly fulfilled. Only when he judged that the right moment had come did he respond to their insistent prodding and lead them to infer that he considered himself the appointed Messiah. And so at last the Sanhedrin had something to complain of. For not only had Jesus, as they understood it, made a claim of startling political danger: he had committed what the Romans would see as blasphemy against the supposedly Divine authority of Tiberius Caesar.[b] And so the ball was now transferred to the Roman court, as Jesus had foreseen all along.

The Lord GOD *opened my ears and I did not disobey or turn back in defiance. I offered my back to the lash, and let my beard be plucked from my chin, I did not hide my face from spitting and insult.*[c]

. . . his form, disfigured, lost all the likeness of a man, his beauty changed beyond human semblance. He was despised, he shrank from the sight of men, tormented and humbled by suffering; we despised him, we held him of no account, a thing from which men turn away their eyes.[d]

Once at the Procurator's palace, the deadly game could recommence. Yet Jesus had made no extravagant statements before the Sanhedrin. At most he had permitted himself an ambiguous reply when charged with claiming the Messiahship, and certainly had not made the claim in so many words. Before

---

[a] Isa. 53:7   [b] Claiming the Messiahship did not, of course, constitute blasphemy against Yahweh, for which the prescribed punishment was in any case stoning, not crucifixion.
[c] Isa. 50:5-6   [d] Isa. 53:2-3

the Judean Procurator, Pontius Pilatus, could act, he would thus require positive evidence of his own. And so Jesus could once again play the game in his own time, choosing the right moment to set the final phase of the action in motion. According to Luke's account, Pilate actually had the prisoner transferred to King Herod for examination, on the grounds that, as a Galilean, Jesus did not come within his own jurisdiction. If the account is to be believed, Herod then returned the compliment and indicated, by arraying the prisoner in a luxurious robe — no doubt one taken from his own wardrobe — that the point at issue was not Jesus' place of birth but his claim to be King-Messiah, which had been made in Jerusalem.

All this, if true, had taken time, and Jesus must take care not to overplay his hand. The execution which he knew was drawing near must occur on the eve of the official Passover Sabbath, so as to coincide with the slaughter of the ritual Paschal lambs in the Temple. His survival, too, as we shall see, would depend on it. On no account must the ordeal be postponed until afterwards.

If John is to be followed at this point, Pilate had Jesus heavily flogged and re-arrayed, then faced him once more with his Jewish accusers, perhaps expecting that they would now be satisfied and withdraw the charge.[a] The guards plaited a crown of thorns and jammed it over his head. General hoots of derision broke out. The prisoner was roughly handled. The still-determined Sanhedrin representatives hastily mustered further supporters, all demanding further action. Increasingly aware that nothing short of acquiescence would satisfy them, Pilate at length gave orders for the prisoner's execution, albeit on grounds of hearsay evidence.

Matthew's account, however, suggests that the prisoner was not flogged until the order had finally been given. And we may assume that it was for this eventuality that Jesus had been planning, since it appears to have been the current custom for the condemned to be whipped unmercifully before execution, as part of a general policy of making capital punishment as slow, painful and thus exemplary a sentence as possible. The relevant prophecy[b], in other words, could safely be expected to be fulfilled.

But now the most critical moment of all was fast approaching. Jesus had, in the event, delayed the moment of execution until the last possible moment. Evidently he judged that there was still sufficient time for the remaining events covered by his life-script as Priest-Messiah to be played out before the Passover Sabbath began — yet not so much time as to prolong his expected agony unreasonably.

Time was still of the essence. But then so, too, was place.

Jesus, as we have seen, had taken good care to be arrested in his secret hideout in the privately-owned Garden of Gethsemane. And if that fact had not given the spark of an idea to Pilate, there were others in high places who could be trusted to see that it did. The prisoner, after all, was the current idol of the masses, now about to start their Passover celebrations in Jerusalem — even though they had apparently shown little real interest in what he had to tell them. For the same reasons which forbade his being arrested in public, he could not therefore now be executed in public. His death, when it occurred, must be both secret and private. Where better and more appropriate, therefore, than in the rebel's very headquarters, the Jasmine Garden itself? (The accounts may speak of a place of public execution known as 'Golgotha', but the word in fact means nothing in Hebrew, least of all 'place of a skull'. At least one commentator interprets the term as referring to the site of a wheelpress[a] for pulverising herbs and flowers[21] — a not inappropriate adjunct to a herb-garden such as Gethsemane, if that is what it was.)

There remained only the problem, therefore, of how to get him there. Once again, any public appearance would risk precipitating a public riot, even though, as the Passover itself approached, the streets would tend to become empty while the citizens busied themselves with preparing for it. Then again, a route could be taken across the Tyropoeon viaduct, past the Antonia (the Roman garrison-fortress) and around the north side of the Temple, well away from the populous poor quarter in the south-east corner of the city, where the prisoner had most of his supporters. The viaduct had been built precisely in order to spare the well-to-do of the upper city any such contact with the lower orders while on their way to the Temple. For safety's sake, of course, the prisoner would still have to be rendered unrecognisable. But then this task could safely be left to his brutal manhandlers. The already half-dead prisoner's grimy, blood-covered face, bowed beneath the weight of a wooden beam, would not be easily recognisable, even to his own mother.

And so the prophecy from Isaiah 53, quoted above, could with a fair degree of certainty be expected to come literally true, and the plan could then go forward to its most critical point.

Yet on himself he bore our sufferings, our torments he endured, while we counted him smitten by God, struck down by disease and misery; but he was pierced through for our transgressions, tortured for our iniquities; the chastisement he bore is health for us and by his scourging we are healed. We had all strayed like sheep, each of us had gone his own way; but the LORD *laid upon him the guilt of us all . . . Without protection, without justice, he was taken away; and who gave a thought for his fate, how he was cut off from the world of living men, stricken to the death for my people's transgression?[b]*

---

[a] *golgeth* ('press-wheel')   [b] Isa. 53:4-6, 8

Already, then, the Priest-Messiah had started to atone for Israel's backslidings. First by being whipped, and now by accepting execution, he was in the very process of laying the foundations for the Kingdom's imminent dawning.

My God, my God, why hast thou forsaken me and art so far from saving me, from heeding my groans? . . . I am a worm, not a man, abused by all men, scorned by the people. All who see me jeer at me, make mouths at me and wag their heads: 'He threw himself on the LORD for rescue; let the LORD deliver him, for he holds him dear!' . . . I tell my tale of misery while they look on and gloat. They share out my garments among them and cast lots for my clothes. But do not remain so far away, O LORD; O my help, hasten to my aid.[a]

They shall look on me, on him whom they have pierced, and shall wail over him as over an only child, and shall grieve bitterly as for a first-born son.[b]

It had been clear all along that the only form of execution that would fully accord with the prophecies was one involving both being stripped naked and being pierced by sharp instruments. In contemporary Palestine these conditions were amply fulfilled by the standard Roman punishment for brigandage, mutiny, treason and rebellion — namely crucifixion. Not that crucified criminals were always nailed to their crosses, but it would take little to bribe the executioners to adopt this method rather than binding the prisoner to the gibbet with ropes. And in view of the charge of *lèse-majesté* which had now been successfully laid against the prisoner, it was therefore a foregone conclusion that the prophecies could be satisfied in this respect.

It needed no prophetic planning, meanwhile, to ensure that the prisoner would be abused and spat upon by his captors, as well as wailed over by his friends and relatives. His own feelings of shame, too — as foreshadowed in Psalm 69 (below) — were inevitable; nakedness was an abomination to any Jew, which was one of the reasons why it was Roman standard practice to add this insult to the sufferings of the crucified.

And if there were casual bystanders along the way who chose to add their voices to the shouts of derision, then they, like Jesus' executioners themselves, were merely fulfilling unwittingly the Teacher's prophetic plan. In a sense, their action was Jesus' own fault. Well might he murmur, as he was assisted with his heavy crossbeam through the streets and out onto the Mount of Olives, 'Father, forgive them; they do not know what they are doing.'[c]

Thou knowest what reproaches I bear, all my anguish is seen by thee. Reproach has broken my heart, my shame and my dishonour are past hope; I looked for consolation and found none, for comfort and did not find any. They put poison in my food and gave me vinegar when I was thirsty.[d]

[a] Ps. 22:1, 6-8, 17-19 [b] Zech. 12:10 [c] Lk. 23:34 [d] Ps. 69:19-21

(Of the Passover Lamb:) *You must not break a single bone of it.*[a]

In these two passages, however, there was a glimmer of hope for Jesus' survival. For, as we shall see, the prophecies went on to insist that he would — indeed must — survive the experience. The eventuality, in fact, was by no means unknown. Men had been known to last as long as three days on the cross, and still to recover when taken down. The historian Josephus, it seems, was himself a later witness to such a case, in which, of three men taken down at his request, one survived.[42] The whole point about crucifixion as a method of punishment was its gruesome slowness.

And so secret plans, we may be sure, had already been made to take advantage of the fact. The Priest-Messiah would indeed be crucified. For a time he would be left in agony on the cross. Heart-rending the spectacle might be, but nothing less was necessary to achieve the predicted atonement of Israel to its God. Jesus must bear the pain as long as he possibly could. But then, before consciousness finally left him, he was to call out for a drink. At this, a female accomplice would come forward with a small sponge full of wine on the end of a stick. It was perfectly normal, after all, for such 'sisters of comfort' to be present at crucifixions. Perhaps even one of the supervising guards might be persuaded to raise it to the prisoner's mouth on the tip of his own spear. *But that wine would be drugged:*[b] the prophetic passage from Psalm 69 required explicitly that some poisonous herb or other noxious substance (*rosh*) be administered to the agonised Messiah.[c]

Almost immediately the drug would render Jesus unconscious. Concocted by the Essene herbalist-physicians, it would be sufficiently powerful to induce almost total paralysis — and, in particular, near extinction of both respiration and heartbeat. With the victim apparently dead, one of Jesus' friends in high places would quickly approach the Procurator for permission to remove the 'body' for burial in a nearby tomb. Even if the request were refused, the approach of the Passover Sabbath meant that, under Jewish Law, the supposed corpse would have to be taken down well before nightfall. But things could not be left so long: the legs of prisoners still alive on the cross before a festival were normally broken well before 6 p.m. in order to hasten their deaths. Jesus must accordingly be removed and entombed well before that time, not least in order that the symbolic conditions laid down by Exodus 12:46 (above) might be fulfilled.

And so at length, in the coolness and privacy of the tomb, those same physicians, armed with the appropriate antidote, could get to work to treat and revive the patient.

In the event, Jesus' secret accomplice must clearly have been alarmed at the

---

[a] Ex. 12:46   [b] Compare Mk. 15:23, 36   [c] In view of the already-encountered Hebrew poetic habit of saying things twice over, the poisoned food and vinegar (i.e. sour wine) of the Psalm did not, of course, necessarily have to be construed as separate substances.

state he was in even before crucifixion commenced. The flogging had taken a heavy toll. When the nails were produced, the appointed bystander evidently rushed forward to offer him the prepared drink forthwith.[a] But Jesus refused, determined to fulfil his predicted role. And so the nails were driven in, the heavy cross hauled upright, then dropped with a sickening thud into its waiting hole. The ordeal had commenced.

For a while the bystanders watched the writhing of the half-suffocating victim, the dripping of the blood. In reply to the jeers and torments of some of the onlookers, the would-be Priest-Messiah offered only groans of agony and despair.

Then, with an effort, Jesus began to speak. 'My God, my God, why hast thou forsaken me . . .' he began, then lapsed into half-audible mumbling, after the approved Jewish manner of reciting the scriptures. Those in the know would have recognised at once that he was reciting to himself the twenty-second Psalm (see above), which in many respects not only foreshadowed his present agony, but also went on to predict his ultimate survival and triumph.[b] Eventually reaching the last verse, he raised his voice again to declaim the final words '. . . that this was his doing' (literally: 'he has done'). As recorded by John at second-hand and in translation, they are better known to us in the form 'It is finished.'[c]

And now the time had come to embark on the most crucial stage of the plan. Almost with his last gasp, Jesus, commending his soul to Yahweh, uttered the pre-arranged cry 'I thirst.'[d] His accomplice ran forward. Jesus took the proffered wine. Almost at once, the drug took effect.[e] His head lolled. Quickly a bystander and Essene sympathiser whose name has come down to us as Joseph of Arimathæa took to his horse and sped to the Procurator's palace in the west of the city.

By all accounts, Pilate was astonished — as well he might have been — that Jesus had expired after a mere three hours or so, and pondered for a while Joseph's request for his *soma* (which, curiously enough, is the Greek for a *living* body) while the report was checked. When it eventually proved correct, he released what he now called the *ptoma* (the word for a corpse) to his petitioner. Meanwhile, at the Jasmine Garden, the guards were already breaking the legs of the two brigands who had, it seems, been crucified with Jesus. Finding Jesus apparently already dead, however, one of them contented himself with making sure by thrusting a lance into his side. At once, according to John, watery blood came out.[f] This detail apparently indicates that the spear-tip had penetrated the pleural cavity, in which blood and fluid are known to accumulate following severe bruising of the chest-cage, as had undoubtedly occurred during Jesus' heavy flogging. On the

---

[a] Compare Mk. 15:23   [b] See below.   [c] Jn. 19:30 A.V.   [d] Jn. 19:28   [e] Compare Jn. 19: 28-30   [f] Jn. 19:34

other hand, it is just possible that John's witness had merely seen the attendant centurion reaching up to Jesus' mouth with the sponge soaked in red wine on his spear-tip, followed by Jesus' clumsy attempt to drink from it, spilling some of it on his chest in the process. Certainly the text is so insistent at this point as to suggest that some doubt was cast on the story at the time.[a, b]

Only now, it seems, did Joseph finally return to claim the body. Possibly the delay while Pilate checked his report had frustrated the whole messianic plan. If John's spear-thrusting account is genuine, the chances that the unconscious Messiah could be revived to fulfil the final stage of his mission had been immeasurably lessened. The Essene physicians could cope with a simple case of crucifixion. Even where nails had been used, there was hope of full restoration, with only limited impairment of subsequent movement. The flogging, however, had possibly been more severe than anybody had expected[b], and had weakened the victim to an alarming extent. If, now, a gratuitous puncture of the lung were thrown in, the patient's chances of survival were distinctly slight. True, the heroic Alexander the Great had survived the removal of an arrow from the lung at around the same age while campaigning in India, but then he had been a fit man before he started. Now, however, as Jesus' tortured body was carefully borne towards the waiting tomb, there was little, if any cause for optimism. For the Essenes, things looked dark indeed.

But the LORD *ordained that a great fish should swallow Jonah, and for three days and three nights he remained in its belly.*[c]

He was assigned a grave with the wicked, a burial-place among the refuse of mankind, though he had done no violence and spoken no word of treachery.[d]

But God will ransom my life, he will take me from the power of Sheol.[e]

I shall not die but live to proclaim the works of the LORD. *The* LORD *did indeed chasten me, but he did not surrender me to Death.*[f]

Come, let us return to the LORD; *for he has torn us and will heal us, he has struck us and he will bind up our wounds; after two days he will revive us, on the third day he will restore us, that in his presence we may live. Let us humble ourselves, let us strive to know the* LORD, *whose justice dawns like morning light, and its dawning is as sure as the sunrise.*[g]

Yet the LORD *took thought for his tortured servant and healed him who had made himself a sacrifice for sin; so shall he enjoy long life and see his children's children, and in his hand the* LORD's *cause shall prosper. After all his pains he shall be bathed in light, and his disgrace shall be fully vindicated; so shall he, my servant, vindicate many, himself bearing the penalty of their guilt. Therefore will I allot him a portion*

---

[a] Compare Jn. 19:35-37. [b] Compare the evidence of the Turin Shroud.[54] [c] Jon. 1:17 [d] Isa. 53:9 [e] Ps. 49:15 (Sheol = Hades, Hell, the land of the dead) [f] Ps. 118:17-18 [g] Hos. 6:1-3

with the great, and he shall share the spoil with the mighty, because he exposed himself to face death and was reckoned among transgressors . . .[a]

I will declare thy fame to my brethren; I will praise thee in the midst of the assembly . . . For he has not scorned the downtrodden, nor shrunk in loathing from his plight, nor hidden his face from him, but gave heed to him when he cried out . . . Let all the ends of the earth remember and turn again to the LORD; *let all the families of the nations bow down before him. For kingly power belongs to the* LORD, *and dominion over the nations is his. How can those buried in the earth do him homage, how can those who go down to the grave bow before him? But I shall live for his sake, my posterity shall serve him . . . declaring to a people yet unborn that this was his doing.*[b]

From the various accounts it would seem that the titular owner of the Jasmine Garden was none other than Joseph of Arimathæa, who had no doubt purchased it for the Essenes, ostensibly as a source of herbs for their healing activities. Previous arrangements had evidently been made for this secret, if influential supporter to prepare a temporary 'tomb' within his garden[c] to cater for the very eventuality that had now occurred. Behind the great wheel-press for crushing herbs and flowers he had had a large cavern hollowed out in the rock. With the wheel in its normal position, the entrance was thus invisible. Only when the season for preparing herbs and essences arrived would its existence become apparent. And by then, if the Essenes' messianic plan was successful — and with all its scriptural support, how could it possibly fail? — it would have served its intended purpose.

Conceivably, then, it was this cavern — this temporary shelter — that had already served as the secret, overnight hideout of Jesus and his associates during the build-up to the Passover. Even if they had been spotted entering the garden, in other words, they would mysteriously have disappeared from view. Now, however, the Messiah's body had itself been brought back to this same hideout, ostensibly for burial in what, now that the wheel had been rolled back, gave the appearance of a large tomb, originally built for himself by the garden's owner.[d] If so, then it was truly 'a burial place among the refuse of mankind', for the Messiah's rightful tomb would, of course, have been on the opposite side of the valley and a little to the south, where the vast royal cave-sepulchre of David was to be found.

And so, in the dark recesses of the cavern, the Essene physicians were already lying in wait for their expected patient. Everything would now depend on their skill. For the prophecies required that he be revived and restored to health 'on the third day' — in other words, by Sunday, the day after the Sabbath. At a stretch, this could be taken to refer to the following Tuesday (the 'third day' of the Jewish week), but even so the requirement

---

[a] Isa. 53:10-12   [b] Ps. 22:22, 24, 27-31   [c] He would scarcely, after all, have prepared one in anybody else's (see note *d*).   [d] Mt. 27:57-61, Jn. 19:41

would place severe demands on their expertise. And in particular it would require that they work during the Passover-Sabbath.

As Essenes, the physicians would, of course, be undisturbed by the Passover-requirements, since they had already celebrated their feast on the previous Tuesday/Wednesday. But unless, as one theory suggests, the Essenes also celebrated a different Sabbath from the rest of society, they would need to display an attitude to Sabbath-healing similar to that already displayed by Jesus himself. Perhaps it was in anticipation of this very fact that he had undertaken his various, well-publicised Sabbath-healing escapades in the first place. The Sabbath, he had declared at the time, was made for man, not man for the Sabbath, and the Son of Man himself was therefore lord over it.[a] The point had no doubt been taken by the Qumran healers. The necessary treatment, consequently, could commence.

But when the tortured body of the Messiah, executed as a common criminal, was borne gingerly into the cave, the physicians were aghast at what they saw. How could they possibly hope to restore *this* last-ditch case to life and health in the time allotted, still less guarantee that he would be able forthwith to take on the burdens of kingly office? How could he ever hope to 'share the spoil with the mighty' and take up again the ancient role of David, when death was so obviously staring him in the face?

On that day his feet will stand on the Mount of Olives, which is opposite Jerusalem to the east, and the mountain shall be cleft in two by an immense valley running east and west . . .[b]

The king rejoices in thy might, O LORD; well may he exult in thy victory, for thou hast given him his heart's desire and hast not refused him what he asked. Thou dost welcome him with blessings and prosperity and set a crown of fine gold upon his head. He asked of thee life, and thou didst give it him, length of days for ever and ever.[c]

With your sword ready at your side, warrior king, your limbs resplendent in their royal armour, ride on and execute true sentence and just judgement . . . Your throne is like God's throne, eternal, your royal sceptre a sceptre of righteousness. You have loved right and hated wrong; so God, your God, has anointed you above your fellows with oil, the token of joy. Your robes are all fragrant with myrrh and powder of aloes, and the music of strings greets you from a palace panelled with ivory. A princess takes her place among the noblest of your women, a royal lady at your side in gold of Ophir.[d]

Notwithstanding the victim's state, however, an assistant by the name of Nicodemus — a sympathetic Pharisee — now appeared carrying a bundle weighing over half a hundredweight. According to John's account, this contained myrrh and aloes, as required by Zechariah's prophecy above.[e] The weight of spices mentioned, however, is far greater than would have been

---

[a] Mk. 2:27   [b] Zech. 14:4   [c] Ps. 21:1-4   [d] Ps. 45:3-4, 6-9   [e] Jn. 19:39

necessary for embalming the body, as John implies — or even for perfuming the predicted kingly robes. What seems clear from the recorded details is that the bundle in fact contained not merely myrrh and aloes, but also the Messiah's golden regalia, armour and royal vestments, ready for his expected triumphal procession into Jerusalem as King-Messiah.

But the chances now seemed virtually nil that Jesus' feet would ever again voluntarily touch the Mount of Olives, let alone (*pace* Matthew's wishful report at 27:51) with sufficient supernatural strength to produce the predicted earthquake. He was on the Mount of Olives, certainly, but on his back, not his feet, and the prospects that things would ever be otherwise now looked almost irredeemably bleak. The great Essene plan to inaugurate the Millennium, drawn up by the Teacher of Righteousness some two centuries earlier, had done more than merely encounter a stumbling-block. It was on the point of collapse, teetering on the brink of disaster, within an ace of foundering altogether.

12

Disaster

Slowly the Sabbath wore on. After the long night followed an even longer day. At some time during it, we may assume, the crucified Messiah regained fitful consciousness, aware even through his searing pain of the dire nature of the crisis that surrounded him.

At all costs the remainder of the world-plan for whose sake he had come so close to death must now be fulfilled. Almost obsessively its details raced through his brain in a never-ending train. The Teacher's blueprint, which he had committed to heart from his earliest youth, seemed to clutch at him now like a drowning man, as though aware that in him lay its only remaining hope of life and fulfilment. His injuries notwithstanding, he must somehow pull himself together, get on with the job.

In that day, says the LORD *of Hosts, I will break their yoke off their necks and snap their cords; foreigners shall no longer use them as they please; they shall serve the* LORD *their God and David their king, whom I will raise up for them.*[a]

My servant David shall become king over them, and they shall have one shepherd . . .[b]

So from the west men shall fear his name, fear his glory from the rising of the sun; for it shall come like a shining river, the spirit of the LORD *hovering over it, come as the ransomer of Zion, and of all in Jacob*[c] *who repent of their rebellion.*[d]

Seventy weeks are marked out for your people and your holy city; then rebellion shall be stopped, sin brought to an end, iniquity expiated, everlasting right ushered in, vision and prophecy sealed, and the Most Holy Place anointed . . .[e]

Pay heed to me, my people, and hear me, O my nation, for my law shall shine forth and will flash the light of my judgement over the nations . . .[f]

The LORD *said to Moses, 'I am now coming to you in a thick cloud, so that I may*

---

[a] Jer. 30:8-9 and see also Isa. 26:19   [b] Ez. 37:24   [c] 'Jacob' = Israel   [d] Isa. 59:19-20 and see Ez. 43.   [e] Dan. 9:24   [f] Isa. 51:4

speak to you in the hearing of the people . . . Go to the people and hallow them today and tomorrow and make them wash their clothes. They must be ready by the third day, because on the third day the LORD *will descend upon Mount Sinai in the sight of all the people . . .' On the third day, when morning came, there were peals of thunder and flashes of lightning, dense cloud on the mountain and a loud trumpet blast.*[a] *Thus Moses completed the work, and the cloud covered the Tent of the Presence, and the glory of the* LORD *filled the Tabernacle.*[b]

I was still watching in visions of the night and I saw one like a man coming with the clouds of heaven; he approached the Ancient in Years and was presented to him. Sovereignty and glory and kingly power were given to him, so that all people and nations of every language should serve him; his sovereignty was to be an everlasting sovereignty which should not pass away, and his kingly power such as should never be impaired.[c]

So ran the ancient texts, the oracles upon which the Essenes' Teacher of Righteousness had based the next section of his extraordinary prophetic blueprint. And what they now required was nothing less than a triumphal progress to take over the reins of Divine government in Jerusalem. Early on the third day, they revealed, the Messiah must emerge from his 'tomb' to be joined by the shining ranks of the Essenes from Qumran, clad in their freshly-washed linen robes of ceremonial white. Donning the same costume over his newly-acquired royal vestments, he would be raised aloft on a portable chair draped in cloth of the same anonymous white. Then the procession would, as previously, cross the Kidron Valley from the east via the Temple Causeway and make its way into the city.

At the same time Yahweh himself, it was confidently believed, would once more start to make his presence felt, as he had formerly done over a thousand years before at the time of the Mosaic Exodus. Even as the 'shining river' of white-clad marchers crossed the ravine, the 'spirit of the LORD' would suddenly be seen hovering over them in the form of a cloud, as it had done during the ancient wilderness-journey. Such inhabitants as were already awake at this hour — as practically all of them would be following the Mount of Olives earthquake — must inevitably be terror-struck at the phenomenon. And even if the Roman guards failed to respond to it, they would doubtless be disinclined to obstruct the progress of what they would regard as yet another boring religious procession connected with the interminable Jewish Passover-festival.

Now the procession, turning south, would make its way through the priests' quarter, attracting more and more hangers-on by the minute, until it reached the great cave-tomb of King David, which lay on the rocky slope opposite Gethsemane, just within the ramparts of Zion itself. Thus, in a

---

[a] Ex. 19:9, 10-11, 16   [b] Ex. 40:34   [c] Dan. 7:13-14 and see Ps. 2:6-8, Jer. 30:21.

sense, the Messiah would truly have 'come home' to his rightful burial-place. While he was ceremoniously borne inside, the rest of the people in Jerusalem and their still-sleepy pilgrim-guests would be summoned by his excited disciples to come surging to the sepulchre to watch what they promised would be a truly miraculous spectacle. For no sooner would a large crowd have gathered than the King-Messiah, having divested himself of his white linen cover-all, would re-appear in the entrance to the sepulchre, seated on what was now revealed to be a portable throne, and wearing the full robes and regalia of his ancient predecessor, in symbol of the latter's rebirth in him. At the self-same moment the Essenes would suddenly produce the shining swords that they had concealed beneath their robes and exultantly wave them aloft.

The crowd would, of course, immediately go wild with delight and revolutionary messianic fervour. Now the full meaning of the earthquake would dawn on them. The Messiah — whether Jesus or David — had indeed risen from the dead and was coming to claim his Kingdom! Amid singing and dancing and delirious shouts of joy, they would fête the procession as it now set out on its final, brief journey to the Temple. And meanwhile, as the news spread — backed up by the visible sign in the sky of Yahweh's presence — the remainder of the city would rise as one in revolt against the Roman oppressors, and Jerusalem would be freed at a stroke from the hated foreign yoke.

33 AD was, after all, the third of the four possible fulfilment-dates for Daniel's celebrated 'seventy weeks' (i.e. 490-year) prophecy — though it is by no means certain that the Essenes could have calculated the date so exactly. And that appears to have been the precise time for which these very events had been arranged.[28, 38]

And so the procession would duly re-enter the already-secured Temple precinct. As they did so, the cloud which overshadowed them would descend upon the Sanctuary in token of the ending of their journey[a], flashes of lightning and peals of thunder would issue from it, and Yahweh would once again take up residence in the Temple which he had so long deserted on the summit of Zion, his latter-day Holy Mountain.

It was at that moment that the King-Messiah himself, having been duly re-anointed as such by the Essenes' priestly leaders, would come forward and go into the Sanctuary. Like Moses before him, he would enter the cloud and come face to face with his God as the nation's High Priest and King, the 'Man' or 'son of man' figure foretold by Daniel, in terms of which Jesus had identified himself throughout his ministry.[b] And from that moment all

---

[a] Compare Ex. 40:36–37, and also the parallel phenomenon at the time of Solomon's dedication of the original Temple. (I Ki. 8:10–11). [b] The term (*bar enash* in Aramaic, *ben adam* in Hebrew) was customarily employed as a sectarian code-word for 'Messiah', especially in northern Palestine, no doubt because it was also widely used to mean simply 'he', 'I' or 'one' (compare German *Mann/man*) — as, no doubt, it frequently was also on Jesus' own lips.[42, 53]

sovereignty would be granted to him. His, in fact, would be the Kingdom, the power and the glory for ever.

Then, in the end, what has been decreed concerning the desolation will be poured out.[a]

Go, my people, enter your rooms and shut your doors behind you; withdraw for a brief while, until wrath has gone by. For see, the LORD *is coming from his place to punish the inhabitants of the earth for their sins; then the earth shall uncover her bloodstains and hide her slain no more.*[b]

The LORD *said to my lord, 'You shall sit at my right hand while I make your enemies the footstool under your feet.'*[c]

And so, from that moment, the great, final showdown between the forces of Darkness and Light, so long foreshadowed by Zoroastrians and Essenes alike — and expected by the latter since at least the great earthquake of 31 BC — would at last commence. The new earthquake would have borne witness to the fact. Cloud-borne, the spirit of Yahweh would go forth to war from his Temple at Jerusalem. It was to be a time of unmitigated world-wide horrors, and during it the Messiah's immediate followers must retire to the fortress-monastery at Qumran — or possibly stay behind closed doors within Jerusalem itself — while the Essene shock-troops, led by their own priests and joined by thousands of disaffected Pharisees, Zealots and other converts, conducted the campaign on the Messiah's behalf. He himself, meanwhile, would act as a kind of magical talisman, very much as the ancient Ark of the Covenant had done before him. He, like it, now embodied the marks of the nation's Covenant with Yahweh, and in token of the fact the cloud of the Divine Presence would continually overshadow both him and them, so assuring them of victory. But the Messiah himself, as a 'man of peace', would take no part in the fighting.

The plan of campaign for the expected war — including details of the King-Messiah's shield[d] — is spelt out with almost ritual precision in the Qumran *War Rule*. But for details of the accompanying period of natural and supernatural catastrophes the Teacher had once more had recourse to the scriptures themselves. And no doubt it is his selection of texts which, duly edited and interpreted, consequently appears on Jesus' lips at Matthew 24.

An end is coming, the end is coming upon the four corners of the land . . . Behold, the day! The doom is here, it has burst upon them.[e]

The end of it shall be a deluge, inevitable war with all its horrors[f] . . .

For the LORD*'s anger is turned against all the nations, and his wrath against all the host of them: he gives them over to slaughter and destruction.*[g]

---

[a] Dan. 9:27   [b] Isa. 26:21   [c] Ps. 110:1   [d] *War Rule*, V[51]   [e] Ez. 7:2, 10   [f] Dan. 9:26 and see Dan. 11:40   [g] Isa. 34:2

Outside is the sword, inside are pestilence and famine . . .[a]

Behold, the LORD *will empty the earth, split it open and turn it upside down and scatter its inhabitants . . . The earth dries up and withers, the whole world withers and grows sick. For the earth's high places sicken, and earth itself is desecrated by the feet of those who live in it, because they have broken the laws, disobeyed the statutes and violated the eternal covenant. For this a curse has devoured the earth and its inhabitants stand aghast. For this those who inhabit the earth dwindle and only a few men are left. The new wine dries up, the vines sicken . . .*[b]

You have no cares now, but when the year is out, you will tremble, for the vintage will be over and no produce gathered in . . .[c]

I will hand them over as plunder to foreigners and as booty to the most evil people on earth, and these will defile them. I will turn my face from them and let my treasured land be profaned; brigands will come in and defile it. Clench your fists, for the land is full of bloodshed and the city full of violence. I will let in the scum of the nations to take possession of their houses . . .[d]

For son maligns father, daughter rebels against mother, daughter-in-law against mother-in-law, and a man's enemies are his own household.[e]

Let your astrologers, your star-gazers, who foretell the future month by month, persist and save you! But look, they are gone like chaff; fire burns them up . .[f]

Tempest will follow upon tempest and rumour upon rumour. Men will go seeking a vision from a prophet; there will be no more guidance from a priest, no counsel from elders.[g]

Take from my hands this cup of fiery wine and make all the nations to whom I send you drink it. When they have drunk it they will vomit and go mad; such is the sword which I am sending among them.[h] *For as the waters fill the sea, so shall the land be filled with the knowledge of the* LORD.[i]

Armed forces . . . will desecrate the sanctuary and the citadel and do away with the regular offering. And there they will set up 'the abominable thing that causes desolation' . .[j]

Lie writhing on the ground like a woman in childbirth, O daughter of Zion, for now you must leave the city and camp in open country.[k]

When the windows of heaven are opened and earth's foundations shake, the earth is utterly shattered, it is convulsed and reels wildly . . .[l]

I will show portents in the sky and on earth, blood and fire and columns of smoke; the sun shall be turned into darkness and the moon into blood before the terrible day of the LORD *comes.*[m]

---

[a] Ez. 7:15   [b] Isa. 24:1, 4–7   [c] Isa. 32:10, and see Isa. 24:17   [d] Ez. 7:21-4, and see Dan. 11:33   [e] Mic. 7:6   [f] Isa. 47:13-14   [g] Ez. 7:26   [h] Jer. 25:15-16   [i] Isa. 11:9   [j] Dan. 11:31   [k] Mic. 4:10   [l] Isa. 24:18   [m] Joel 2:30-31 and see Isa. 13:10-11, 24:23.

At that moment Michael shall appear, Michael the great captain, who stands guard over your fellow-countrymen; and there will be a time of distress such as has never been since they became a nation till that moment. But at that moment your people shall be delivered, every one who is written in the book: many of those who sleep in the dust of the earth will awake, some to everlasting life and some to the reproach of eternal abhorrence. The wise leaders shall shine like the bright vault of heaven, and those who have guided the people in the true path shall be like the stars for ever and ever. [a]

All the host of heaven shall crumble into nothing, the heavens shall be rolled up like a scroll and the starry host fade away . . . for the sword of the LORD *appears in heaven.* [b]

Then he will raise a signal to the nations and gather together those driven out of Israel; he will assemble Judah's scattered people from the four corners of the earth . . . [c]

All you who dwell in the world, inhabitants of earth, shall see when the signal is hoisted on the mountains and shall hear when the trumpet sounds. [d]

Such, then, were the oracles of things to come, so clear that hardly any explanation was necessary. The destruction of city and Temple, the advent of false prophets, wars, plagues, famines, earthquakes and worse, persecution, deportation, near-genocide, betrayal by former friends and relatives — all were clearly predicted, and the only ones to survive would be those who, during the interim, remained totally faithful to the Covenant, whose terms must now be proclaimed world-wide. Well might Jesus' own disciples pray, then, and constantly watch their every act.

Then, finally, when the Sanctuary was desecrated anew, those survivors must forthwith take to the hills. And there, amid all manner of celestial signs and portents, they would at last see again the resplendent cloud of the Divine Presence overshadowing the Messiah — not to mention the clouds of celestial angels who would have flocked to his support in his final campaign[f] — as he made his way back over the mountains of Judea, rejoicing in his ultimate triumph over the forces of Darkness. In his train would be the teeming masses of the nation's long-lost exiles, gathered together by his angelic messengers. And at the same moment the ancient Jewish dead would miraculously be raised to life once more in order to learn their fate. For now at last the final age of everlasting peace, prosperity and righteousness would be about to begin. For those worthy of it, immortality would once again be the birthright of everyman, as it had once been in the Garden of Eden. And so the Messiah would finally have entered the Kingdom long promised him.

Arise, Jerusalem, rise clothed in light; your light has come and the glory of the LORD *shines over you . . . and the nations shall march towards your light and their kings to*

[a] Dan. 12:1-3   [b] Isa. 34:4-5   [c] Isa. 11:12   [d] Isa. 18:3   [e] Mk. 13:33   [f] Compare *War Rule,* XIX[51]

your sunrise.[a]

Here is my servant, whom I uphold, my chosen one in whom I delight, I have bestowed my spirit upon him and he will make justice shine on the nations. He will not call out or lift his voice high, or make himself heard in the open street . . .[b]

I will take you out of the nations and gather you from every land and bring you to your own soil . . . I will give you a new heart and put a new spirit within you . . . and make you conform to my statutes, keep my laws and live by them.[c]

Thereafter the day shall come when I will pour out my spirit on all mankind; your sons and your daughters shall prophesy, your old men shall dream dreams and your young men see visions; I will pour out my spirit in those days even upon slaves and slave-girls.[d]

They shall beat their swords into mattocks and their spears into pruning-knives; nation shall not lift sword against nation nor ever again be trained for war . . .[e]

. . . and each man shall dwell under his own vine, under his own fig-tree, undisturbed.[f]

All mankind shall come to bow before me, says the LORD; *and they shall come out and see the dead bodies of those who have rebelled against me; their worm shall not die nor their fire be quenched, and they shall be abhorred by all mankind.*[g]

On that day the burden they laid on your shoulder shall be removed and their yoke broken from your neck . . .[h]

But for you who fear my name, the sun of righteousness shall rise with healing in his wings, and you shall break loose like calves released from the stall.[i]

Then shall blind men's eyes be opened, and the ears of the deaf unstopped. Then shall the lame man leap like a deer, and the tongue of the dumb shout aloud . . .[j]

The LORD *feeds the hungry and sets the prisoner free. The* LORD *restores sight to the blind and straightens backs which are bent . . . The* LORD *shall reign forever, thy God, O Zion, for all generations.*[k]

They shall live in the land which I gave my servant Jacob, the land where your fathers lived. They and their descendants shall live there for ever, and my servant David shall for ever be their prince. I will make a covenant with them to bring them prosperity; this covenant shall be theirs for ever. I will greatly increase their numbers, and I will put my sanctuary for ever in their midst.[l]

The sun shall no longer be your light by day, nor the moon shine on you when evening falls; the LORD *shall be your everlasting light, your God shall be your glory.*[m]

Via these and a myriad similar texts, the Teacher's *Book of Meditation*

---

[a] Isa. 60:1, 3 [b] Isa. 42:1-2 and see Isa. 11:10 [c] Ez. 36:24, 26, 27 [d] Joel 2:28-29 and see Isa. 32:13, 15, 18-19 [e] Isa. 2:4, Mic. 4:3 [f] Mic. 4:4 and see Zech. 3:10, Ez. 34:22-23, 25 (p. 109), Ps. 96:13 [g] Isa. 66:23-24 [h] Isa. 10:27, and see 11:1, 4, 6 (p. 107) [i] Mal. 4:2 [j] Isa. 35:5-6 [k] Ps. 146:7-8, 10 [l] Ez. 37:25-26 [m] Isa. 60:19

concluded by detailing the secrets of the coming Kingdom. Restored, rebuilt, re-peopled with the Jewish exiles, and with the Temple in its midst newly reconstructed to Ezekiel's design as described in Chapters 40 to 44, Jerusalem would become the Divinely-sanctioned capital of the world, with the Messiah acting as Yahweh's appointed vicar on earth. He it was who, without any need for self-display or self-promotion, would judge the wicked, separate the 'sheep' from the 'goats', and admit the faithful to their rightful glory. It is almost as though he were expected to be installed by popular consent, rather than asserting his authority by force. Under his protection the land would grow rich, the crops flourish, the people multiply. All disease would be banished, all hunger and want satisfied. Even the ageing process would stop, and Messiah and people alike would for ever enjoy the prosperity and peace long promised them as their eternal inheritance.

But when would all this happen? How long must elapse between the Messiah's revival in his lonely tomb and his eventual, triumphant return to inaugurate that final era of bliss? How long was the great War and its concomitant period of disasters to last before the New Age dawned?

On this question the Essene oracles were in no doubt what-soever.[a] Impossible as it clearly was to name the exact day and hour[b], the texts assembled by the Teacher made quite clear the destined duration of the intervening time.

Forty days you spent exploring the country, and forty years you shall spend — a year for each day — paying the penalty of your iniquities. You shall know what it means to have me against you.[c]

For forty years I was indignant with that generation . . .[d]

When you have completed all this, lie down a second time on your right side, and bear Judah's iniquity for forty days; I count one day for every year. Then turn your face towards the siege of Jerusalem and bare your arm, and prophesy against it.[e]

For four decades, then, the Time of Wrath would devastate the world, yet the text from Psalm 95 specified that it was to be a single generation that would suffer it all. Jesus and his followers, in other words, could expect still to be there at the end, and so to inherit the ultimate Kingdom as the texts required.[f]

Such were the secrets of the Kingdom that had already been expounded by Jesus to his disciples during the run-up to the fateful Passover. What he had not explained to them, however, was the detailed plan for the initial messianic takeover. His appearance as David returned at the head of an

---

[a] Compare the Qumran *War Rule* and *Damascus Rule*, VIII[51]   [b] Compare Mt. 24:36.
[c] Num. 14:34   [d] Ps. 95:10   [e] Ez. 4:6-7   [f] Compare Mt. 24:34

Essene army, the subsequent popular rising and his triumphal entry into the Temple were matters which were probably known only to Jesus himself and the inner cabinets at Carmel and Qumran. Any inadvertent leak of the plan would, after all, result in immediate Roman counter-measures.

Consequently, Jesus' instructions to his disciples had been simply to stay in the upper room on the Ophel over the Sabbath, and then to send two of their number to the Jasmine Garden on the Sunday morning as soon as it was light. Only then would he give them their marching orders to summon the people to assemble in front of King David's tomb in expectation of a miracle.

Such calls were nothing new. Numerous would-be Messiahs had in the past summoned the people forth to witness Divine prodigies, both up-country on Mount Gerizim and out in the east on the banks of the Jordan. All had been brutally dealt with.[42] No doubt the authorities' evident suspicion of John the Baptist had been based on just such antecedents. But this time the miracle would happen under their very noses. The people would have assembled and the magic worked before either they or the Roman garrison had time to organise and take effective counter-measures. And so the Messiah would proceed to take over his rightful throne.

It was therefore with a mixture of eagerness and trepidation that two of the disciples hurried to the 'tomb' that Sunday morning. The accounts disagree as to exactly who they were. But what they do agree on is that the disciples found not a waiting Messiah but an empty grave-slab, not a king in gorgeous robes smelling of myrrh and aloes, but an empty shroud devoid of either. And in their place a young man clothed in gleaming-white, newly-laundered clothes — the ceremonial white robes of the Essenes.

In Luke, Mark's gleaming youth has become two men, in Matthew an angel, in John two. All, however, bear witness to a fact and — as befits an angel[a] — a message.

The fact was that the despairing Essene physicians, conscious of the enormous prophetic responsibilities that now rested on their shoulders, had made a vital decision almost as soon as the official burial-party had left the tomb on the Friday evening. Folding back the bloodstained shroud, and aghast at the patient's injuries, they had immediately concluded that Jesus had no hope of fulfilling his predicted role within the three days allowed for his recovery. Indeed, he would be lucky to survive at all. It was not a question of mere revival and first-aid. What he needed — and needed urgently — was a period of intensive care and nursing in an environment where such treatment was available. And that could mean only one thing. He must be transferred to Qumran as soon as possible.

For the Essenes, 'as soon as possible' meant, at the earliest, Saturday evening. For twenty-four hours their hands would be tied by the very Law

[a] Grk. *ággelos* = messenger

for whose sake Jesus' survival was so vital. It was an almost archetypal cleft-stick situation. And yet, being strict Essenes, they could only wait. Even among the comparatively lax Pharisees, emergency life-saving on the Sabbath was one thing, defying the laws restricting Sabbath-travel quite another. And so, in the dusk of the Saturday evening, we may imagine, one of the physicians eventually slipped out of the tomb and, stumbling and falling in the darkness, hurried down the familiar Kidron ravine towards the shores of the Dead Sea.

The distance involved was fully twenty miles of very rough going. But in all probability the panting physician never got that far. Somewhere in the lower reaches of the deep, twisting *wadi* he heard the sound of movements ahead of him in the darkness. Soon, thanks to the full, Passover moon that had now risen high enough to strike down into the very depths of the valley, he could make out a long line of gleaming white figures coming to meet him. It was the army of Essenes from Qumran, secretly moving up the ravine under cover of darkness to make their predicted rendezvous with the Messiah by the light of dawn.[a]

Breathless greetings were exchanged. Then, crestfallen, the physician broke the dreadful news. The Essene leaders held an urgent consultation. Inevitably, they were incredulous at the apparent failure of the prophecies. Only after further, specific details from the physician did they eventually decide that the plan must be temporarily abandoned. And so the main body of the army set off back down the valley to Qumran, while a guard and stretcher-party were sent ahead to rescue the dying Messiah.

Dawn must already have been close when the little group of Essenes eventually reached the tomb in the Jasmine Garden. At any moment, Jesus' disciples might arrive. At all costs, the news of the setback must be concealed from them, lest such 'weaker souls' should be diverted from their purpose and spread alarm and despondency among the people. Since the disciples had not been made privy to the plan's immediate details in the first place, they must somehow be convinced that all was well.

Perhaps it was at this moment that the lips of Jesus started to move. Whispering was not the word for it — his punctured lung alone had seen to that. 'Tell them,' he seems to have mouthed, 'that I am going on before them into that which is perfect (*kalil*)'. By this he presumably meant the perfection of the promised Kingdom. But his listeners, hearing his agonised, unvoiced 'k', assumed that what he had really intended to say was the voiced 'g' of *Galil* (Galilee), and it is in this version that the message has come down to us in Mark and Matthew.[a]

And so one of the newly-arrived Essenes was delegated to stay behind — still clad in the newly-washed robes prescribed by Exodus 19 — to await the

[a] Mk. 16:7, Mt. 28:7

arrival of the disciples' emissaries and deliver the message. The remainder of the party hurriedly tidied the 'tomb', left the shroud folded up in a corner in token of the Messiah's successful escape from death, and collected up the spices and royal regalia for possible later use. Then, leaving the tomb wide open, and carrying the recumbent and scarcely-breathing Messiah with them as gently as they could, they set off for Qumran by the way they had come.

13
Second Thoughts

The assembled disciples, inevitably, were shattered by the news. If what their emissaries reported was correct, the great messianic plan, as already explained to them in general terms by Jesus, had misfired. All their hopes and expectations had been dashed. Instead of an imperishable Kingdom, all they had for their pains was some vague message to the effect that Jesus was 'going before them into Galilee' — a message which in any case made no sense, since it contradicted Jesus' own earlier instruction to them to stay in Jerusalem until the Kingdom dawned.[a]

Clearly, the report was untrustworthy. The 'angel' in the tomb had been either a figment of the imagination or, more likely perhaps, one of a party of grave-robbers, surprised in the half-light of dawn by the first disciples' arrival.[b] That he might have been a Qumran Essene seems not to have occurred to the disciples since, thanks to Jesus' habit of keeping his cards close to his chest, they were totally unaware of the Essenes' planned involvement in the revival-plan and subsequent popular coup. And in any case, no Essene — indeed, no right-minded Jew of any persuasion other than the deceased's female relations — would have risked defilement by entering a tomb containing what was supposed to be a corpse.

Yet who would have wanted to steal the body? Had they been attracted by the expensive spices? Had the robbers' unexpected break-in baulked the anticipated miraculous resurrection-process? And if so, where was Jesus' body now? Certainly the resurrection itself could not have occurred for, if Jesus had survived, he would have been there, arrayed in his kingly robes, to meet them as he had promised. The fact that he was not could only mean that he was indubitably and finally dead, his body either reburied who knows where or unceremoniously dumped among the perpetually-burning city garbage in the adjoining valley of Hinnom, better known as 'Hellfire' or *Gehenna*. The latter possibility, at least, would have had the merit of fulfilling

[a] Acts 1:4 [b] Compare Jn. 20:13

the prophecy at Isaiah 53:9.[a]

The disciples' understandable despair and despondency were no doubt mirrored, although for different reasons, among the Essenes at Qumran. For the sectaries had other, equally daunting aspects of the problem to consider. On the one hand there was the immediate, if forlorn battle for the Messiah's still-ebbing life to be waged with all the resources at their disposal. On the other, there was the need for an agonising re-think of their plans, and in particular a re-appraisal of the requirements of the prophetic timetable.

Consequently the main need was for time. Time to think, to study, to interpret, to discuss. The Essenes' foremost prophetic interpreters must be assembled. The word of God must once more be sought on the people's behalf, as it had been once before by Moses on Sinai. And so, just as Moses had required forty days to fulfil that task, so the same period must now elapse before the results of the Qumran deliberations were finally decided. There would then remain the task of conveying the decisions made to Jesus' own disciples and announcing them to the Essene movement at large. The obvious time for this would be some three weeks later, at the Feast of Weeks, or Day of Pentecost, when the Essenes customarily held their annual general assembly precisely in order to celebrate Moses' reception of the original Covenant, admit new members and assess each member's progress during the year. And by then, of course, the Messiah's physical fate would in all probability be known, for better or for worse.

For several days, it may be, the stricken patient lay at the point of death. Then, slowly at first, the unbelievable happened. He started to rally. Soon he was conscious, his mind feverishly re-running the events of the last few weeks and days. Perhaps, to while away the hours, he even dictated penitential hymns or psalms on the subject to an amanuensis, much as David himself had done to console himself during his darkest hours, and as the sect's own Teacher of Righteousness had likewise done to such moving effect in the existing poems of the sect's Hymn-scroll.[51] David's celebrated Psalm 23, indeed, seemed to sum up both his present circumstances and his still unextinguished hopes, almost as though it were the natural sequel to the starkly prophetic twenty-second Psalm already quoted above (pp. 144, 148).

Since the Qumran *Hymns* are not signed or dated, we cannot, of course, be sure who wrote each of them. Certainly the first seven of the twenty-five extant compositions contain strong evidence of the Teacher's own authorship. But in Hymn 8[51] we start to find passages such as

I thank Thee, O Lord,
    for Thou hast not abandoned me

[a] See p. 147 above.

whilst I sojourned among a people [burdened with sin]
. . .but Thou hast saved my life from the Pit.
. . . Thou hast caused me to dwell with the many fishers
who spread a net upon the face of the waters
and with the hunters of the children of iniquity . . .

This clear reference to Ezekiel's apparent vision of the future Dead Sea Community[a] leads on to the words:

For Thou, O God, hast sheltered me
from the children of men
and hast hidden Thy Law [within me]
against the time when Thou shouldst reveal
Thy salvation to me.

The next six hymns show evidence of having been composed by the same author, almost as though he had taken it upon himself to add a further chapter of seven pieces to the Teacher's original seven. They are marked by alternating moods of black despair and religious exaltation:

I thank Thee O Lord,
for Thou hast not abandoned the fatherless
or despised the poor . . .
[All who have ea]ten my bread
have lifted their heel against me,
and all those joined to my Council
have mocked me with wicked lips.
The members of my [Covenant] have rebelled
and have murmured round about me;
they have gone as talebearers
before the children of mischief
concerning the mystery which thou hast hidden in me.

Whether quite recently or at an earlier stage, in other words, the author had been rejected by his own designated followers, even to the extent of being 'betrayed' after the manner of Judas. But there is more to come:

. . . so do they let fly [their poisonous darts],
viper's [venom] against which there is no charm;
and this has brought incurable pain,
a malignant scourge
within the body of Thy servant,
causing [his spirit] to faint

[a] Ez. 47:1-12

and draining his strength
so that he maintains no firm stand.

What could thus be seen as a direct reference to the unforeseen effects of a throwing-spear or javelin is followed by a further passage of unmitigated hopelessness:

I am clothed in blackness
*   and my tongue cleaves to the roof* [*of my mouth*] . . .
The light of my face is dimmed to darkness
*   and my radiance is turned to decay* . . .
I eat the bread of wailing
*   and drink unceasing tears;*
truly, my eyes are dimmed by grief,
*   and my soul by daily bitterness.*
[*Groaning*] *and sorrow encompass me*
*   and ignominy covers my face.*
My bread is turned into an adversary
*   and my drink into an accuser;*
it has entered into my bones
*   causing my spirit to stagger*
*   and my strength to fail.*
According to the mysteries of sin,
*   they change the works of God by their transgression.*

Apparently unable to take the food or drink necessary for his recovery, the author thus seems to indicate that his terrible wounds have in some way thwarted the predicted purposes of Yahweh, much as we might expect had he been Jesus.

The deeps resound to my groaning
*   and* [*my soul has journeyed*] *to the gates of death.*
But I shall be as one who enters a fortified city,
*   as one who seeks refuge behind a high wall*
*   until deliverance* [*comes*] . . .

However, it is not long before overwhelming depression once more descends on him:

As for me, I am dumb . . .
*   * [*my arm*] *is torn from its shoulder*
*   and my foot has sunk into the mire* . . .
All the foundations of my edifice totter
*   and my bones are pulled out of joint;*
my bowels heave like a ship in a violent tempest
*   and my heart is utterly distressed.*

> A whirlwind engulfs me
>   because of the mischief of their sin.

The picture is of a wounded man suffering the after-effects of crucifixion, deserted by his fellows, despairing of his own recovery and weakened by nausea and dizziness. From the evidence one might possibly conclude that his wounds had become infected. That he was in fact Jesus is thus not entirely beyond the realms of possibility, especially as the Hymn Scroll itself has been confidently dated by scholars, on the evidence of its script, to the first century A D[51], and could thus have included hymns first composed at this time.

Whether or not this supposition is correct, we may well imagine that, thanks to the unceasing efforts of the Essene physicians and the sheer willpower of the patient, the still-prostrate body of the Messiah did at length begin to show signs of mending. The improvement was inevitably a slow one, but eventually sufficient strength had returned for him to be taken — no doubt at his own insistence — into the community's dining-hall to attend the Essenes' sacred meal, extending his hand in blessing over the bread and wine as the sect's *Community Rule* and *Messianic Rule* had long anticipated, and as he had already done among his own disciples. Perhaps it was a memory of this occasion that was to underlie the account of just such a physical appearance at Luke 24:36-43.[a] But in the event the effort seems to have proved too much. As so often happened to warriors with chest-wounds acquired in battle, no sooner had he sat up for the first time — adding to the stress on the wound by raising his arms in blessing — than he suddenly coughed up a pool of blood and slumped back, dying, into his litter. As Luke's gospel actually specifies, he 'blessed them with uplifted hands; and in the act of blessing he parted from them.'[b]

The assembled sectaries were naturally horrified. For some days now they had begun to believe that the impossible could, after all, happen. Now they knew, starkly and brutally, that they had been deluding themselves all along. Their plans would henceforth have to take account of the fact that the physical Jesus would no longer be with them.

Reverently, the body was laid to rest in the sect's cemetery, in fulfilment of the apparent double prophecy at Isaiah 53:9 — *He was assigned a grave with the wicked, a burial-place among the refuse of mankind* — which now seemed to the ever-flexible Essene interpreters to indicate that he must be buried *twice*, the second time among their own company of exiled 'drop-outs'.[c] Among the mourners, in all probability, was the immensely respected James the Just, the younger brother of Jesus. Already no doubt summoned secretly to Jesus'

---

[a] 'Touch me and see,' he is alleged to have challenged them; 'no ghost has flesh and bones as you can see that I have'.   [b] Lk. 24:50-51   [c] The obvious interpretation — that the body must indeed be dumped among the rubbish of the valley of Hinnom, much as the disciples themselves may earlier have concluded — would doubtless have been too much for them to contemplate.

bedside as his closest surviving male relative and one of the leaders of his cell of close followers, he was now invited to remain at Qumran until the sect's deliberations were concluded. In this way there could be no risk of his disclosing prematurely to the world at large the news of the Messiah's death and the plan's apparent failure.

But the fact that Jesus was dead did not, for the Essenes, necessarily mean the end of the matter. The immortality and rebirth of the soul were, as we have seen, prominent among their beliefs. And so the realisation seems gradually to have dawned that King David could still be reborn to claim his Kingdom — whether in the person of Jesus or in some other form. The scriptures, therefore, must be combed for indications of whether this was destined to happen, and if so how and when.

The LORD *said to my lord, 'You shall sit at my right hand while I make your enemies the footstool under your feet.*[a]

Here, for a start, was a familiar prophetic passage which could be interpreted to mean that, if Jesus' body had, at death, been consigned to Hell (*sheol*, Hades or even *Gehenna*), his soul had been transferred to Heaven (i.e. the sky), there to remain at Yahweh's side until the expected time of war and calamity was over. It was to be at that time, in other words (and not, after all, during the next few days), that he would first take his kingly seat in the Temple, overshadowed by the cloud of the Divine Presence, and empowered to pass judgement on the already-defeated kingdoms of the world. And what had been expected to be a kind of 'second coming' — his eventual triumphant return at the end of his victorious military campaigns — would, in reality, be his first.

In view of this, it was now actually easier to understand how, despite the predicted time of war, the Messiah-to-be would be a 'man of peace'. For he would, in fact, not be present at all while the fighting took place. The inherent contradiction was now not merely something to be carefully avoided: it was actually impossible.

Meanwhile, the manner of his coming now also had to be reinterpreted. But this, in view of the poetic ambiguity of the relevant texts, was not a difficult task. In particular, Daniel's vision of the Messiah as 'one like a man coming with the clouds of heaven' and being presented to the 'Ancient in Years' could now be seen as referring directly to his celestial presentation to Yahweh. His eventual re-descent from the sky would thus presumably take a similar form. Like Yahweh himself, in other words, he would take the clouds for his chariot and ride on the wings of the wind.[b] Indeed, under the terms of

[a] Ps. 110:1 [b] Ps. 104:3

the next verse of the familiar Psalm, he would also go on to make the winds his messengers, and flames of fire his servants.[a]

I will not trust in my bow, nor will my sword win me the victory; for thou dost deliver us from our foes and put all our enemies to shame.[b]

Neither by force of arms nor by brute strength, but by my spirit! says the LORD of Hosts.[c]

As for the expected war itself, the prophetic texts clearly implied that, since Yahweh himself would now be taking over personal responsibility for routing the Messiah's enemies, the Qumran Essenes would not, after all, have physically to go to war on his behalf. Instead, they could wait confidently in the wings, prodding and manipulating as opportunity permitted and the spirit guided. Others, no doubt also goaded directly by Yahweh himself, would unwittingly do all the dirty work for them, and the role of the Essenes would thus be limited to stepping into the eventual political power-vacuum once their enemies had reduced each other to impotence and ruin.

And so the only serious question remaining was one of timing. The forty-year expectation of course remained unaltered. Jesus' predecessor, the sect's original Teacher, had, after all, quite clearly expected the same period to ensue between his own death and the end of the period of ordeal.[d] Yet he had been wrong. Indeed, there were worrying indications in the scriptures that the Divine timescale was not commensurate with the human one at all. Psalm 84, for example, contained the suggestive verse: *Better one day in thy courts than a thousand days at home[e]*, almost as though time differed according to where you were. Then again, the prophetic texts already used to predict the forty-year interim period contained not only the phrase 'a year for each day'[f], but also the reverse — Yahweh's clear statement, 'I count one day for every year.'[g] And so the expected 'forty-years' of Divine wrath could be as short as forty earthly days, while only the apparent assurance of Psalm 95:10 that its calamitous events would all befall a single generation ruled out the possibility that the period might be as long as 40 x 360 traditional *years* — an unimaginable timespan of 144 centuries — or even a thousand times longer than that.

Similar considerations naturally affected the various 'third day' prophecies relating to the Messiah's expected resurrection. For now, applying the same mathematical criteria as above, it became clear that 'on the third day' could mean either 'during the third year', 'in three thousand days or more' (taking due account of the psalmist's use of the word 'better') or even 'during the

---

[a] Ps. 104:4, and compare Heb. 1:1-14, where this verse is specifically brought into relationship with Ps. 110:1. [b] Ps. 44:6-7 [c] Zech. 4:6 [d] *Damascus Rule*, VIII[51] [e] Ps. 84:10 [f] Num. 14:34 [g] Ez. 4:6

third millennium'. Thanks to the 'single generation' idea, however, the choice seemed once more to narrow itself down to the first two — either three years, or a minimum of eight or nine.

Somehow these apparently conflicting possibilities would eventually be reconciled by Yahweh. Either the 'three-day' period would be extended, or the 'forty-year' period shortened, or both. In this way the messianic return would coincide, as the Essene interpreters now fully expected, with the ending of the time of wrath. All that was needed was scriptural confirmation of the idea. And in the event, the vital text was duly discovered.

Thou, our God, hast punished us less than our iniquities deserved and hast allowed us to survive as we now do — shall we again disobey thy commands . . . ? Would not thy anger against us be unrelenting, until no remnant, no survivor was left?[a]

Rarely as the sectaries were wont to take their prophetic oracles from the text of Ezra's history of the refounding of Jerusalem, they were doubtless much gratified by the results of their researches. The period of wrath was, despite everything, to be shortened for the sake of the 'precious remnant' of their own Elect. No firm conclusion was possible as to the exact extent of the shortening. All that could be said with any certainty was that the crucial moment would occur soon — not within the next three years, but certainly within forty.

And so fresh plans must be laid to watch the developing world-situation carefully and prayerfully as it developed. In accordance with the composite oracle at Daniel 11:31, Micah 4:10 and Daniel 12:1-3 (see pp. 155-156 above), the Essenes in the neighbourhood of Jerusalem must be ready at a moment's notice to leave for the relative safety of the wilderness as soon as the prophesied destruction of the city and profanation of its Temple loomed. And it was out there in the open country that they would at last see the signs and portents that would herald the Messiah's imminent, cloud-borne return from the skies.

The revised prophetic scenario, then, was finally agreed. On the fortieth day after Passover, as had been arranged, the supporting oracle-scroll was promulgated in witness of the fact. Possibly it is this document which, in reality, underlies the so-called 'Little Apocalypse' placed by Matthew on Jesus' own lips at chapter 24. And so it only remained to announce the crucial findings to the assembled Essenes in Jerusalem — and, in particular, to Jesus' own disciples, who now constituted the *de jure* interim messianic government — at the coming Feast of Weeks or Day of Pentecost, the central festival of the Essenic year.[52]

The meeting of the sect's elders with the disciples was duly fixed for the early morning on the first day of the week (for the Essenes' Pentecost

[a] Ezr. 9:13

always fell on a Sunday[52]). The Qumran delegation was, understandably, a high-ranking one, as befitted the announcement of such portentous tidings. Any one of them would have qualified to preside over such a gathering, having been specifically trained, as their *Damascus Rule* required — and as far as was practically possible — in 'all the secrets of men and the languages of all their clans.'[a] The disciples themselves were no doubt tense, on edge, at once excited and apprehensive. Still dejected and disillusioned as they indubitably were, they had the feeling that something electric and astonishing was in the air. In silence they assembled in the familiar upper room of the house in the priests' quarter, and prepared themselves to welcome their exalted visitors. As the appointed time approached, more and more of the Essenes currently in Jerusalem for the festival turned up at the house. Soon they were lining the stairs, packing the downstairs rooms, spilling out into the street. By the time the Qumran delegation arrived, it had to make its way through a milling throng of Jews drawn from all the multifarious national sub-cultures of the Middle East, each of which had its own special quarter in Jerusalem.

As the meeting commenced, a breathless hush fell over the house and the street outside. Ears strained to catch some hint of what was being said in the upper room. First on the agenda was the appointment of officers and the admission of new members to the group, as was the custom at such annual conventions. The position of treasurer having fallen vacant with the suicide of Judas, Peter (whom Jesus had apparently appointed acting chief of the twelve until he returned) asked for nominations for the post, arguing, not untypically, that the new appointment was required by the prophecy relating to the Messiah's betrayer. *May his days be few*, ran the text of Psalm 109:8; *may his hoarded wealth* (or '*his charge*') *fall to another!* Either way, it was clear that someone else must be appointed to take charge of the community's funds. In the event, two names were proposed and, after lots had been drawn, the appointment was, it seems, conferred on Matthew — who, as a former tax-gatherer, was clearly well-qualified for the task.[b]

Now came the main business of the meeting — the announcement of the findings of the Qumran enquiry. In deference to the relationship of James the Just both to the deceased Messiah and to his surviving followers, we may imagine that it was to him that the task of revealing the outcome was finally allotted. Flanked by the white-robed ranks of the sectaries, the revered ascetic stood up to speak. The Messiah, it seemed, had succeeded in emerging from his tomb alive and so, by fulfilling the last of the relevant prophecies, had finally clinched his claim to the Priest-Messiahship. By the same token, all Israel's past sins were now forgiven. And so the way was now clear for the Son of Man to inaugurate the Kingdom of God on earth.

---

[a] *Damascus Rule*, XIV   [b] Compare throughout the possibly mutilated account at Acts 1.

True, the physical Jesus had been taken to Qumran and, despite the physicians' valiant efforts, had subsequently died there. But that had been merely in order to allow his soul to ascend into Heaven, there to be presented to Yahweh amid the clouds of Heaven in accordance with Daniel 7:13, and to sit at his right hand, as Psalm 110:1 required, until the Time of Wrath was past and his enemies defeated.

Such had been the conclusions arrived at by the assembled sectaries, under the guidance of the spirit of Truth, on the fortieth day after Passover, and the appropriate document — the so-called 'Little Apocalypse' — was produced to prove it, setting out in detail all that was to come.[a]

And so now the words of Psalm 104 could clearly be applied to the Messiah who, like Yahweh himself, *takest the clouds for thy chariot, riding on the wings of the wind; who makest the winds thy messengers and flames of fire thy servants.* Cloud-borne as he had departed, cloud-borne he would return. And moreover, that advent was likely to occur sooner rather than later, for the time of ordeal had been shortened by Yahweh for the sake of his Elect. The disciples, then, and all the faithful with them, must be constantly on the alert, constantly at prayer until the Messiah returned — as return he assuredly would within the lifetime of those present.

For a moment the disciples sat spellbound, hardly believing their ears. Then, as James sat down, the room suddenly erupted with cheering, with stamping of feet, with shouts of exultation. Quickly the word was passed down the stairs by those nearest the door. The Messiah had risen. He had taken his seat in heaven. The time of wrath had been shortened. The Messiah was returning on the clouds of heaven.

Like a hurricane the news swept through the house and out to those waiting in the street. With it, the well-known words of the relevant scriptural oracles were passed, as proof-texts, from mouth to mouth. Especially did the magnificent imagery of Psalm 104 fire the imagination of the excited crowd. The Messiah had made the very clouds his chariot, had taken the wind for his messengers, flames of fire for his servants! Soon it became impossible in the hubbub to distinguish what had happened from what had been said, the words of James from the words of scripture. The Messiah had actually spoken to the Qumran messengers in a rushing, mighty wind; flames of supernatural fire had settled on his servants, the disciples.

Meanwhile, both the Hebrew (or Aramaic) and the Greek that were the crowd's common tongues used a single word for both 'wind' and 'spirit'. In both languages, too, the words for 'angel' and 'messenger' were identical. Amid the bedlam of voices, consequently, a new rumour quickly spread. The 'new spirit' long predicted for the onset of the Millennium had already descended on the assembly in the upper room.[b] The Messiah's angelic army

[a] Compare Mt. 24-25, Acts 2:14-36. [b] Compare Acts 2:14-17, as well as the preceding text.

was already at hand, and he himself could not be far behind.

The impression was strengthened as the disciples, clearly ecstatic, emerged from the house and hugged and kissed everybody in sight. It made no difference that Peter, quoting what he could remember of the 'Little Apocalypse', tried valiantly to set the record straight.[a] Clearly his strongly Galilean Aramaic was not being understood by a large part of the crowd. Realising this, the various multilingual Qumran dignitaries, who by now were leaning out of the upstairs windows observing what was going on, endeavoured to help out. In language after language they proclaimed the good tidings to the various national sections of the crowd. Jews from Greece, Egypt, Persia, Arabia and even Rome heard the new interpretation of the prophecies not in the accepted *lingua franca*, but in their own mother-tongue. But even this effort tended to be counter-productive. Agog at such a rare display of linguistic dexterity, the majority of the simple crowd — unable, in the nature of things, to understand most of what was being said — merely took it as further evidence that the speakers, if not actually drunk, were 'speaking in tongues', newly inspired by the Essenes' spirit of Truth.

And so a myth was born — the myth that the Messiah had sent a spiritual go-between to mediate between himself and his waiting followers on earth until such time as he should return. The myth grew, subsequently winning for the 'spirit' in question the status of a third member of a kind of heavenly tribunal. The idea which, three centuries later, was to become basic to the Christian doctrine of the Holy Trinity had started out on its long pilgrimage through history.

Meanwhile the same belief was to add immeasurably to the disciples' own moral stature. As repositories of the Messiah's holy spirit of Truth, they had, like the Messiah himself, become as it were all Light and no Darkness. From normal human beings they had suddenly been transformed into exalted, almost godlike personages. The belief, naturally, worked wonders, both for the disciples and for those who now started to come to them for leadership, encouragement and healing.[b] Like Jesus himself, his followers very soon actually turned into what they were believed to be. The result was a true demonstration of that human faith which Jesus himself had so prized. The disciples positively exuded charisma. They could move mountains. They could transmit their newly-acquired powers to others. And who could be sure that, given time, they might not also succeed in transforming the world?

As the idea of the Holy Spirit spread, so, naturally, did its sphere of presumed influence. All manner of new beliefs and doctrines could now be held to be validated by its workings. Where previously the extent of the presence of the Essenes' spirit of Truth in any individual was to be carefully assessed and scrutinised by the community's Master, now the operation of

[a] Compare Acts 2:17-36   [b] Compare Acts 2:43

the Holy Ghost came to be widely regarded as mòre or less autonomous and self-validating. The Spirit had been de-controlled and de-institutionalised; it had broken free of all restraints, taken control of its own destiny. And, in particular, it could now be trusted, independently of all other evidence or rational argument, to reveal the truth or otherwise of incoming reports and rumours.

It was not long, for example, before stories started to circulate claiming to be direct evidence that what the Qumran interpreters had asserted had actually been observed. Jesus had been seen standing outside the tomb.[a] He had walked and talked with two of his followers on the road to Emmaus[b], with several at a time, with hundreds at once.[c] As formerly, beginning 'with Moses and all the prophets', he had 'explained to them the passages which referred to himself in every part of the scriptures.'[d]

That the names and places differed in these various accounts was of little importance. His final meal at Qumran was soon transformed into a meal with his assembled disciples in Jerusalem or by the Sea of Galilee.[e] Albeit in locations as disparate as Jerusalem, Bethany and (by implication) Galilee, he was reported as actually having been seen rising on a cloud into the sky, in logical anticipation of the expected manner of his return. Moreover, as might be expected, the alleged date of this spectacular elevation coincided exactly with the promulgation of the Qumran document affirming the Messiah's ascent to heaven. And so for Christians, to this day, Ascension Day comes forty days after Easter (Passover).

The fact that the stories appeared to back up the new doctrine was, of course, already seen as evidence of their probable truth. Thereafter it needed only the supposed inspiration of the Holy Spirit to convince their various collectors of it. And so, in due course, these stories came to be regarded as indisputable facts, and thus as direct evidence for the very suppositions from which, curiously enough, they had actually derived in the first place. The time was to come when merely to doubt such accounts was to be guilty of heresy against the Church, and thus worthy of death. Wishful hindsight had finally come into its own.

And so a new process entered the field of prophetic interpretation. Henceforward, for some years at least, prophecy was to be regarded by the faithful as if it were actually more real than reality itself, and the truth of a story was, thanks to the concept of Divine inspiration, to depend more on its relationship to the scriptural predictions than to actual events. The results were, as we shall see, disastrous for the cause of factual truth, but of inestimable benefit to the larger myth to which, increasingly, that truth was to become subservient.

---

[a] See Jn. 20:14-18   [b] Lk. 24:13-32   [c] 1 Cor. 15:5-7   [d] Lk. 24:25-27   [e] Lk. 24:33-43, Jn. 21:1-14

14

Prophecy as Alternative Reality

And so the years passed in Jerusalem. In the house in the priests' quarter, Jesus' disciples, under the paternal guidance of James the Just and John the Priest, addressed themselves to the task of ministering to the growing numbers of supporters who were daily flocking to their cause. These included not only Essenes from communities throughout Palestine, but also Pharisees, Zealots and other Jews of no particular affiliation. Only the Sadducees remained resolutely aloof.

Within a matter of weeks of the celebrated Pentecost assembly, if the accounts are to be believed[a], the Nazarenes must already have become easily the largest religious sect in Palestine. Both in their organisation and in their general way of life, they continued to display clear Essenic trademarks. Apparently governed by a central council of twelve laymen and three priests — one of whom admittedly, was temporarily present in spirit only — they sold all their property and handed over the proceeds to the community's funds. Meals were taken together, and a strict regime of prayer and religious observance maintained.

Meanwhile, the growing power and reputation of the movement's 'alternative Sanhedrin' naturally started to rankle with the Sadducean establishment. Before too many years had passed, a programme of systematic persecution was set in train. Selected Nazarenes were arrested, questioned and charged with sedition, heresy and even blasphemy. Some were flogged, others stoned to death. The persecutors were unremitting in their task. During the early AD 40s one young man in particular — a Greek-speaking expatriate Pharisee from Cilicia named Saul — took upon himself the mantle of chief inquisitor and executioner, apparently motivated by a psychological aversion of extraordinary violence. Some have put this down to an underlying belief on his part that Jesus had usurped the messianic role that was rightfully his own[42], others merely to a fundamental

[a] Compare Acts 2:41, 47

disagreement with the Essenes' interpretation of the prophecies. Certainly, whatever the cause, his aggressive attitude was flatly contrary to the advice of the celebrated Gamaliel, his own Pharisaic tutor.[a]

Eventually Saul's persistent enquiries led back, as inevitably they had to, to the sect's main stronghold, the 'land of Damascus'. And it was while on his way north to persecute the Nazarenes of this increasingly hostile region that he was suddenly struck by a blinding realisation. His persecution of the movement, it was obvious, was merely strengthening it. For every member martyred, hundreds more were clamouring for admission. His own reputation was going down, not up. By allowing himself to be goaded by the Nazarenes' mere presence into attacking them, he was merely banging his head against a brick wall. If, therefore, he wished to put matters right, he must become more canny and less a tool of his emotions. He must use the movement, not oppose it. Since merely damming the river was increasingly proving to be an impossibility, it must be diverted, made to flow in the channel which it should have followed all along.

Thus, in a flash, Saul's true destiny revealed itself to him: instead of trying to beat the movement, he must join it.[b]

Throughout Palestine the Nazarenes were shocked, even horrified, at the news of Saul's professed conversion. With him as a friend, they seem to have felt, who needed enemies? Yet the inexorable process had already begun whereby the diminutive Saul, who had now renamed himself Paul ('Little One'), was to replace Jesus' teachings with a new mystery-religion of his own devising. Incorporated into it were elements of Pharisaic occultism, Greek mysticism and the Zoroastrian doctrine of the perpetual war between Darkness and Light, apparently adopted during a stay in one of the Essene encampments in the eastern desert immediately after his sudden illumination.[c] Basic to his message was the conviction that the heavenly Messiah whom he had never known in life had, through the operation of the Spirit, chosen him, Paul, to be his vessel and mouthpiece on earth until he should come again. In view of Isaiah's prophecy at 11:6 — 'And a little child shall lead them' — he had thus chosen his new name shrewdly, especially as *naar*, the Hebrew word here translated as 'child', was more often used to mean 'young man'.

In token of his commission Paul was authorised — or so he claimed — to preach a totally new doctrine. The sacrifice of Jesus, it seemed, had cancelled out all sin, whether past, present or future. All who believed this and underwent the same, Essenic baptism that Jesus had undergone were thus perpetually freed from guilt and, by the same token, automatically filled with his spirit — the New Spirit long prophesied for the coming Kingdom. They

[a] Acts 5:33-39, Acts 22:3 [b] Compare the various versions of the experience at Acts 9:1-30, 22:1-21, 26:12-23, Gal. 1:13-23. [c] Compare Gal. 1:17.

themselves, consequently, would henceforth constitute the physical body of Christ on earth.[a] And so they could now regard themselves as ritually pure for the few years until the Messiah returned and the Kingdom actually dawned. Adherence to the provisions of the ancient Law was no longer either necessary or relevant, for a new, spiritual Law had, under the terms of Jeremiah 31:31-34, been written on their hearts. And so the new doctrine was as appropriate to non-Jews as to Jews. Paul's gospel could, and should, be preached to all and sundry. And eventually, when the Messiah returned, the miraculously-transformed faithful, both dead and living, would be raised to meet him in the clouds, the physical earth would be destroyed, and a new, spiritual dispensation would dawn throughout the universe.

Although formulated with total disregard for the views of the original disciples who had actually known Jesus, the new doctrine certainly had a remorseless logic about it. Like the teachings which it was intended to supplant, it could be squared with the messianic and millennial prophecies. Moreover, it clearly had its attractions, both for Paul and for his new-found followers. He himself could adopt a powerful role as the virtual mouthpiece of God, in opposition to the apostles at Jerusalem whose Jewish converts he could hope to swamp by sheer force of gentile numbers. At the same time his followers — soon to be dubbed 'Christians' by their opponents, significantly after the Greek, not the Jewish, word for Jesus' office — were freed, not only from the burden of their accumulated guilt-feelings, but also from the onerous demands of the Jewish Law. Almost for the first time, perhaps, they felt themselves to be free men and women, forgiven in advance for anything they might do, justified in their every thought and action by the inner spirit's presumed response to their sincere faith. Convinced that they could now do no wrong, many of them forthwith gave up their regular jobs in view of the imminence of the Kingdom, and surrendered themselves to vices and excesses of the most refined extravagance while there was still time . . .

Paul, who, despite his adventurous religious ideas, had been brought up a strict Jew, was obviously aghast at the forces that he had inadvertently unleashed. The resultant scandalous publicity was rapidly discrediting his cause in Jewish and Gentile eyes alike. And so most of the rest of his career was given over to fighting with one hand a running battle against such excesses (to which we owe most of the eloquence of his surviving epistles) while fending off with the other the indignant Nazarenes at Jerusalem, who were no doubt immensely relieved when some of their opponents managed to get him handed over to the Romans as a Nazarene trouble-maker. During his subsequent time in custody, specially-commissioned Nazarene envoys spared no pains to correct the misleading ideas that he had by then spread

[a] I Cor. 12:27

abroad throughout the Eastern Mediterranean.[43, 44] In their eyes, indeed, he was one of the 'false prophets', predicted by the Essenes' Pentecost Declaration, who would claim Jesus' name and 'mislead even God's chosen, if such a thing were possible.'[a] And so it is perhaps no surprise that, at the time of his eventual appeal to Nero and reported execution in Rome, only three Jewish followers of the Messianic cause were prepared to offer him support.[b]

Paul's infuriating and subversive antics abroad were not without their effects even on the Jewish home-community, and the Nazarene leaders were much concerned at the fact.[c] It was, after all, vital that the Nazarene faithful should maintain their strict state of ritual purity and their total adherence to the Law for the whole duration of the interregnum if they were to prove worthy of the Kingdom when it finally dawned, for the self-sacrifice of the Priest-Messiah — contrary to Paul's view — had been effective only in respect of sins already committed. What they had entered was nothing less than a time of trial designed to sort out the men from the boys, or rather — to use the more familiar, prophetic analogy — the sheep from the goats. On them had fallen the long-prophesied role of the 'faithful remnant', and if they were to fail in their task the whole nation would go under.

For a young, expatriate Pharisee to suggest, therefore, that Jesus' Passover sacrifice had been not merely retroactive but effective for all time, and that their efforts were therefore unnecessary, was to undermine the whole rationale of their way of life. His claim of exclusive messianic authority did nothing, either, to reinforce the Nazarene council's own efforts to counteract the suggestion. And as for the now-spreading popular view that heaven was just around the corner, this, too, needed to be assiduously played down. A great deal could happen yet, and the time of ordeal, though shortened, might still be longer than most people thought.

A number of surviving texts seem to bear witness to this concern among the Nazarene leadership in Jerusalem. A purported letter from Peter points out, no doubt on the basis of Psalm 84:10, that 'with the Lord one day is like a thousand years and a thousand years like one day'.[d] Another from James, criticising the 'anything goes' mentality, asks tartly, 'Can you not see, you quibbler, that faith divorced from deeds is barren?'[e] The fact that both letters were written in Greek suggests that they were intended mainly for the endangered, hellenised Jews of far-flung parts of the Empire, as both texts confirm. But we can also be sure that the faithful at home were constantly given similar admonitions.

Yet the activities of Paul were by no means the only problem confronting

---

[a] Mt. 24:24   [b] Col. 4:10-11, and compare Schonfield's analysis of Paul's activities.[43]   [c] Compare Acts 21:20-25   [d] 2 Pet. 3:8   [e] Ja. 2:20

the Nazarene council by the AD 60s. Another was the curious prophetic phenomenon which we have already dubbed 'wishful hindsight'.

It was, after all, axiomatic among the Nazarenes of whatever persuasion that Jesus, by fulfilling the messianic prophecies, had proved himself to be the promised Messiah. That assumption, indeed, was now regarded as beyond question. And so, in a sense, the argument could now be reversed. Since Jesus was the Messiah, *ergo* he had fulfilled all the relevant prophecies. And so prophecy could now be seen almost as an alternative form of reality. In order to establish what Jesus had done it was sufficient to delve into the ancient predictions.[a] 'Consult the book of the LORD and read it,' Isaiah had written:[b] 'not one of these shall be lacking.' Henceforth, actual reports and concrete evidence started increasingly to be regarded, especially by those at the periphery, as of little account, while it went without saying that any story or rumour, however uncorroborated, that agreed with the predictions was, *ipso facto*, proved.

This argument, of course, ignored two important facts. One was that the still-surviving disciples actually knew at first hand what Jesus had done. The other was that those less privileged newcomers who were now claiming to use the prophecies as a short cut to the truth, or even to get behind what they may have regarded as an official screen of silence, were not necessarily the best-qualified to determine what the relevant messianic prophecies were, much as they might claim to justify the process in terms of Divine inspiration.

But soon the prophetic game had caught on, and a synthesis of rumour and half-baked biblical scholarship had started to produce a whole rash of startling and, frankly, quite unrealistic reports and ideas. On the basis of Isaiah 7:14, for example, Jesus' mother Mary was held to have been still a virgin at the time she bore him. (The fact that the original Hebrew text required no such suspension of the natural laws is a clear indication that some at least of the latter-day embroiderers of the Jesus-story were Greek-speaking converts, in all probability largely ignorant of the true Hebrew background, and basing their speculations on the unreliable Greek translation of the Old Testament of the third century BC known as the Septuagint, which originally appeared in Egypt.) By the same token — and since, under the terms of Psalm 2:7, Jesus had been dubbed 'God's son' — Joseph had not, after all, been his father. At the same time, texts such as Isaiah 11:1 apparently required that he be a descendant of David, and so — despite Jesus' own denial of the requirement at Matthew 22:41-46 — at least two genealogies were duly invented to demonstrate his Davidic descent.[c] Oddly enough,

---

[a] The astute reader will not of course be slow to realise that something of the same process underlies my own researches. I would merely ask him to judge the results on the basis of inherent probability.   [b] Isa. 34:16   [c] Compare Mt. 1:1-17 with Lk. 3:23-38.

these turned out to be mutually contradictory, and blithely traced the succession back through the man who was supposedly not Jesus' father in the first place.

Various prodigies were now adduced to embellish his birth-story, possibly out of the feeling that it ought at least to measure up to the nativity-myths of the existing Middle-Eastern gods and god-men whose authority he had, in a sense, usurped. In fulfilment of Numbers 24:17 — and in apparent ignorance of the fact that the Star of David had always been simply the symbol of the Messiah — a special star was said to have appeared at his birth. Led by it, Chaldean Magi from the east had come bearing gifts for the new-born god-king, no less than they had recently done at the birth of the similarly divine and regal emperor Nero, the embodiment of the sun-god Mithras.[42] One tradition even had it that they had actually been kings, apparently thanks to a superficial reading of the prophecy at Isaiah 60:3 concerning Jerusalem — 'The nations shall march towards your light and their kings to your sunrise.' Also in deference to the Mithras-legend, shepherds had appeared to pay tribute to their new lord and master in the sacred cave of his nativity.

Next had followed a 'massacre of the innocents', with Herod the Great familiarly cast in the role of the ancient pharaoh of the Egyptian oppression. Jeremiah 31:15 required, after all, that Rachel weep for her dead sons. Since the scriptures stated that this semi-legendary matriarch had been buried near Bethlehem[a], it followed that the children of Bethlehem must have been massacred soon after the nativity, with only the infant Jesus escaping, just as the river-borne Moses had done before him.

After astonishing the elders in the Temple with his knowledge at the age of twelve — the incident described by Luke seems to have been borrowed from the autobiography of Josephus, one of Luke's main sources of local colour[42] — Jesus had been baptised by John at the age of around thirty. During the course of the ritual the spirit of Yahweh had actually been seen to descend upon him, in fulfilment of Isaiah 11:2; in token of his role as a man of peace (Isaiah 9:6, 7, Micah 5:5, Zechariah 9:10), it had taken the form of a dove; and a celestial voice had actually been heard misquoting a selection of words from Exodus 4:22, 2 Samuel 7:14-16 and 1 Samuel 16:22.

Subsequently, after a triple series of temptations by Satan in the wilderness which had reflected with curious precision three of the main themes of the prayer which Jesus had bequeathed to his followers (the supersubstantial bread, the coming test and the Kingdom), he had gone on to perform a whole series of miracles. On the basis of texts such as Isaiah 25:6 and 62:4-5, with their familiar prophetic imagery of the coming Messianic Banquet and the marriage of Yahweh to his people, Jesus had, it seemed, attended a

[a] Gen. 35:19

wedding-feast in the hill-country near 'Nazareth', at which he had actually transformed ordinary water into well-matured wine. This rather pointless display of magical powers had been followed by a flood of other prodigies, many of them clearly based on the subsequent, millennial predictions which it had not even been the task of Jesus, in his limited role as Priest-Messiah, to fulfil in the first place.

Thus, in fulfilment of Isaiah 35:5-6, he had healed the blind, the deaf, the lame and the dumb. No less than the contemporary Galilean Hasid, Hanina ben Dosa, he had actually cured at least two of them at a distance — for Hanina's reported remote healing of the son of Gamaliel himself was by now on everybody's lips.[53] Not to be outdone, either, by the ancient prophet Elisha[a], Jesus had even healed such lepers as had been presented to him during his travels — notwithstanding the fact that, in Jesus' time, lepers were strictly confined to remote camps and caves which there is no record of his ever having visited. Again like Elisha[b], he had also fed multitudes with a few loaves of bread and still left plenty to spare — thus also fulfilling Psalm 146:7 and Isaiah 25:6. As apparently envisioned by Ezekiel 47:9, he had miraculously increased the catches of his fishermen-disciples — though whoever dug out this particular prophecy seems to have been so unfamiliar with Palestine as to be unaware that Ezekiel was describing the fishless Dead Sea, not the Sea of Galilee. Moreover, since fish are normally caught for eating, the 'multiplication of fishes' story was in due course assimilated to the 'multiplication of bread' theme just mentioned, so that the crowds were eventually held to have been fed on bread *and* fishes. And a variety of details — names, places, times and numbers — were then added to the stories for added verisimilitude, much as still happens today during the transmission of folk-tales of the more everyday variety.

The numerous predictions that the Messiah would 'free the prisoners'[c], meanwhile, proved a harder nut to crack. But, in the event, numerous reports of cast-out devils and restored paralytics seemed to provide at least a figurative fulfilment. So, too, did the rumours that Jesus (again like Elisha[d]) had restored dead people to life. And a number of stories to the effect that corpses had been seen to rise from their graves at the time of Jesus' own emergence from the garden-tomb seemed to confirm the various prophecies of a resurrection of the dead at Isaiah 26:19 and Daniel 12:2.

Least convincing of all, however, were the anecdotal attempts to show that the Messiah had, as prophesied, brought peace to the world.[e] Here a story had to be adduced on the basis of Psalm 65:7, Psalm 89:9 and Psalm 107:23-32, in all of which Yahweh is described as stilling the fury of the sea. There should, of course, have been no confusion here between Yahweh (for whose

---

[a] 2 Ki. 5:1-14   [b] 2 Ki. 4:42-44   [c] Compare Ps. 146:7, Mal. 4:2, Isa. 10:27.   [d] 2 Ki. 4:18-37
[e] Compare Isa. 32:17-20, 2:3-4.

name the Jews, in speech, generally substituted the word *Adonai* — 'Lord' — because of the strict taboo on pronouncing it) and Jesus (actually called by his followers *Adon*, in token of the fact that he was their lord and master). Yet both words were traditionally rendered into Greek by the single word *kyrios*. Moreover, such was the remoteness of the story's inventors from the original Jewish tradition that the distinction between the man and the God he served was by now becoming more than a little woolly. The Essenes had themselves not helped to clarify the issue by taking non-specific scriptural allusions to Yahweh out of context for use in their prophetic anthologies. Yet they had never applied *explicit* 'Yahweh'-statements to the expected Messiah: at most they had freely interpreted the personal pronouns within them. The Greek-speaking converts of the Empire, however — with all their cultural traditions concerning men who, like Achilles and Alexander, had become gods — had no such compunctions. And so Jesus, usurping Yahweh's place, was duly made to still the apocryphal storm. For good measure, he was even made to walk on the water after the apparent prescription of Psalm 77:16-19, and to save his leading disciple from disaster while attempting to follow suit, in the spirit of Psalms 69:1-2 and 18:16.

The resulting, often colourful accounts were in due course incorporated by their largely foreign authors into the collections of stories and sayings which were by now being written down in the far-flung parts of the Empire for the benefit of converts who had never known Jesus or even visited Palestine. Out of the process were to emerge at least twenty different purported 'gospels', or accounts of Jesus' life[20], from which the familiar four were eventually to be selected for general use nearly two hundred years later. Most of the rest were subsequently either lost or deliberately destroyed, presumably in the interests of doctrinal consistency.

Yet what the miracle-reports on which many of these would-be biographies were largely based tended to ignore was the real sense of the predictions, as understood by their original anthologisers, the Essenes. What the prophets had been referring to, as they saw it, was a future time of idealised human existence in which there would be no more disease or deformity, no more hunger or death, no more war or oppression by foreign invaders. There would not even be any more day or night, for the powers of Darkness would have been abolished for ever.

But that era would not come until the Messiah returned at the end of the time of ordeal. And since, clearly, he had not yet reappeared, it was pointless to suggest that Jesus had already fulfilled such prophecies. To suggest that he had done so by merely healing the odd blind person here, curing the odd cripple there, or producing food out of thin air for one, or at most two, hungry crowds was wilfully to misunderstand what the prophecies were about. They were concerned with the inception of a whole new world-order, not with turning a man — even the Messiah himself — into a common miracle-worker or, worse still, some kind of a god. And it is for this reason that we can safely regard any gospel-stories which clearly attempt to do just this as later accretions, rather than factual reports.

What would be less safe, however, would be to assume, on this basis, that Jesus was necessarily devoid of 'abnormal' powers. On the contrary, the stories and rumours about his activities as a healer may quite well have had some basis in fact. As one of the highly-revered Hasidim — and a prominent one at that — he could scarcely have been credited with less abilities than they. And so it was axiomatic that people would come to him for healing, as they did to others of his ilk, believing that merely touching the hem of his garment would act as a powerful talisman against sickness. As they believed, so it naturally tended to be, especially where psychological or psychosomatic conditions were involved. And so, even though — as Jesus himself often pointed out — it was his petitioners' own belief that had healed them, he himself received all the credit for such cures, a fact which in turn tended to strengthen even further the faith of subsequent patients.

Moreover, if the reports of Jesus' healing-activities had at least some basis in fact, the same may have applied, if at a different level, even to some of the more flamboyant miracle-rumours. 'Prophetic archaeology' — the systematic unearthing of prophetic texts — may, once again, not have been entirely to blame. But in this case the fact at the basis of the stories is more likely to have been Jesus' own use of parable in his teaching. Just as Jesus' fig-tree parable at Luke 13:6-9 was in due course to be turned into an incident in which he had allegedly cursed a literal fig-tree for failing — not unreasonably — to bear fruit out of season[a], so various of the miracle-accounts may originally have been based on similar parables of his on the subject of the coming Millennium. And so teaching-stories about how the returning King-Messiah would turn the water of everyday life into the wine of Yahweh's millennial wedding-banquet, or how he would feed the world's hungry with bumper crops from land and sea alike, duly became transmuted into the miracle at Cana, the feeding of the five thousand and the miraculous draught of fishes. Parables on the millennial raising of the dead to life duly received similar treatment, not merely in such stories as the account of the raising of Lazarus, but also in the apocryphal accounts of his having miraculously infused life into clay sparrows as a child.[20]

Jesus himself, in other words, had — if unwittingly — supplied some at least of the grist for the tale-spinners' mill. But the result was, paradoxically, so incredible a series of stories as eventually to raise serious doubts among many of the sober-minded of our own time as to whether the man could ever

[a] Mt. 21:18-22

have existed at all. And if the effect of the stories was increasingly to turn him into a god rather than a man, this tendency was increased, rather than lessened, by surviving reports of his actual teaching. So overawing had Jesus' impact clearly been, so acute and highly-developed his wisdom, that it had evidently produced a kind of culture-shock among his followers. Unable to measure up to his advanced level of consciousness, the temptation was all too great for them to turn him into a super-being, and then saddle him with personal responsibility for their own spiritual destiny.

Even among the Nazarenes at Jerusalem, this tendency was already strong enough. But among the new converts in Greece and Rome, with their Hellenic background of divine saviours and supernatural god-men, the temptation to turn Jesus into a god was irresistible. In such an atmosphere the combination of the new miracle-reports and Paul's new theology could only be disastrous. The vital role of the 'faithful remnant', the intense personal efforts to prove worthy of the Kingdom, were alike abandoned. The message was falsified, the Covenant inevitably betrayed.

And so the original Nazarenes could only fight such developments for all they were worth, while intensifying all the more their own efforts to observe the strict conditions laid down by the scriptures and the Teacher's book of oracles.

15
Twilight of the Gods

As the time for the Kingdom's expected dawning neared, the Nazarenes' overriding task of self-purification was made increasingly difficult by the continually deteriorating political situation at home.[a] Following Pilate's recall to Rome in AD 36, and the death of the emperor Tiberius in AD 37, Caligula had succeeded to the Imperial throne. Even at this early stage, a national revolt was only just avoided when he proposed to erect a statue of himself as God in the Jerusalem Temple. The plan, as luck would have it, was thwarted at the last moment by his own death.

Claudius, his successor, appointed the relatively sympathetic Herod Agrippa as King of Judea. But, almost as sensitive as his illustrious former namesake to the possibility of plots against his life, the latter reacted to Nazarene criticism by beheading one of the sect's members and then arresting Peter himself. At once, the Zealot underground swung into action and, evidently acting on inside information gleaned through an effective spy-network, succeeded in rescuing the eminent disciple from his captors' clutches.[b] For Agrippa's subsequent sudden death poisoning cannot be ruled out as a possible cause.

A reversion to direct Roman rule followed under the procurator Cuspius Fadus. But to this development the popular reaction was naturally a bitter one. Guerrilla fighting broke out. A would-be prophet called Theudas appeared, and was only prevented from attempting to lead his followers dry-shod across the Jordan, after the manner of Joshua, by a military action in the course of which he was brutally decapitated.

Matters were now made ten times worse by the great famine of AD 46. This was immediately followed by a Jewish sabbatical year which meant that no work could be done to make good the deficiency, as well as a Roman census and the arrival of a new procurator, Tiberius Alexander. This constellation of

[a] Compare Schonfield's account[43], from which most of the following details are taken. [b] Compare Luke's idealised version of the incident at Acts 12:6-17.

calamities led to further revolts in various parts of the country. Guerrilla leaders were captured and crucified, and even the peace-loving Nazarene leaders in Jerusalem found things becoming so difficult for them at home that many of them set out on missionary journeys to the Jews of the Dispersion, dedicated to spreading the news of the coming Kingdom and to setting straight the exaggerated ideas about Jesus which by then had started to multiply in foreign parts. With them they seem to have taken copies of two reference-documents prepared by Matthew — one a selection of messianic proof-texts from the Old Testament, no doubt culled from the Teacher's *Book of Meditation*, and the other a collection of the sayings of Jesus. As Papias records: 'Matthew compiled the Oracles in the Hebrew language, and each interpreted them as he was able.'[43] It is these documents which are nowadays thought by biblical scholars to underlie our four familiar gospels.[42]

Meanwhile a different kind of propaganda was also being circulated. This was designed primarily to demoralise the Roman occupiers. Purporting to be the product of the Sybilline Oracle, it repeatedly pronounced doom on the Empire at the hand of a vengeful Yahweh.[43] Thanks to the lines of communication which Rome had thoughtfully provided, it was not long before this literature and its bearers were spreading their message of disaffection and sedition among Jewish populations throughout the Empire. Funds were amassed, arms secretly collected. To the increasingly unnerved and superstitious Romans, even Paul's innocent proclamation of the 'resurrection of the Messiah' (*anastasis Christou*) seemed to be a reference to some kind of 'messianic uprising'. Soon the emperor Claudius himself reacted to the spreading alarm and despondency by closing the Roman synagogues, expelling all foreign Jews from Rome and appointing a new procurator in Judea. At the same time he sounded a note of warning against Jewish sedition throughout the eastern Empire.

In Palestine, too, the tension was mounting as the expected Day of Judgement loomed. Nazarenes and Essenes daily intensified their efforts at national purification, Zealots threatened death to impious gentiles. A government official was mugged, and a Roman soldier who tore up and burnt a copy of the scriptures during the ensuing reprisals had to be beheaded at the insistence of a furious mob. A national disaster followed when, during a further disturbance at the Temple during the Passover festival, twenty thousand people were crushed to death.

In AD 51, further reprisals were taken by the new governor, Cumanus, when hostilities broke out between Galileans and Samaritans. This time the public reaction was so intense that a national uprising was, once again, only just avoided. Despite a series of exemplary crucifixions, and the replacement of Cumanus by Antonius Felix, widespread guerrilla activities now became an accepted daily occurrence.

The result was, of course, even more crucifixions. In reaction, the Zealots

— now increasingly militant, despite Nazarene attempts to restrain their ardour — took to mingling with the crowds in Jerusalem and other cities, wearing curved daggers under their cloaks, and assassinating in broad daylight any Jew currently suspected of being a collaborator.

With the death of Claudius in AD 54, the tension was redoubled as the infamous Nero succeeded to the Imperial throne. Now the guerrilla-actions started to broaden into general class-warfare. Private armies representing rich and poor, the established and the dispossessed, confronted each other in the streets. The ordinary priests, who had sided with the common people, were deprived by the Sadducean authorities of the rations to which they were entitled. And it was ostensibly for speaking up on their behalf that James, the brother of Jesus, was now seized by agents of the ruling High Priest, pushed over the parapet of one of the eastern pinnacles of the Temple and finished off by stoning in the Kidron valley below.

The Nazarenes were shocked to the core by the ghastly news. Surely, now, the end could not be far off. The conviction, it seems, was soon to become universal. As the year AD 62 progressed, reports started to come in of supernatural phenomena in the vicinity of the Temple. A semi-deranged peasant named Jesus ben Ananias continually unnerved the citizens of Jerusalem by appearing in the streets day and night, dolefully proclaiming the city's doom. Battalions of celestial cavalry were even seen coursing through the clouds, evidently presaging the imminent return of the cloud-borne royal Messiah.

Now followed a further Roman census and a collection of taxes during which Nero's new procurator, Lucceius Albinus, helped himself to considerably more than his due. It soon transpired, in fact, that he was open not only to discreet bribery, but also to offers of a hand in selected protection-rackets. To this the Zealots responded virtually in kind by seizing hostages and using them as a bargaining counter for a variety of demands, not least the release of imprisoned terrorists.

The subsequent replacement of Albinus by Gessius Florus merely worsened the situation, for what Albinus had indulged in privately Florus now committed quite openly, almost as if he were deliberately trying to provoke a revolt. But the last straw was added for the Jews when news suddenly arrived of the Great Fire which had virtually destroyed Rome in the summer of AD 64. For the sadistic Nero had reacted to the disaster by impartially rounding up all the Roman messianists, Jewish and gentile alike, and putting them to death in the most excruciating and barbarous manner, on the grounds that they, who had been predicting Rome's downfall, had actually conspired to cause it. The charge, in other words, had been the use of the familiar prophetic technique of deliberate fulfilment.

What now resulted in Judea was a virtual collapse of law and order. In consequence, it became clear to the Nazarenes that a massive Roman clampdown could not be far off. Rome, it was obvious, was now both alarmed and incensed at the spreading messianic canker, and was merely awaiting a pretext to mount a massive and exemplary hammer-blow against Jewish civilisation in general — and the regime of Florus seemed intent on provoking that final showdown.

It was at this critical juncture that James's successor and first cousin, Simeon ben Cleophas, acceded to the Nazarene leadership. Having assessed the increasingly threatening situation and noted the movement's powerlessness to influence events in Jerusalem any longer, he succeeded in persuading his colleagues that the moment long spoken-of by the Essenes' original book of oracles had finally arrived. The predicted world-wide woes had so far, admittedly, been somewhat less dramatic than might have been supposed — though, heaven knew, they had been bad enough. But if it was in Yahweh's power to shorten the Divine Day of Wrath for the sake of the Elect, then it was equally within His capability to mitigate its effects for the same reason.

Now, however, the final crunch had come. At any moment the wrath of Yahweh would descend upon apostate Judea in the form of the dreaded Romans themselves. Jerusalem would be destroyed, its Temple pillaged and desecrated. Accordingly, the time had arrived for the faithful to leave Jerusalem for the relative safety of the open country while the Divine Wrath passed by, as Isaiah 26:20-21 and Micah 4:10 required.

Significantly, the moment of departure was fixed for the festival of Passover, as it had been once before for the departing Israelites of the Egyptian Exodus, when the Divine Wrath had similarly passed over the land. The assembled Nazarenes, accordingly, packed their communal belongings and, leaving their beloved city behind them for the last time, headed out across the Jordan into the desert region beyond Pella. Thence, it may be, some of them carried on northwards and westwards, and so eventually returned, after many trials and tribulations, to the original fount of their inspiration amid the sacred groves of Mount Carmel.

The inevitable upshot was that, by the spring of AD 66, the Qumran Essenes were left in sole charge of the messianic cause in Jerusalem and its surrounding area. For some thirty years they had waited patiently in the wings for this very moment. And now the massive opposing forces were, as anticipated, at long last poised to attack, ready at the drop of a hat to tear each other to pieces. And so the Essenes could now arrange to supply whatever provocation was needed at a moment of their own choosing. They would then need only to sit out the final scene, safe in what they believed to be their secure refuge, prior to stepping into the ensuing power-vacuum and assuming final control on the Messiah's behalf.

Among the assumptions upon which the Essene *War Rule* was based was that the final battle between Darkness and Light would be fought out somewhere in the 'Desert of Jerusalem'[a] — i.e. the Judean desert in the vicinity of the Dead Sea. It followed, therefore, that a similar condition would apply to the proxy-war which was now, under the terms of the later Pentecost Declaration, to be fought by others on their behalf. Accordingly, the armies of the opposing forces had to be drawn into the area at the onset of the fighting by some act of military violence.

At this point, therefore, the Essenes, newly galvanised into action by the Nazarene departure, secretly informed the Zealot leaders of their prophetic conviction that the time had at last come for large-scale action. So, at least, it would appear on the basis of subsequent events. The effect of this unexpected communication was both immediate and electric. The Qumran Essenes, after all, normally kept themselves very much to themselves, but when they did venture to give voice to their views, they were renowned for their prophetic accuracy. And now here they were suggesting that the time had come to mount a concerted and determined attack on Herod's former desert-fortress of Masada, an isolated and almost impregnable rock-citadel by the shores of the Dead Sea some thirty miles south of Qumran, and regularly manned by a Roman garrison.

The Zealots quickly saw the logic of the idea. As a result of their surprise attack, Roman forces would no doubt be drawn off from Jerusalem, so allowing the people, already in the midst of a tax revolt, to stage a successful coup in the capital itself. As the news spread, the whole country would soon be up in arms, and so in no time the invaders would be massacred and the kingdom of Israel finally restored to its former glory.

The assault-force of over a thousand guerrillas duly set off, no doubt under cover of darkness. In a commando-type attack, the watch was silently overpowered, the fortress infiltrated, the sleeping garrison massacred almost before they had had a chance to buckle on their armour. The operation was a total success.

As soon as the news reached Jerusalem the population, as expected, went wild with delight. At once there was a call to arms, a massive revolt ensued, and any plans the procurator might have had to dispatch a relief force to Masada were quickly abandoned. As it happened this was to make no difference to the success of the plan. For the beleaguered Jerusalem garrison, too, were quickly pinned down, and managed only with the greatest difficulty to smuggle out an urgent plea for assistance to the Roman governor of Syria. By now the revolt was spreading like a forest-fire. From Jerusalem the flames quickly fanned out across the hills of Judea, then north into Samaria and on into Galilee. By the time the Syrian governor had assembled

[a] *War Rule*, I[51]

his two legions, the partisans were ready and waiting for him. In a bloody engagement in Galilee the Roman relief-column was routed and put to flight.

At this juncture there was a curious and unhelpful diversion. A Zealot descendant of the famous resistance-leader Judas of Galilee, one Menahem by name, decided that the moment had come to provide the people with the victorious anti-Roman king whom they had long been expecting. He, in other words, would take over the role of the long-promised Messiah. Apparently oblivious of the incompatibility of what he was doing with the now-accepted interpretation of the ancient prophecies, he therefore assembled a small army, equipped them from the Masada armoury, and set out for Jerusalem, which he duly entered in the style of a king.

In a crisis, any friend is naturally better than none, and so at first the nationalists welcomed his help in evicting the Romans from the former Herod's palace. With only the two flanking towers left to capture, however, Menahem, having slaughtered the reigning High Priest and his brother, set off in a triumphal progress to the Temple, arrayed in kingly robes presumably taken from the royal wardrobe. This the populace found altogether too much to stomach. The cavalcade was fiercely attacked, and Menahem, having fled to the Ophel, was tortured and done to death as an obvious false Messiah, while those of his followers who still survived drifted back to Masada.

The resistance-forces now concentrated on consolidating their hold on Palestine in anticipation of the inevitable Roman counterblow. This duly came the following year, when the Roman general Vespasian, assisted by his son Titus, appeared in the north with a formidable army of sixty thousand men. Battle was joined in Galilee, and the Romans succeeded in subduing the whole northern province during their first year's brutal campaign. Reports describe a virtual massacre, with the Sea of Galilee red with blood and littered with floating corpses.

In the following year, AD 68, the campaign was extended into Judea. By the summer, the invading forces had reached Jericho. Jerusalem seemed likely to be next on the list. Yet suddenly the advance was checked. Evidently the Roman commander had extracted from captured Zealots under torture the news that the Essenes had been behind the insurrection. Furious, he ordered the attack to be diverted to Qumran, where he evidently expected to encounter stiff resistance. The unprepared sectaries, however, suddenly forewarned of the army's imminent descent upon them, and pessimistic of their chances against such unexpectedly overwhelming odds, at once got ready for a hurried departure. Placing their precious manuscripts in tightly-sealed jars, they hid them for safe-keeping in the surrounding caves against their eventual return. Then all but a few who, believing in an imminent Divine intervention, resolutely refused to budge, set off north-eastwards across the Jordan in the wake of the earlier Nazarenes, bearing with them such communal possessions as they could carry, together with their Teacher's irreplaceable oracle-scroll.

The Romans, consequently, found only a virtually-deserted monastery, which they had little difficulty in entering and occupying. Quickly subduing such light resistance as presented itself, they led off the survivors to torture and execution, looted such articles of value as they could find, and then put the buildings to the torch. The Essenes' long occupation of Qumran was over.

It was not until the spring of AD 70 that the long-awaited siege of Jerusalem itself began. The Romans, having already laid waste much of the surrounding country, had astutely chosen a moment just before that year's Passover to mount their final assault. In this way they had contrived to ensure not only that their chief opponents (the surviving devout Jews), drawn to the Temple festivities like flies to a jam-pot, would be trapped within their net; but also that the little city, now packed to overflowing with Passover-pilgrims, could be starved into submission with minimum effort and delay.

In the event, the capital still managed to hold out for some months — and that despite a minor civil war within the walls between militants and moderates during the early days of the siege. But conditions soon became horrific in the extreme. Looting broke out, and eventually even cannibalism was reported. Captured defenders were daily crucified below the walls in their hundreds. Would-be escapers were summarily disembowelled for the sake of any valuables they might have swallowed.

Yet, curiously, the three thousand or so Zealots securely ensconced at Masada made no move to intervene. Perhaps it was out of resentment at Jerusalem's rejection and execution of Menahem, or possibly they felt that any further action by them would simply not be welcome. Conceivably, indeed, they were merely awaiting what they believed to be the now-imminent intervention of the heavenly Messiah. Not until the city had all but fallen did a force of two thousand or so at last leave Masada for the capital, but by then it was too late.

For in September the Romans finally succeeded in breaching the inner defences. Soon the Temple was in flames and the starving defenders were being pursued towards their last refuge in the Ophel. But this last stand was of no avail. Mercilessly they were hacked down, and the city itself, already piled high with the corpses of those who had starved to death, was set ablaze and reduced to ruins.

Now a witch-hunt was set in train. Throughout Judea all Jews of Davidic descent were hunted down and executed, lest a new would-be Messiah should ever again arise from among their ranks.[a] And meanwhile, the still-surviving defenders of Masada gazed impassively down from their

---

[a] Thus Eusebius.[43]

rocky eyrie as the Roman legionaries patiently constructed a huge siege-ramp in the valley below — a massive work of engineering which still survives today. It was two-and-a-half years before the besiegers were at last ready to begin their final assault. Then, on the night before it was finally launched, flames were seen spreading across the summit of the citadel. By the light of dawn the Roman attackers burst in to find a scene of utter horror. Amid the charred remains of the buildings that had once surmounted the rock lay the 965 bodies of the fortress's defenders. During the night virtually the entire body of men, women and children had, in an act of unparalleled communal defiance, committed suicide.[21]

It was 14th April, AD 73 — forty years, almost to the day, since the crucifixion of Jesus the Priest-Messiah.

But if the date itself proclaimed that his expected return as King-Messiah was finally due, other events were by now pointing even more dramatically to that fact. The predicted wars and famines, false messiahs, massacres and betrayals had indeed occurred. Jerusalem had fallen, the Holy Place been trampled underfoot by barbarous enemies. And even while Judea was under attack a blood-curdling piece of news had rocked the entire known world.

The emperor Nero had committed suicide.

Such was the cloak of mystery and secrecy that surrounded this doom-laden event that many refused at first to believe it. Others feared that the maniacal despot had magically survived and would return. Omens and prophecies soon abounded. Signs and portents were seen in the heavens. In Rome, tens of thousands of citizens were carried off by a great plague. The surrounding countryside was suddenly laid waste by a disastrous flooding of the Tiber. Similar floods affected Lydia, while several eastern cities were flattened by earthquakes. Comets, eclipses and meteors terrified the ignorant. Vesuvius and other volcanoes erupted into new life, their volcanic ash blotting out the sun and turning the moon red. There were skies of terrifying crimson, suns which set in a sea of blood.[a]

With all these frightening fulfilments of the Jewish prophecies, then, how could the Messiah now fail to appear? Surely the new World-King must shortly reveal himself?

And then, suddenly, came the electrifying news that he had.

There in the heart of Palestine, he had been discovered and acclaimed by the shining ranks of his faithful followers. Already he was in the midst of destroying his enemies for ever. Already he had performed miracles, curing the lame and restoring sight to the blind.[b] He had even made solemn sacrifices at Elijah's open-air altar on Mount Carmel, source of the Essenes' inspiration, and there received oracular confirmation of his regal status.[c] With the collapse of the Julian dynasty, the old World Order had at last come

---

[a] Details from Tacitus and Seneca.[43]   [b] Thus Tacitus and Suetonius.[43]   [c] Thus Tacitus.[24]

to an end, and the new universal ruler, the godlike 'restorer of the world' (as he was later to be called), had come to claim his own.

As the news spread, a sigh of relief went up across almost the whole of the known world. Amid shouts of exultation, the new monarch set out on his triumphal progress home to his devastated holy city, upon whose ruins his new world-capital was already being rebuilt.

But among the still-fleeing Essenes it was a day of black despair, marking the ultimate failure of the great Essenic plan. For his destination was not Jerusalem, but Rome.

And his name was Vespasian.

16
Ironies of Fate

If we have considered in some detail our story thus far — the prophetic saga which, starting with Moses and the Old Testament prophets, was eventually taken up by the Essenes and deliberately brought to a head in the Jesus initiative — then it is not without good reason. For in the telling of it we have repeatedly been able to observe both the laws and the tricks of prophecy in action. In the course of it, too, we have succeeded — albeit by spanning a number of gaps in the evidence with a bridge of informed hypothesis — in constructing a picture which differs radically from the established view of what occurred, and so helps to cast new light on a matter of perennial controversy.

More to the point, however, we have been able to place in better perspective what was arguably — and almost literally — the most epoch-making collision between the worlds of prophecy and reality that has occurred during the whole of man's recorded history.

The claim may at first sight seem a large one. There have, after all, been other such collisions. The fall of much of Central America to Spain in the early sixteenth century was, it is said, due in large measure to the influence of Aztec omens and prophecies. These forecast the end of the established order and the coming of victorious invaders from the east (headed, according to some accounts, by their own long-lost, bearded god Quetzalcoatl) in or around 1519 AD — the very year when Cortés and his Conquistadors appeared off their eastern coasts.[a] Yet the Spanish Conquest was to be of relatively localised importance.

The Jewish prophetic drama, by contrast, was to reverberate not only right through history until the present day, when our modern thought and institutions — even those of non-Christian countries — continue, as we shall see, to

---

[a] Suggestions that the Aztec prophecies actually envisaged a fair-haired Quetzalcoatl in a black beret and gown arriving precisely on Maundy Thursday of the year in question may owe more than a little to what we have termed 'retrospective prediction', both contemporary and modern.[50]

be governed by its paradigm in ways of which we are all but unaware. It was also, thanks to later Christian missionary activity, to echo all around our planet with a force apparently out of all proportion to the extent of its geographical origins.

That it was able to do so with such apparent ease was due very largely to a single, extraordinary fact. For the same paradigm — or something remarkably like it — was already in existence in many of the major cultures to which the ideas of Christianised Judaism were subsequently spread. Again and again, the ancient religions of East and West — of Europe, Asia, Africa and even America — spoke of a god-man who had suffered for his people, who had departed for other realms, who could still be contacted through sacrifice and ritual, and who would one day return to save his people in their hour of need. The legend was already active in ancient Egypt, Persia and Central America, and persists right down to our own time in the traditions of Hinduism and Buddhism. In Osiris, Zoroaster, Mithras, Quetzalcoatl, Vishnu and the Buddha Maitreya the messianism and millennialism of first-century Judaism was mirrored in parts of the world which, by rights, should never even have heard of them — to such an extent that the early Christian missionaries came to regard such traditions as fiendish caricatures planted there by the Devil in order to undermine their efforts in advance.

If we are to explain this phenomenon, then it has to be in terms of a kind of tide, or 'standing-wave' in the evolution of the human psyche which, at certain points in man's development, throws up a vision of a time of ordeal followed by a once-and-future golden age, initiated by a transcendent human entity of supreme enlightenment. In Jungian terms, this pattern would be seen as an archetype — specifically, the 'archetype of initiation' — a kind of inherited psychic instinct which affects not only the race as a whole, but also individual human beings within it. As a result of its coming into play, certain actions then follow as a means of manifesting the vision and, to the extent that vision and physical reaction are in harmony, a new order of consciousness — whether individual or collective — eventually results.

In these terms messianism and millennialism can be seen as psychic evidence of a readiness for change, as an indication of an imminent quantum-jump in the quality of human consciousness. Unfortunately the tendency of religious establishments is to institutionalise such visions, holding them forever in a kind of fossilised limbo lying somewhere in a future which recedes almost as quickly as it is pursued.

It was the unique contribution of the first-century Essenes to attempt deliberately to take that future by storm; and that their efforts to do so were to have such thunderous consequences bespeaks a considerable measure of right timing on their part. As Victor Hugo was later to put it, 'There is no greater power than an idea whose time has come.'

The sources of that sense of timing may well give us pause for thought. To an extent, the Essenes' actions seem, as we have seen, to have been geared to a specific world-scenario that had already been spelt out by the biblical prophets. Yet that scenario had apparently already arisen several times before, to no apparent effect. That the Essenes chose to act when they did may thus point to the use of independent sources of knowledge. As I have indicated elsewhere,[27, 28] both received zodiacal wisdom and the internal design of the Great Pyramid of Giza seem to bear witness to an awareness on the part of their originators that a 'change of epoch' was due during the last century or so BC. Moreover, it is now clear that the Essenes were privy to the secrets of astrology and possibly, through their Egyptian connections, also acquainted with the Egyptian mystery-teachings. If this connection is assumed, it is not too surprising to find that the Essene movement proper was established in around 150 BC — almost exactly the year marking the notional beginning of the current age of Pisces (the Fishes) — and that their own literature goes on to represent them as 'fishers of men'.[a] Jesus' own use of the term, his apparent life-long association with fishermen, his constant use of fish-imagery and the apocryphal fish-miracles then follow quite naturally, as do the subsequent Christian use of the fish as a secret sign, the use of ritual immersion as a symbol of initiation, and the use of the term *episkopos* (overseer) — a Greek word containing within it the Latin root for 'fish' — to designate the leaders of the early Christian communities.[27]

If the Essenes made full and effective use of such esoteric sources in timing their extraordinary initiative, however, they were clearly less successful, at least in respect of post-Crucifixion events, in their application of the laws of prophecy themselves. Not that they alone were at fault in this regard. Their prime sources, the biblical prophets, had already started to fall foul of the Third Law (*Preconception and prophecy do not mix*) long before the Essenes appeared on the scene. They were, after all, consciously aware of the millennial prophecies of Moses, not to mention those of their own immediate predecessors[b], before ever they began their prophetic careers. In their prophecies — emerging, by contrast, from largely intuitive levels of consciousness — they then attempted to flesh out and give substance to the bare bones of the pre-existing Mosaic framework. The result was an incompatible mixture, a clash of wavelengths, which inevitably tended to distort the resulting image. In neurophysiological terms, the activities of the two relatively specialised hemispheres of the brain were attempting to interfere with each other's functioning, and the result was a decline in overall efficiency.

But now the Essenes proceeded to compound the problem by specialising in precisely that area adversely affected by the Sixth Law (*Prophecy and*

---

[a] Compare *Hymn* 8.[51]   [b] Note, for example, how Micah and Zechariah both take up the imagery of Isaiah 2:4 at Mic. 4:3-4 and Zech. 3:10.

interpretation are incompatible activities). To the Teacher of Righteousness, prophecy and interpretation were one. It was precisely through his own oracular exegesis of the scriptures that the future was to be divined.

True, insofar as it was within their control, the Essenes at least managed to counteract the First and Second Laws (those of Surprise Fulfilment and Thwarted Expectation) by actively co-operating with the Fourth (*Prophecies tend to be self-fulfilling*). Indeed, their policy of deliberately bringing the ancient prophecies to pass not only enabled them to keep a firm hand on the manner of their fulfilment, but also proved, in the event, to be astonishingly effective as far as it went, apparently adding enormous, unseen power to their elbow during the first half of the Jesus initiative.

At this point, however, things once again started to come unstuck. The purpose of their deliberate fulfilment of the messianic prophecies, it will be remembered, had been to satisfy all the conditions for the inception of the promised millennial Kingdom. Up to that point, events had been almost entirely within their control. But now, suddenly, everything depended on the miraculous intervention of an unpredictable God in establishing a new dispensation based apparently on little more than magic. The whole enterprise had, in a sense, been an attempt to tie down Yahweh, the celestial magician, and hold him to his alleged promises. Not surprisingly, perhaps, Yahweh — or the laws of nature — declined to co-operate.

But then, in any case, the Essenes had apparently mistimed the advent of the King-Messiah. This problem, accordingly, they had attempted to rectify by a hurried re-think of their predictions. Unwittingly, they now ran into problems arising out of the operation of the Fifth Law (*A prophecy's accuracy decreases as the square of the time to its fulfilment*). The forty-year delay, in other words, had the effect of falsifying what — but for the centurion's spear-thrust — might have been a reasonably valid expectation on their part. And meanwhile, as their own control over events progressively weakened, the long-suppressed First and Second Laws now swung back into operation with a vengeance.

The results were disastrous. Thanks to the long delay, the predicted 'false prophets' — Paul among them — had ample time seriously to undermine the Essene cause, and so to compromise the conditions of ritual and legal purity on which the coming of the Kingdom totally depended. Towards the end of the period particularly the expected wars and catastrophes tended increasingly to take a different course from that predicted. Worse, at the last moment, the Essenes' courage apparently deserted them, and Qumran was abandoned in the face of a massive assault by Vespasian's armies.

Yet the force of the prophecies was far from spent. The Fourth Law (that of Self-Fulfilment) was still alive and kicking. Even though the Essenes' hand was no longer on the helm, the time of ordeal duly produced the new world-ruler, as had been predicted. But the newly-resurrected First and

Second Laws contrived to give the result a virtual 180-degree twist. Far from the expected Messiah, or Christ, it was his antithesis, the Antichrist, who now ascended the sacred throne.

In the language of John's Revelation, the Beast had been cured of his deadly wound and given authority to mount a grotesque parody of the expected Kingdom. He had been permitted to make war on the saints (i.e. the faithful), and to bear rule over all the world's peoples. The best that could be hoped for, therefore, was that the setback was only temporary. Given time, Rome the 'Great Whore' would meet her just deserts, the Empire would be destroyed, and a shining new Jerusalem would, like the Messiah himself, descend ready-formed from the skies upon the ruins of its devastated predecessor.

Such views were not confined to the Christian fringes. Amid the ravages of Palestine, too, the bitterness was intense and the hope of salvation still not dead. But if the foreign successors of Paul tended increasingly to paint the coming of the Kingdom in semi-magical, other-worldly colours, the native Jews, for their part, remained convinced that the prophecies meant exactly what they said. The Messiah would still return in flesh and blood, the invaders would at long last be expelled, Jerusalem rebuilt and the land restored to physical peace and prosperity.

It seems to have been some considerable time before Rome began to realise that it had not, after all, succeeded in excising the messianic canker at source. Destroying Jerusalem and its Temple had admittedly deprived the Sadducean leaders of their spiritual power-base, but the Nazarenes were still active on the periphery of Palestine, while within it the Pharisees, whose activities were based on local synagogues rather than focussed on the Temple, were able to adjust to the changed circumstances and revive the ancient expectations. As life and institutions gradually recovered from the disaster so, too, did the resistance to the Romans — if anything, with renewed zest.

And so, in due course, further unrest ensued. During the reign of Trajan a further revolt among foreign Jews had to be put down, while the now-centenarian Simeon ben Cleophas was murdered as a member of the messianic dynasty. Eventually, in a rising tide of renewed Roman exasperation, the emperor Hadrian decided to rub the Jews' faces firmly and finally in the dirt by flattening the site of Jerusalem and building on its ruins a new city renamed Aelia Capitolina and sacred to Jupiter Capitolinus, whose shrine would occupy the former Temple-site.

To the ever-more-indignant Jewish messianists this was not merely an intolerable affront, but the ultimate fulfilment of Daniel's well-worn prophecy that the setting up of an 'abomination of desolation' in the Holy Place would mark the beginning of the end. Moreover, Daniel's text made it abundantly clear what was to happen next. *The people who are faithful to their*

God, it proclaimed, *will hold firm and fight back.*[a] The resulting war would be prolonged and bloody, but eventually the re-appearance of the Messiah would settle the issue for good and all, and the invader would be exterminated. Then would follow the long-awaited Golden Age.

If Hadrian and his advisers were unacquainted with the burden of the Hebrew scriptures, a Jewish guerrilla-leader by the name of Shimeon bar (or ben) Kosiba certainly was not. As the spirit of revolt rapidly grew, the celebrated Rabbi Akiba proclaimed Bar Kosiba to be the Messiah, and changed the latter's name to Bar Kokhba (Son of a Star) to reflect the fact, in the spirit of Numbers 24:17: *A star shall come forth out of Jacob, a comet arise from Israel.* Ignoring the fact that his enemies were performing a similar transformation to call him Bar Koziba (Son of a Lie — i.e. Antichrist), the new leader rapidly organised his forces and launched a major attack, as the scriptures clearly required.

Apparently taken by surprise, the Romans throughout Palestine were quickly routed by the growing forces controlled by the man who, in effect, was the Pharisees' Messiah. Within a few months of the beginning of the rebellion in AD 132, the Jews were once again in control of much of Palestine. Under Bar Kokhba the country was divided into districts, each ruled by a military governor. Documents were issued and Roman coins re-stamped bearing dates such as 'the second year of the liberation of Israel by Shimeon ben Kosiba'. Religious laws and festivals were strictly observed. And so successful were the freedom-fighters that the Romans had to recall their ablest general, Julius Severus, from Britain before they were able to start recovering the territory lost.

At length, however, the strength of the Imperial armies started to prove too much for the liberation-forces. One by one, the latter's strongholds were reduced. Eventually, in AD 135, the beleaguered Bar Kokhba himself was killed in a fierce engagement near Jerusalem. The war was finally lost. The inevitable reprisals quickly followed. This time the Romans, still smarting under their heavy losses, and determined that this most troublesome of subject races should never again threaten the peace and stability of the Empire, embarked on a deliberate programme of enslavement, deportation and genocide. Nearly a thousand villages were razed to the ground, and upwards of half-a-million Jews put to the sword. In Judea particularly, the population was to all intents and purposes exterminated, while even in Galilee the survivors were pitifully few.

At this juncture, if the prophecies were to be believed, the true Messiah should at last have intervened to rescue his 'precious remnant' of faithful followers and found the New Jerusalem. Whether because they had not been faithful enough, or because the prophetic interpreters had once again got

[a] Dan. 11:32

their timing hopelessly wrong, he failed conspicuously to do so. Admittedly, Jerusalem's every valley was in due course exalted, its every hill brought low, and on its ruins Aelia Capitolina was duly completed. Yet Jews were actually forbidden to enter it, and if this citadel of the pagan god Jupiter was the New Jerusalem, then it was a travesty of the one that had been promised. To the injury that was the Roman false Messiah of the First Revolt had been added the insult that was the false Jerusalem of the Second. Once again, it seems, the First and Second Laws of Prophecy had done their baleful work.

For those in foreign parts, therefore, the conclusion was inevitable. The expectation of the Messiah's imminent return — whether after three days or forty years — had been wildly wrong all along. No precise timing, in fact, could be put to the event. Instead, the millennial timetable must be based on a curious figure arrived at by the author of John's Revelation (the last book of our current Bible), apparently on the basis of a garbled, second-hand account of the Essenes' emergency deliberations following the death of Jesus (compare page 168). The Second Coming (as it gradually came to be termed) would occur when the number of the Jewish faithful reached the magic figure of 144,000.[a]

Since there was, of course, no objective means of discovering exactly when this figure had been reached, the room for flexibility was now considerable. The possibilities could even encompass the clear suggestion by the author of 2 Peter 3:8-9 that the Messiah's return could be delayed until as late as the third millennium A D. And meanwhile there was no way in which the Jewish guardians of the faith, whether Essene or Nazarene, could now control either this growing tide of revisionism or the seductive Pauline theology which increasingly tended to accompany it. For such of their members as had survived the holocaust — and they were few enough — had now been scattered to the four winds. Their chain of command had been broken, their channels of communication closed to them, their very presence in any of the Empire's cities made illegal. And if the promise that 'this generation will live to see it all'[b] was to be fulfilled, then it was now clear that some kind of reincarnation or resurrection would have to be involved.

Pauline Christianity, on the other hand, had succeeded in adapting much more successfully to the hostile Roman environment. Thanks to its spiritualising of the messianic expectation, it was already seen to pose less of a threat to public order than its more physically-orientated Jewish counterpart. A determined effort to keep its head down and to oppose the Jewish militants in times of trouble was in due course to earn for it a considerable measure of tolerance from the Roman authorities. And eventually its leaders managed to impose sufficient internal discipline on their members to excite the approval and even the admiration of respectable Roman society.

[a] Rev. 7:4, 14:1, 14:3   [b] Mt. 24:34

And so Paul's brainchild survived. As time went on, it was to absorb many of the ideas and practices of the religions with which it came into contact. From the religion of Isis it absorbed the cult of virgin and child. From Mithraism it took its nativity (December 25th), its holy-day (Sunday), its priestly organisation, the form of its communal buildings and even, in many cases, their actual sites. Its regular sacred eucharist of bread and wine may owe more to Mithraic than to Essenic influence. Its very headquarters on Mount Vaticanus was eventually to be built atop the central shrine of the pagan cult in Rome.

And in the process the new religion and its beliefs came to be regarded as increasingly 'normal'. Early in the fourth century AD, indeed, it was eventually proclaimed the official religion of the Empire by Constantine the Great. And so the transmuted messianism and millennialism of ancient Judaism came to be incorporated into the institutions of the very Empire which had destroyed them in their original form. Albeit spiritualised and deferred in their fulfilment to an impossibly remote future, the ancient prophecies were still accorded a real force. Indeed, that force was now to be effectively recharged by the belief of growing millions of new adherents. The old, physical order would fall, the Messiah would come, the new, heavenly order would be inaugurated — but not while the Emperor himself took on the role of Christ's vicar on earth, thus making such celestial interventions unnecessary.

It was to be another century before the Jews' original expectation at last came true, and Rome finally fell — though still in the absence of any Messiah. As for the expected millennium, the First and Second Laws of prophecy once again contrived to exert their ironic spell. For Rome's Eastern Empire, albeit much reduced in size, now entered a period of almost unparalleled magnificence, with government and religion working hand in hand. It was almost exactly a further thousand years, in fact, before Constantinople, its last, resplendent bastion — already weakened and looted by the Christian Crusaders of Western Europe — at last crumbled before the onslaught of the Muslim Turks.

False Messiah, false Jerusalem and, now, false Millennium — all, it seemed, had put in their respective appearances. The prophecies had succeeded in working their magic, but in strange, perverted ways. The first two Laws of Prophecy were still rampant, almost irrepressibly on the loose. Was there to be no end to this saga of tragic, prophetic irony?

17
The Resurgent Archetype

In Europe, meanwhile, an age of darkness had descended upon the former Western Empire. During it, the ancient Judeo-Christian beliefs and expectations were carefully preserved by remote groups of cave-dwelling monastics, and subsequently institutionalised in stone-built monasteries of growing size and power. In seventh-century Arabia, they were even revised and revivified by the prophet Muhammad, who — apparently thanks to belated Essene, Nazarene or even primitive Christian influence — had the perspicacity to see them for the historical misrepresentations they were, and attempted a virtual return to source. Yet here, too, the spiritual quest soon turned into worldly empire-building and, by the time Constantinople finally fell in 1453, both the Arab Caliphate and the Church of Western Europe had become wealthy political organisations in their own right, exercising temporal power much as the Roman emperors had done before them. Indeed, the identification became complete when the Roman pope himself crowned Charlemagne the first temporal head of what was actually to be known as the 'Holy Roman Empire' on Christmas Day, 800 AD. More striking still, that Empire was to last almost exactly a thousand years, until it was abolished by Napoleon Bonaparte in 1806.

In all this there was a curious, and almost exact, parallel with the history of the original Essenes. Their early years in the wilderness, their establishment of the monastery at Qumran, the expectation of the Qumran sectaries that they would eventually gain political power and initiate the millennium, exercising their priestly authority through a subservient, kingly Messiah — all these ideas were directly reflected in the development of Western Christianity. One group of monastics, indeed, had even gone so far as to establish its base on Palestine's own Mount Carmel, living in separate huts around a central chapel much as the Essenes had done before them, and so inviting the inevitable label 'Carmelites'. History, it seemed, was repeating itself — or possibly the Fourth Law of Prophecy was merely continuing to exert its effects in a more or less cyclic wave-pattern.

But clearly it had still not produced the kind of millennium that had been expected. True, there had been a few anxious moments (particularly in beleaguered Anglo-Saxon England) as the numerically beguiling year 1000 approached. But the crisis had been weathered, no Messiah had appeared, and life was able to return to normal. Yet now, as the Turkish pressure on Constantinople mounted, there was a growing feeling throughout Europe that a New Order was only just around the corner, and that the political dispensation which was currently parodying the millennial expectation might soon give way to one that actually embodied it.

Not that contemporary hopes were expressed in so many words. Yet there could be no doubt that a new spirit was abroad, even if nobody associated it with the prophecy of Ezekiel 11:19. To some extent, it was the Crusades which, by exposing the European mind to Arab culture and to the considerable influence which it had already absorbed from Eastern and classical sources, had begun to open the floodgates of European consciousness. But now, as Constantinople fell in 1453, and its classical scholars fled with their precious documents to Italy, the rediscovery at first hand of the ancient cultures, with all their artistic revelations and their philosophical and scientific wisdom, produced a sudden explosion of cultural vigour from whose effects no department of human life seems to have escaped. Moreover, as a result of the consequent closing of the ancient overland spice- and silk-routes to the Far East, mariners now set out to circumnavigate the globe with a view to reaching the East by sea. And so, to the explosion of knowledge based on documentary sources, a similar explosion based on the explorers' direct experiences now ensued. Geography, cartography, ethnology, astronomy and the various biological and maritime sciences all progressed by leaps and bounds. And, thanks to the recent invention of the printing-press, this knowledge could now be disseminated to the public at large. The Renaissance was born.

If, then, there was ever a chance of a physical millennium on earth, this, clearly, should have been it. Yet where was the promised Messiah? The knowledge of the 'new gospel', admittedly, was now reaching the furthest corners of the globe, and prosperity, thanks to colonial looting and exploitation, was certainly on the increase at home — yet what of the promised era of peace and freedom? Instead of being overthrown by the new forces of revolution, the institutions of the Old Order somehow contrived to weather them. Wars, every bit as brutal as before, continued to be fought by old-style monarchs who had simply turned themselves into Renaissance tyrants. Such was the gulf between millennial ideal and physical reality that it did not seem to have occurred to anybody to attempt to make the connection.

And so, in religious circles and among the heirs of the Jewish tradition — not least Nostradamus — the messianic and millennial dream continued to lurk, unexorcised, somewhere in the far lands of misty expectation. But now, suddenly, the advent of the printing-press made possible a dramatic sharpening of that awareness, and resulted in a considerable increase in scriptural knowledge generally. For copies of the Bible now started to be made available to the common people in their own respective tongues. For the first time in Europe, even the relatively uneducated could see for themselves what the scriptures actually said and assess for themselves what the message of Jesus had really been.

The result was what we now know as the Reformation, and its conse-quences for man's millennial expectations were to prove immense. As the new, Protestant sects set themselves up in revolt against the worldly and corrupt ecclesiastical regimes, the biblical message was analysed and spelt out with new and urgent clarity. Its words were accorded interpretations which were, if anything, even more literal than those placed upon them by the first-century Essenes and by the Jews in general. Veering away somewhat from the emphasis on personal hell-fire after death with which the former ecclesiastical dispensation had blighted human consciousness throughout the Middle Ages, the new preachers looked forward to a coming era of living ordeal on a world-wide scale which would precede the coming of the Messiah, the raising of the dead, the awful day of judgement and the translation of the righteous to an idealised heaven either on a transmuted earth or somewhere in the clouds. The physical world and its institutions alike stood condemned, and would inevitably be destroyed. Chief among them, indeed, were the Church of Rome and its various vassal rulers. The anti-Roman rhetoric of John's Revelation thus started to make sense again for the first time for centuries and to be seen as directly relevant to the general theme.

And so now the detailed beliefs and expectations which had been basic to the Essenes' messianic initiative of the first century started to be spread to a public many times larger than had ever been possible before. Moreover, thanks to the growing world-network of trade and colonisation, the new-found missionary zeal — whether Protestant or Catholic — also disseminated the various forms of the message to parts of the world that had not even been heard of in the Essenes' day. Christian beliefs were imposed on subject-populations who were told to forget what the missionaries termed their 'primitive superstitions'. Where the latter survived at all, it was often because they largely mirrored the new paradigm, and so could successfully adapt to it. As a result, enormous areas of the globe now stood in expectation of some kind of eventual messianic return and the inception of a miraculous Golden Age.

Nevertheless, Renaissance thinking had freed men's minds not merely to re-interpret the scriptures, but also to disagree with the re-interpretations of others. There was a new confidence in the validity of human reason as a tool for discovering the truth. As a result, not only were old dogmas discarded and opposed but, as time went on, a multitude of warring Protestant sects arose. Inevitably, some of their systems of belief were themselves turned into virtual dogmas, and before long there were recriminations and persecutions. It was largely as a result of these that the celebrated Pilgrim Fathers set out in 1620 with the deliberate intention of founding a Puritan 'new world' in North America. The millennial reference was, it seems, quite deliberate. For when the USA eventually obtained its independence during the following century, its Great Seal was to bear the image of a pyramid capped by a resplendent apex-stone in apparent reference to Psalm 118:22, surrounded by the legend NOVO ORDO SECLORUM — 'a new order of ages'. And ever since, whether explicitly or otherwise, its institutions have paid lip-service to Christian ideals, and to the intention of establishing a just and ideal society on the soil of America.

In Europe, meanwhile, rational thinking had advanced to the point where it had started, paradoxically enough, to doubt the power of unaided reason to reveal the truth at all. Thanks to increasing contacts with primitive cultures and totally different traditions, thinkers such as Voltaire and Rousseau started to realise that there were hidden depths within human consciousness which also demanded their say. The result was the Romantic Movement, whose mainspring was also a form of millennialism — but this time one which saw the inception of the Golden Age in terms of a return to the innocence of the Garden of Eden, a dispensation in which, as in the Heavenly City of John's Revelation, there would be no need of any Temple, nor of religious institutions, since man, the Noble Savage, would once again be at one with the primal Deity.

In due course the movement was to produce both its Time of Wrath and its would-be Messiah. The French Revolution was merely the beginning of a sixty-year period of upheaval and war throughout Europe, and in Napoleon Bonaparte it threw up a man dedicated to fulfilling the role of world-ruler and initiating a new dispensation based on order, reason, prosperity and justice. The ancient millennial dream had once again burst out into actuality and, in the event, it took all the forces of the established order to force it back underground again.

Yet the archetype, if such it was, merely responded to this repression by redoubling its strength. Still using reason as its primary tool, it was already propelling Western man pell-mell into the machine-age. But now the growing storm of the Industrial Revolution finally broke in all its materialistic frenzy. Transport, communications and production were alike galvanised into unprecedented vigour. As the new influence spread, science in general and, latterly, medicine in particular, made giant strides. Materially, Western man advanced more in the last fifty years of the nineteenth century than he had done in the rest of his known history put together. It began to seem that nothing was impossible for him. Given only time and persistence, he could unlock the secrets of the universe, harness them all to humanity's benefit. And so a physical Golden Age would soon be established on earth by the sweat of man's own unaided brow.

The new ethic spread rapidly across the far-flung and less privileged parts of the globe with all the force reserved for some new kind of magic. Almost universally, the subject-populations started to abandon their former philosophical systems to climb on the new, materialist bandwagon. Temporarily unaware that it relied to a remarkable degree on their own willingness to be exploited as a source of cheap labour and materials, they longed for the day when the benefits of the new technology would become theirs, and increasingly bowed down to the new god of material progress, while paying only cautionary lip-service to their ancestral systems of wisdom.

Once again then Europeanisation with its substantial underlay of Christian ideology had dealt a heavy blow to the indigenous cultures of the rest of the world. And, in particular, its millennial convictions were soon to become accepted as almost axiomatic to any reasonable view of man's destiny. Thanks in part to science-fictionists such as Verne and the later H. G. Wells, the myth of progress and perfectibility was finally to come into its own. Man was heading into a bright, unknown future, and only time stood between him and it.

Inevitably, this view duly became reflected in the various systems of thought which now started to arise in Europe. The general climate of expectation made it possible, for example, for Darwin to develop his celebrated theory of evolution, which might never have seen the light of day in 1859 but for the fashionability of the now almost universal 'progressist' outlook. His contemporary and admirer, Karl Marx, was similarly inspired to evolve a scheme for human advancement which echoed to an astonishing degree the messianic and millennial format of ancient Judaism.

In view of Marx's heredity and upbringing, this similarity is perhaps not altogether surprising. Casting himself (as his photograph alone amply suggests) in the prophetic role of Moses, he and Friedrich Engels proposed in their *Communist Manifesto* of 1848 the existence of a remorseless historical process — a concept curiously similar both to Darwin's theory of natural selection and to the 'psychic standing-wave' or 'archetype' already proposed above — whereby feudalism inexorably gives rise to a capitalist, bourgeois regime and then, following a bloody revolution, to a new order of society entirely, governed initially by a 'dictatorship of the proletariat'. The scheme — which was eventually expected to apply on a world-scale — thus corresponded exactly to the Time of Wrath and the messianic inception of the New Age already basic to Jewish millennialism, with the sole exception that the Messiah was here to be seen as a collective, rather than an individual manifestation, somewhat after the style of Moses' 'kingdom of priests' and

·'holy nation'.[a]

As the nineteenth century wore on, the 'progressist' climate seems to have had its effect even in the religious sphere. Here, too, it soon became apparent that there was a growing number of devotees who were convinced that the millennium, if not already here, was not far away. In deference, therefore, to Jesus' apparent promise at Matthew 24:14 that the New Age would dawn as soon as the Gospel had been preached throughout the world[b], there now developed a positive ferment of scriptural and missionary work. Between the years 1803 and 1833, over seventy Bible Societies were formed, specifically dedicated to propagating the Christian message across the globe. One of them alone, the British and Foreign Bible Society, was in due course to publish the Bible, either in whole or in part, in over a thousand languages. And of more recent years the Jehovah's Witnesses have taken this particular world-mission very much to heart.

Implicit in the millennial scheme, nevertheless, was the added conviction that the New Age would not dawn until Armageddon had overtaken the nations and the Messiah had reappeared. It followed, therefore, that the present order, for all its apparent millennial promise, was doomed. This apparent contradiction was partially resolved by a growing conviction in certain somewhat zany Anglo-Saxon quarters that Britain and the USA would, after all, be saved from the expected holocaust, thanks to the extraordinary revelation that their inhabitants were really the descendants of the lost Ten Tribes of Israel, and therefore qualified for special redemptive treatment.

Such improbable exegetical squirmings were grandiloquently eschewed, however, by a contemporary Persian religious prophet who took for himself the name Bahá'u'lláh ('Glory of God'). Patiently restating the ancient teachings of Islam, Judaism and Christianity, this Shi'ite Muslim pietist, born in 1844, let it be known that the millennium had indeed already come, and that he was its Messiah. The apparent absence of the physical tell-tale 'signs of the times' he and his successors contrived to explain by insisting that such phenomena were to be understood allegorically rather than literally. The coming of the Messiah amid the clouds of heaven, for example, merely indicated the appearance of the light of truth amid the clouds of darkness and delusion. Meanwhile the outlines of a new social order were sketched out — including freedom of religion, sexual equality, an international parliamentary forum and court of justice — and subsequent followers of what was to become the Bahá'í faith (one of whose main centres was, appropriately, established on Mount Carmel) were to point to the fact that many of these ideas have since been adopted as a justification for Bahá'u'lláh's considerable claims. Possibly this view ignores the fact that Bahá'u'lláh was by no means the only thinker of his time to propose such views. Possibly,

---

[a] Ex. 19:6   [b] Compare the O.T. prophecies listed in chapter 12.

too, it pays too little attention to the apparently inevitable operation of the Fourth Law of Prophecy (*Prophecy tends to be self-fulfilling*).

The new and growing movement did set a trend, however. For in the course of the next century or so a whole rash of self-professed Messiahs was to appear, most of them curiously ignorant of what the title really meant, and unaware of the strict conditions which by now had, thanks again to the Fourth Law, become virtually inseparable from the underlying archetype. Thus, none of them appeared in the clouds, none seriously attempted to destroy all the unfaithful, none succeeded in abolishing hunger, disease or death, none produced an age of everlasting peace, and none seemed in the least concerned to rebuild Jerusalem or its Temple.

Moreover, if the idea was abroad that the millennium was here already, and that man had somehow managed to avoid the necessity for an initiatory Time of Wrath, then he was in for a rude shock. For, just as late nineteenth-century society, immensely proud of its science and technology, had reached the apogee of its daring and self-confidence, the world was rocked by a series of events which threatened to destroy its achievements for ever. In Jungian terms, the collective hero-archetype had overreached itself.

Perhaps the supreme symbol of this obvious 'change of epoch' was the sinking of the *Titanic* in 1912. Billed as 'the largest, the tallest, the most magnificent ship in all creation', this pride of the world's premier passenger-fleet collided with a lurking, unseen iceberg on a perfectly clear night during its maiden Atlantic crossing, taking with it to the bottom a glittering array of prominent personalities. The shock was, and still remains, profound. 'God', as one of the survivors is said to have remarked, 'went down with the Titanic.' There could scarcely have been a more appropriate omen for what was to follow.

For in just over two years the world was at war. During the course of four years of carnage on the battlefields of Europe, over six million lives from all over the world were lost. The authority of politicians and generals alike was discredited. The basic assumptions of existing society were irrevocably undermined. The Old Order, if not dead, was on the point of collapse. The resurgent human unconscious was once more in the process of bursting through the hypocritical veneer of rationalist civilisation.

But the same spirit of revolution that was now abroad had struck on other fronts too. China had revolted against its rulers in 1911, Russia was to follow suit in 1917. Dynasties were tumbling all over Europe. In the world of ideas, Einstein had produced his Special Theory of Relativity in 1905, and would publish his General Theory ten years later, thereby turning on their heads the orderly, established assumptions of Newtonian science on which the whole of nineteenth-century scientific optimism had been based.

The religious, quick to identify the First World War with Armageddon, the final battle between Light and Darkness predicted by St John's

Revelation[a], were possibly surprised to find that it was over so quickly. Could there, after all, have been a change of Plan? If the thought ever occurred to them, it was quickly dashed.

As early as 1912, the young Adolf Hitler had started to immerse himself in the irrational, pseudo-occult dreams of world-destiny on the basis of which he now proceeded to startle the nations in the nineteen-thirties. By 1933 he was firmly in power, welding together the German nation in a sense of dynamic purpose which owed its power almost entirely to the still-slumbering, still-waiting millennial archetype within the soul of Western man. The degree to which his language and ideology matched that of the ancient Jewish dream was extraordinary. All foreigners, all those of impure blood must be expelled from the sacred soil of the Fatherland; its exiles must be given the chance to return to the fold; war must be waged world-wide against the Fatherland's enemies until they were beaten into submission; all nations would then recognise the new, rebuilt Berlin as the eternal capital of the world; and thus would ensue a thousand-year kingdom, a millennium of purity and peace, prosperity and justice.

It was Hitler, the new world Messiah, who would thus initiate and supervise the programme whose product would be a kind of collective Nietzschean Superman — a race whose blood was pure, whose determination was boundless, whose powers were infinite, whose right to rule was therefore unquestionable. That race would be both Aryan and German, and it would succeed in fulfilling the millennial destiny which the Jews had tamely betrayed. The new Messiah would be a man of resplendent action, not a meek rabbi who tamely submitted to crucifixion.

Ill-informed as Hitler inevitably was about the true nature of the Essenes' messianic initiative, his prejudice in this regard may perhaps have been understandable. But in time it was to become obsessive, even pathological. In the name of his millennial ideal, the German Fuehrer, aided by the Japanese imperial war-machine, in due course embarked upon a second world-conflict even more extensive than its predecessor. Sixteen million lives were afterwards estimated to have been lost on the Russian front alone. Thanks to aerial bombing and rocketry, even civilian populations at home were involved in the fighting. Europe was devastated, Germany itself reduced to rubble. Determined, if possible, to drag the whole, unworthy world with him in a kind of *Götterdämmerung*, the defeated Fuehrer committed suicide. Only then was it finally discovered that his by-now maniacal anti-Jewish obsession had resulted in the deaths of some six million imprisoned Jews. And the conflict concluded on the Far Eastern front with the explosion of the first nuclear weapons, whose mushroom clouds cast a dark shadow over man's very continued existence on the planet.

[a] Rev. 16:16

Here surely, then, was the promised Armageddon, with Hitler fulfilling the role of the biblical Antichrist. And, that being so, could the Messiah himself now be far behind? Such, at least, appeared to be the view in religious circles. As if in answer to the question, reputed Messiahs now started to pop up with alarming frequency, just as they had during the first century or so B C.[42] Increasing numbers of Eastern gurus and leaders of obscure Western religious sects vied for the souls of bewildered youth, who were — paradoxically enough — starting to become disillusioned by the very phenomena which, some *forty years* after the holocaust of 1914, were now apparently fulfilling almost literally the ancient millennial predictions. The hungry were being fed, the sick were being made whole, and prosperity was starting to return to a partially devastated world. More specifically, thanks largely to medical technologies recently developed under the impetus of war, sight was actually being restored to the blind, hearing to the deaf, speech to the dumb and mobility to the lame. In not a few instances, patients who in former times would have been declared dead were, with the aid of new intensive-care techniques, even being restored to life. Under new, enlightened policies of penal reform the prisoners, too, were starting to be released and put to work under less barbarous schemes of community service. And soon, thanks to the advent of the machine age, work itself would be abolished, so removing the grinding curse which had been laid on mankind ever since the Garden of Eden.

And yet, while established Western societies began to look hopefully towards a man-made millennium constructed on the basis of the apparently boundless possibilities of modern science and technology, a spirit of disillusionment and revolt increasingly affected the younger generation, who seem to have sensed that the proposed New Order threatened to become a mere extension of the Old, with all its inequalities, injustices and hypocrisies. The world's rich would get richer, the poor poorer, the privileged more powerful, the oppressed weaker.

Even the apparent millennial manifestations themselves were already starting to turn sour. Thanks to the improved medical technologies, a world population-explosion was in train, with all its concomitant pressures on the environment. These pressures were merely added to by the growing demands of affluent Western societies, with their armies of insatiable machines. A world resources-shortage loomed, a pollution-crisis threatened, hunger stalked the southern hemisphere. And even among the industrial nations the imagined blessing of freedom from work soon started to turn into the curse of unemployment, which could now not even be exported, as it had been hitherto, to the indulgent poor of the Third World.

In time, consequently, Western leaders, both political and religious, began to lose their former overwhelming conviction of their own rightness. From about 1968, a spirit of uncertainty started to become apparent throughout the developed world, as the young revolted against the imposed norms and values of their elders and as the sheer vastness of the world's problems at last started to be realised. As the Third World watched, and the oil-producing nations organised themselves to demand their fair share of the world's wealth, the West's vision of a bright, new, affluent future started to fade, its optimistic expectations to crumble into the dust. Economic ruin threatened, social unrest lurked menacingly beneath the surface, and even the still-persisting shadows of the war-clouds seemed to be massing more thickly.

But then, in religious circles, no less had been expected. True, messianism and millennialism had been unsuccessfully invoked so many times in the past that the religious establishment was now starting to play down both ideas as serious possibilities. Perhaps, it was suggested, there were dangers in taking the prophecies — and even religion itself — too literally. The ancient Sadducees would have sympathised. But in less 'official' circles, and notably among the rapidly swelling numbers of evangelical Christians, there was a return to the words of the scriptures no less sincere and whole-hearted than that of the Essenes and Pharisees two thousand years earlier. In particular, the commandments were now re-emphasised, the New Testament promises repeated, the prophecies revised and re-expounded in loud and unambiguous terms.

For a typical exposition of the current expectations one could do far worse than take Hal Lindsey's immensely readable and entertaining *The Late Great Planet Earth*, published in 1970.[30] Lindsey's proposed timetable is complex, and not always easy to follow. Yet first on the list, it seems, is to be the return of the exiled Jews to Palestine, in accordance with the repeated predictions of the Old Testament prophets to this effect.[a] Since, Lindsey argues, the independent state of Israel was refounded in 1948, and exiles have been returning to it ever since, this prediction is already in course of fulfilment. Its natural consequence, the re-occupation of Jerusalem, has likewise now occurred, and it is therefore only a matter of time before the Temple is rebuilt atop its ancient mount, possibly following a natural catastrophe which will destroy the existing Muslim Dome of the Rock. This reconstruction will be the essential precondition for a renewed setting up of the prophesied 'abomination of desolation' within the Holy Place.

Meanwhile, the nations of the world will be organising themselves into four confederacies — Russia and its satellites, the Arab and Black African states, the Chinese and their allies, and a ten-nation confederacy of Europe. Under the stress of growing world-problems, a potential world-leader will then arise from among the last mentioned (which was formed, be it noted, in 1981!), subsequently forming a coalition of seven out of the ten states. Thanks to his recovery from an apparently mortal injury — a 'counterfeit of

---

[a] Compare the predictions listed in chapter 12.

the resurrection', according to Lindsey — this leader will come to be worshipped as God by a new, non-Christian world-religion which will by then have developed on the basis of astrology, drugs, black magic and devil-worship — and which will, paradoxically, include the established Churches. Identified by Lindsey as the Antichrist, this figure will be supported and sponsored by a so-called False Prophet or Second Beast — a Jew who will control the world's economic system, issuing everybody with a mark or number for the purposes of financial transactions, and who will use magical means to force the world to worship his master.

The Antichrist will now install himself as God in the newly-rebuilt Jerusalem Temple, at the same time guaranteeing the safety and religious traditions of the Jews. This event will mark the beginning of a seven-year countdown to Armageddon. Nevertheless, for three-and-a-half years there will be world-wide economic prosperity, and the Antichrist will be universally acclaimed as world-ruler.

Towards the end of this period, however, he will destroy the religious system which brought him to power, and persecute the 144,000 Jews who will by then have suddenly accepted Christ. The persecution will not affect existing Christians, who will in the nick of time have been suddenly and miraculously removed from the earth to meet Jesus in the clouds, together with the Christian dead of previous generations. This process, described as 'the Rapture', will nevertheless, it seems, be only a temporary one while the earth itself is 'cleansed'.

Now all the forces of evil will be let loose upon the earth. The Arab/African confederacy, headed by Egypt, will invade Israel from the south, and Russia will use this as a pretext to invade the Middle East by land and sea, double-crossing its erstwhile African allies. To this, the Roman dictator (the Antichrist) will respond with a nuclear attack, and the Russians, having temporarily based themselves on the Temple area in Jerusalem, will be wiped out. After a short breathing-space, the now-rampant Chinese will advance with two million troops across the Euphrates, and will meet the Antichrist's forces on the Palestinian plain of Jezreel (Armageddon) — which lies, curiously enough, just below Mount Carmel.

A dreadful carnage will then follow around Jerusalem and in the area south of the Dead Sea. A sudden earthquake will devastate the earth's cities, one-third of the Jews will suddenly acknowledge the Christian Messiah and, at the critical moment, Jesus will return from the sky. As his foot touches the Mount of Olives, the latter will split open, and the newly-converted Jews will shelter in the crack as a thermonuclear blast sweeps across the world, destroying all ungodly kingdoms.

Then will follow the long-awaited millennial Kingdom on earth, subsequently leading — after a brief rebellion — to an everlasting dispensation during which every atom of the galaxy will be disintegrated and re-assembled in a new form.

Lindsey's scenario, culled largely from familiar prophecies in the books of
Isaiah, Ezekiel and Daniel[a], as supplemented by the related pronouncements
of John's Revelation — all of them, in their turn, books of mixed preconception and prophecy — is nothing if not dramatic. Its ingenuity in weaving
together all the unfinished loose ends of messianic and millennial business
into a continuous thread of events is little short of amazing. Yet it is not
untypical of what is widely believed in evangelical circles. Indeed, Lindsey,
oblivious of the Law of Divided Functions, goes on to link it with today's
world via a series of minor predictions of his own. There will, he says, be
a growth of ecumenism, a tendency towards religious semi-political super-
organisations and, at the same time, a falling-away of congregations and a
desertion of the Church by the young. Instead, they will return to primitive
forms of Christianity in a sort of religious underground movement. Tension
will meanwhile mount in the Middle East, Israel will become richer, Western
Europe will supplant the financially weakened USA as the leading power in
the West, and its coalition of ten European nations will go on to become the
mightiest power on earth. The papacy will become more political, and there
will be a growing desire for a single world-ruler; there will also be a limited
nuclear war (possibly between Russia and China), a population-explosion,
widespread famines, and an increase in crime, unemployment, poverty,
illegitimacy, mental illness and drug-addiction. Astrology, witchcraft and
oriental religions will increasingly flourish.

What Lindsey has done, of course, is to mix together a number of
prophetic and pseudo-prophetic techniques in a way which, while by no
means new, incurs several grave risks. Like the prophets of ancient times, no
less than the members of modern think-tanks, he has endeavoured to sense
the *Zeitgeist* or mood of the moment, and in the light of it has extrapolated
existing trends into the future to produce his personal, short-term
predictions. To this extent he is probably fairly safe.

But he also falls into the same trap as the Essenes, in attempting to mix
prophecy and interpretation in defiance of the Sixth Law. And, more
specifically, he runs grave dangers in trying to descry the details of what lies
ahead through the opaque stained-glass of Christian expectation.
Preconception and prophecy, as the Third Law has it, *do not mix*. The task, after
all, is difficult enough even through *clear* glass.

Almost inevitably, therefore, the First and Second Laws will take their
usual toll of Lindsey's predictions. The ultimate fulfilment of the prophecies,
left to themselves, will take a form that nobody had so far even thought of,

---

[a] Compare chapter 12 above.

least of all Lindsey himself. And yet — and this is the constant paradox of prophetic interpretation — his writings, and others like them, will in due course themselves acquire something of the force of prophecy. The extent of that force will depend very largely on how many people read them and how fervently they believe his conclusions. And so there will be a tendency, under the terms of the Fourth Law, for them to be self-fulfilling, albeit distorted in their turn by the operation of the Laws of Surprise Fulfilment and Thwarted Expectation.

The final outcome will thus tend to reflect not only the familiar, original predictions themselves, but also the various, often conflicting constructions that have been put upon them over the course of the centuries. Those points on which the prophets and their various interpreters agree are likely, thanks to the Fourth Law, to be fulfilled with especial force. Those on which there is disagreement will also be fulfilled, but in minor and contradictory ways. And, thanks to the First and Second Laws, the only prophecies to be borne out exactly as expected will be those that are fulfilled quite deliberately by people who are convinced that the time has come for their fulfilment.

Anybody who does so, however, is walking on dangerous ground. For a prophecy is like a time-bomb. Over the centuries it accumulates enormous psychic power. With the explosive force of any great idea, it will do its job with great efficiency, but the person who places it needs to be very sure of his timing, and even more careful to obey its manufacturer's instructions. Otherwise the device may well blow up in his face. Even if he succeeds in placing and detonating it, he can never be sure that the explosion may not be bigger than he expects, or even perhaps set off some kind of chain-reaction.

One conviction, however, seems to be almost universal among students of the millennial prophecies — namely that the latter's ultimate fulfilment is now very close. That, admittedly, has been the view ever since the Passover of AD 33. Yet now the world-scenario appears to be moving daily into closer alignment with the conditions laid down by the original prophecies. Almost world-wide unrest, lawlessness, war, starvation and economic collapse stare man in the face. Many Jews are returning to their ancestral homeland. Major seismic activity seems to be on the increase. And if celestial portents are needed to complete the picture, even Halley's Comet, as we noted earlier, is due to return in early 1986.

Perhaps it is significant, then, that the designer of the Great Pyramid appears to have seen the end of the present century as a time of significant change.[28] Nostradamus, too, seems to have shared that view.[5] And astrology — *pace* Hal Lindsey — identifies the beginning of the twenty-first century with the inception of the Age of Aquarius, the Water-Carrier.[27]

In which case, it is intriguing to note that the ancient Essenes, familiar as they appear to have been with Egyptian and astrological wisdom alike, seem to have had more than a suspicion that the Kingdom of God might be synonymous with the Aquarian age. It is not merely that the prophet Joel appears to use a water-pouring analogy in his memorable description of the Kingdom — *I will pour out my spirit on all mankind*[a] — or that Peter appears to suggest that 'on the third day' might in fact mean 'during the third millennium.'[b] Jesus, similarly, associates the New Age with the appearance of the 'sign of the son of man' in the sky[c], and elsewhere identifies it with the 'sign of the prophet Jonah.'[d] Yet Jonah was the biblical fish-man — and in the Babylonian schema from which our present zodiac evolved the 'fish-man' was the sign which we now divide into Pisces and Aquarius. Again, the 'ruler' of Aquarius is traditionally held to be Uranus (= 'heaven') — yet Matthew's gospel persists in calling the expected Kingdom itself *basileia ouranou* — literally, the kingdom of the heavens, or Uranuses. Finally, Jesus, it seems, carefully arranges his symbols to match the astrological model. The man who leads the disciples to the upper room where the Last Supper is to be held — prefiguring the exalted reality of the future Messianic Banquet — is, once again, to be a man bearing a pitcher of water.

An Aquarian Kingdom of Heaven, in short, can certainly be squared in many respects with the expectations of Jesus and his contemporaries, if these apparent veiled hints are anything to go by. But fortunately we have other sources of prophetic insight which claim to spell out the future openly and in quite specific detail. It is to the leading modern seers, in short, that our attention must now be turned.

[a] Joel 2:28   [b] 2 Pet. 1:8-9   [c] Mt. 24:30   [d] Mt. 12:39-40, 16:4

18
Seers of our Time

As in any age, the number of modern seers whose predictions can be treated with any degree of trust is small. On the basis of already borne-out forecasts, there are few who measure up to Moses' definition of a true prophet as quoted in chapter three. Too many have not only fallen foul of the Third Law of prophecy — that of Prejudicial Interference — but have also ignored the Law of Divided Functions, which warns against the mixing of prophecy and interpretation. Indeed, it could be said that they have had little choice but to do so. Short of being brought up in a cultural vacuum, all (as we saw earlier) must necessarily have been aware from an early age of the great themes of biblical prophecy and their subsequent interpretations, and most have also come to know the purported forecasts of Nostradamus. The result has been an inevitable implanting of prior assumptions about the world's future. In consequence, much of the output of the modern seers has, in effect, amounted to commentaries on those assumptions rather than prophecies in their own right.

Even the greatest of present-day prophets have to be regarded with some suspicion on this score, for there is not one of them who has escaped entirely from the effects of the problem. On the other hand, they are distinguished from their lesser brethren by a distinguished record of past successes in other prophetic spheres, a fact which has added sufficient psychic force even to what we may term their 'contaminated' predictions to ensure that, unlike those of their colleagues, they will tend to be fulfilled, albeit subject to the operation of Laws One and Two (those of Surprise Fulfilment and Thwarted Expectation). Their pronouncements will, in other words, have been transformed (not least by the force of shared public belief) from mere minor predictions into true prophecies, capable of invoking the Law of Self-Fulfilment.

In our own century, there have so far been a mere handful of psychics capable of measuring up to this general yardstick. Three in particular stand out as pre-eminent in their field, and of these two are still living.

The first, however, was Edgar Cayce (1877-1945), an American small-town photographer who had the extraordinary ability, whilst in trance, to gain access to almost unlimited information on any topic raised simply by tapping-in to what he described as the 'Universal Mind' — possibly cognate with Jung's 'collective unconscious'. Over fourteen thousand 'readings' (as he termed the results of these sessions) were taken down by stenographers from the 'sleeping' Cayce during his lifetime, and are today stored at the A.R.E. (Association for Research and Enlightenment) at Virginia Beach, Virginia, which was founded in 1932 expressly to permit research into these materials. Prominent among the topics treated are medicine, religion, reincarnation, the 'undiscovered past', and future events.

A point of considerable interest to our present enquiry is that Cayce was totally unaware at a conscious level of what he was saying during his 'readings'. The 'self' who spoke in trance was a different Cayce from the waking photographer, who was frequently unable to understand the technical terms used by his 'sleeping' counterpart. Indeed, as a devoted fundamentalist Christian and Sunday-school teacher who read the whole Bible once a year, he was so shocked, one day in 1923, to discover that his 'deeper' self had been expounding the supposedly 'heathen' doctrine of reincarnation, that he came very close to refusing to conduct any further sessions. It was only when friends assured him that there was no necessary conflict between the two views, and presented him with the appropriate biblical evidence,[17, 25] that he consented to continue.

This incident is of considerable importance to us in assessing his various predictions, since it appears to demonstrate that the 'sleeping' Cayce was, to some extent at any rate, free of the prior cultural and religious assumptions of his conscious counterpart. One has the impression from his commentators, in fact, that his revelations stemmed from the very source of Truth itself. Yet this view is almost certainly an exaggerated one, not least because there is worrying evidence in the readings to the contrary. On numerous occasions it is clear, with the benefit of hindsight, that Cayce's revelations coincided rather more than one might expect with contemporary theories and ideas rather than, say, with those of the nineteen-seventies. His 'source', for example, seems to be unexpectedly in tune with the views of the Theosophists, Pyramidologists and British Israelites — views which were much more fashionable at the time than they are now.

This would suggest that Cayce's actual source could have been what, in Theosophist circles, is known as the 'akashic record' — a kind of permanent trace left on the warp of spacetime (or alternatively, perhaps, on the collective unconscious) by every thought, word and known event that ever occurs. This record would, of course, contain not only the true trace of history, but also all the erroneous theories and beliefs that have ever been held, whether about history, the nature of existence or the destiny of man. A mind capable of tapping it might, it is true, be able to achieve some kind of concensus of probability, but there would still be a considerable risk of error. And, in particular, it would be possible for a large weight of past or present prophetic agreement on any given topic to result in false predictions and datings — partly thanks to the First, Second and Sixth Laws, and partly because the preponderance of evidence could be due to nothing more than mutual influence among the seers concerned. Perhaps we should at this point also admit to an additional difficulty, so clearly apparent from the story of millennial prediction so far that it deserves to be formulated in the form of a Seventh Law:

Clairvoyance foreshortens the future.

This law might well be termed the *Law of Prophetic Foreshortening*, and is the almost inevitable result of trying to assess temporal reality through a non-temporal medium — rather like trying to map the heavens by looking up the chimney.

Certainly, Cayce did contradict himself, if only on rare occasions. He asserted at different times, for example, both that Jesus' mother Mary was herself immaculately conceived and that she was not. Moreover, his predictive datings seem particularly prone to error, much as the proposed Seventh Law would require. Nevertheless, it has to be said that the 'sleeping' Cayce did not present himself as the proponent of any particular set of prior prophetic assumptions — whether biblical, Nostradamian or otherwise — even though there is reason to suspect occasional Pyramidological and British Israelite influence, especially in the matter of datings. Consequently his predictions for the future deserve serious, if cautious attention, not least on the basis of his past record. For, although Cayce's 'trance' style is laborious, circumlocutious and often plain vague, it is clear that he succeeded in predicting with considerable accuracy such events as the end of the Great Depression of the thirties, the Japanese attack on Pearl Harbour, America's entry into World War II and the end of the same war. His remarkable success in the field of medical diagnosis likewise gives cause for optimism about his diagnostic abilities in other fields.

And it was Cayce who, many years before the discovery of the ruined monastery at Qumran and the long-lost Dead Sea Scrolls in 1947, had detailed the Essenes' way of life in terms which went far beyond the surviving descriptions by classical historians. Archeology subsequently went on to bear him out in large measure, but it has still to catch up with his further revelations about the movement's headquarters on Mount Carmel[24], just as established Christian scholarship has yet to come to terms with his assertions about the relationship between the Essenes and the first-century Jesus-initiative.[37]

Cayce's predictions for the future[3] concern themselves mainly with future geological and seismic upheavals, the rediscovery of the artefacts of long-forgotten civilisations (notably the fabled Atlantis) and the timing of the Second Coming. Jeane Dixon, by contrast, the second of our three main contemporary prophets, concerns herself more with personal prediction, international politics and the geo-political aspects of biblical eschatology.[9] Using a variety of techniques ranging from prayer and meditation, via dreams, to psychometry and crystal-gazing, Mrs Dixon is what may be termed a 'gossip-prophet', much given to appearing at social functions and on television chat-shows. This unpromising milieu does not, however, appear adversely to affect her sincerity or predictive ability, and she is humble enough to admit that she is not necessarily the best person to interpret her own visions — a fact which nevertheless does not prevent her from making the attempt.

The point is well taken, for Mrs Dixon's personal prejudices are strong and unmistakable. Not only is she a devout Roman Catholic, ardently espousing Vatican dogma. She is also strongly pro-American and anti-Communist, given to using the words 'we' and 'our' in her predictions wherever American interests are concerned. Thus, although her predictions are liable to be adversely affected by the Third and Sixth Laws — those of Prejudicial Interference and Divided Functions — Mrs Dixon's pronouncements can be of great prophetic value, simply because her prejudices are so obvious and thus so easy to discount.

And certainly her past accuracy bodes well in this regard. Her correct forecasts of political and international events, as well as of personal tragedies and of problems in the United States space-programme, are so numerous and so well-known as to need no detailing here.[9, 13, 15, 55] So legendary are her abilities that she was even consulted professionally by President F. D. Roosevelt. Perhaps her best-known subsequent predictions concerned the deaths of President J. F. Kennedy, his brother Robert, and the black civil-rights leader Dr Martin Luther King.

Mrs Dixon's approach, it could be said, is curiously similar to that of the Old Testament prophets. Her output consists largely of a torrent of political and personal warnings backed up by statements of religious principle. In this there are similarities with the youngest, and possibly most astonishing, of the three major modern seers — the Frenchman Mario de Sabato. Born in 1933, the illegitimate son of an Italian father, de Sabato is a man of great religious piety and devotion whose frugal life is dedicated entirely to the prophetic art. Like Jeane Dixon a Roman Catholic, his methods of divination, too, are not dissimilar. But de Sabato is much less tied than his American counterpart to received Catholic dogma. His published ideas,[39, 40] indeed, go far beyond established religious bounds, and appear to be only moderately affected by national chauvinism. Both facts augur well, therefore, for his likely future accuracy in the spheres of religion and international politics.

Certainly de Sabato, like Jeane Dixon, has been remarkably successful to date. Independent estimates of his accuracy range from 85% to 90%, and he is besieged each New Year by the French national press for his predictions for the coming twelve months. But many of his forecasts are much more long-term. Among his predictions made in 1971, for example[39], were grave political and economic crises in Italy, together with floods and earthquakes; Britain's entry into, and disruption of, the European Common Market; the fall of the Shah of Persia; the end of the war in Vietnam followed by its total communisation; crises in Pakistan and Korea; troubles in Angola and Mozambique; an Ethiopian revolution; and the success of heart-transplant surgery from 1974. With hindsight, the record is impressive. Moreover, de Sabato's predictions seem to be catholic in the best sense of the word, and thus of great potential value to assessing the likely course of future events.

All three of our major psychics, then, seem capable of providing reliable data, provided that we can discount the various preconceived notions to which all three are subject. This should not be a very difficult task, since we have already established the areas in which caution needs to be exercised. Moreover, as it happens, we have at least two major 'controls'. For, as I pointed out in my earlier books *The Great Pyramid Decoded*[28] and *Gospel of the Stars*[27], both the Great Pyramid of Giza and the apparent precession of the signs of the Zodiac can likewise be used as sources of prophetic insight. The passages and chambers of the Great Pyramid, in particular, can be interpreted as a kind of blueprint for the evolution of the human soul or psyche. It was precisely this function, it will be recalled, that was assigned to it by the ancient Egyptian funeral rites, as reflected in the Saïte Recension of the celebrated Book of the Dead. The only difference is that the ancients of classical times apparently saw the process as a post-mortem one applying to the soul of one man, whereas the view I propose (and, I suggest, the original one) sees it as a continuing process applying to the whole of living humanity — i.e. to the psyche of man collectively — and lasting from generation to generation.

This view, of course, is not new. It was espoused, in particular, by the nineteenth and early twentieth-century Pyramidologists to whose ideas Edgar Cayce apparently had access. Yet when the Pyramidological approach is freed from the narrow religious preconceptions and blinkered biblical fundamentalism which so often characterises it, the result is a plan of great universal power and impact, and one, moreover, which appears to date its various phases with great precision. Its chronograph, spanning the period from the third millennium B C to the fourth millennium A D and even beyond, appears to predict with complete accuracy the Mosaic Exodus, the Jesus-initiative, the Renaissance and Reformation, the revolutionary period between 1767 and 1848, the enormous expansion of human knowledge in the late nineteenth century, the collapse of the Old Order and its cultural and scientific assumptions in or around 1914, the rise and decline of Hitler and the general economic circumstances surrounding both World Wars. The designer of the Great Pyramid, it seems, was aware (whether consciously or subliminally) of precisely the 'standing wave' in the human psyche to which we referred earlier — the archetypal, evolutionary paradigm which, as we saw, has expressed itself through human history since at least the time of Moses, often through the language of messianic ideal and millennial quest. This pattern the architect duly incorporated into the design of his building, using geometry in place of words. And since he was necessarily free both of biblical and of Nostradamian preconceptions (the Pyramid dates from at least 3600 BC), his apparent ideas can thus serve as a useful yardstick against which to measure the predictions of our modern prophets.

The Zodiac, too, appears to have been devised by ancient sages who were far more concerned with characterising the succeeding ages of our planet than with mere personal prognostication. The original Zodiac, it seems, was established primarily in order to map the progress of the Harvest Moon as it gradually migrated from constellation to constellation at the beginning of succeeding ancient agricultural New Years. Only later was the system re-orientated to its present solar reference point. The result was a cycle of divination lasting no less than 26,000 years (the duration of the Earth's precessional cycle), which — such is the permanence of the stars — we can still read perfectly clearly today.[27] Its stages mark out, for example, the transition from the physically-orientated, bull-centred megalith-cultures of the third and fourth millennia BC to the more spiritually-orientated, ram-centred civilisations of the last two millennia BC, with their multiplicity of inspired initiates shepherding and disciplining the recalcitrant flocks of their compatriots. They also anticipate the switch to the more dangerous freedoms of the first two millennia AD, with their symbolism of fish, net and trident, and go on to map out the likely characteristics of the new age that is almost upon us. This larger framework too, then, can be regarded as independent of more recent religious and eschatological preconceptions, and so can, like the Great Pyramid, serve as a helpful control in assessing the more recent prophets' view of human destiny. Only the intervening interpretations (including, of course, my own) need to be regarded with a certain amount of caution, lest the interpreters' prior assumptions may themselves have coloured the outcome.

And so where does our future lie? In attempting a detailed and consecutive answer, our best plan seems to be to take as a starting-point a date already somewhat in the past, so as to help us to assess events already in train in better prophetic perspective. Accordingly, since the date is mentioned specifically by Cayce, I propose that we take 1958 as our *terminus a quo*, and then proceed to summarise predicted events as they follow in more or less chronological order, using our three major psychics as prime sources and adducing evidence from other quarters as appropriate.

1958, it seems, is marked out as the beginning of a potential forty-year period of increasing geological and seismic disturbance on a world-wide scale.[2, 3] The actual starting-date of the upheavals, however, is not fixed, though it will be identifiable by the simultaneous occurrence of earth-movements or volcanic activity in the South Pacific and in the Mediterranean basin, notably in the area of Etna. These upheavals will reach major, even cataclysmic proportions towards the end of the present century.

First, however, events in the religious sphere are to occupy centre-stage. For 1962 (theoretically February 5th, the date of a remarkable conjunction between partially-eclipsed sun, moon and five planets[36]) marks the birth of a future world religious leader of enormous power and wisdom somewhere in the Middle East.[9, 36] Sybil Leek even appears to identify the child as one David Morris, the son of a Jerusalem dentist.[26] At an early age, it seems, he was sometimes observed to lapse into a trance-like state and to babble to himself in what turned out to be ancient Hebrew — on one occasion while actually building a model of what appeared to be the ancient Jewish Temple. At the same time he constantly referred to himself in the first person as King David. If reincarnation is adduced as a possible explanation, the implication is clear — that the child is King David returned and thus, by definition at least, the long-awaited King-Messiah. The fact that Mrs Dixon, revising her original view, has now branded the figure in question (however identified) as the 'Antichrist' may reflect more on her received religious beliefs than on the truth of the matter — which, as we shall see, may even so not be quite what it seems. Significantly, perhaps, no future Messiah appears to be otherwise pinpointed by her.

The spotlight now shifts to the period between 1968 and 1974, which the Great Pyramid appears to see as characterised by sudden setbacks to civilised societies.[28] On the material level, the oil crisis of 1973-1974, with all its disastrous economic consequences for the world at large, fits this prediction perfectly.

A further sharp economic decline, virtually to subsistence level, is marked out by the Pyramid for the latter end of the period 1975-81, following which world commercial conditions will not change dramatically until around the end of the century.[28] Kinsman's psychics, however, predict that the slump, which they say will last until 1990, will be most severely felt in 1984.[23] Whether or not they have been subconsciously influenced by George Orwell's ideas, its initial effects are certainly already with us.

Events in the religious sphere, meanwhile, will not be standing still. 1973 will have seen an important development in the life of Jeane Dixon's 'Antichrist', leading to the formation of a cell of close followers, possibly somewhere in Egypt.[9] The same year marks the start of a 25-year period during which several psychics expect the birth, or re-appearance, of 'the Messiah'.[3, 36, 39]

But it is not long before the darkening clouds of political and economic gloom start to overshadow the picture once more. From 1975 to 1985 de Sabato predicts severe problems for the West, coupled with what he describes as 'the revolt of the orient'.[40] And if there is to be a brief period of relief between 1985 and 1993, this merely provides a glaring contrast to the even darker period that is to follow.

De Sabato's predictions for the interim make fascinating reading.[39, 40] The Arabs, he predicts, will wage a financial war against the West from whose effects Europe will take ten years to recover. Yet the Arab confederacy will fall apart in feuds and wars in which desert oil-wells will be set alight. This prediction, indeed, has already borne fruit. Only the new Arab prophet and conqueror predicted by de Sabato (and subsequently to be assassinated) is so far missing. Saudi Arabia, meanwhile, will expand its power and influence, while its ruler, like the Shah of Persia and King Hussein of Jordan, will be overthrown, as will Colonel Gaddafi's Libyan successor.

De Sabato foresees near chaos and anarchy in Spain leading to the overthrow of King Juan Carlos, but relative stability for France under a left-wing but non-Communist government.[a] Russia will invade part of Yugoslavia, but will have to grant a measure of autonomy to various of its satellites. Western Europe, united in a Common Market of up to twelve or even fourteen nations, will never again be devastated by wars though, equally, Germany will never be reunited. Berlin, it seems, will become an international city on 'neutral ground'.

There will be attempted left-wing take-overs or uprisings in Italy, Portugal, Spain and the United Kingdom (which will also experience a dramatic change of political direction), and republics will eventually be proclaimed in Belgium, Holland and Britain, whose last king will be the present Prince Charles. Northern Ireland will be ceded to Eire, while Scotland eventually becomes independent. Gibraltar will be handed over to Spain and the Channel Islands ultimately to France. In the Middle East, Israel, after a sudden change of political complexion, will suffer from persistent wars, eventually becoming a mere mini-state, with a further world-wide scattering of the Jews. Peace will come to the area only when the Palestinians are granted their homeland. Meanwhile there will be successive coups in Saudi Arabia, Syria and Lebanon, with Egypt remaining stable and Iraq strongly influenced by the USSR.

But then war will seldom be absent from the world-scene during the last

---

[a] This leftward swing duly became apparent in the French presidential elections of May 1981, in which the socialist François Mitterrand was elected.

twenty years of the century. There will be numerous local conflicts in the Far East, the Middle East and Africa. A hair-raising nuclear confrontation in Korea may, towards the end of the period, threaten man's very survival. And, above all, there will be the great Chinese War.

Kinsman's psychics date the beginning of this epoch-making conflict — also envisioned by Lindsey and a host of biblical interpreters[30] — to 1988.[a] According to de Sabato, the initial skirmishes will take place in South-East Asia and India. Then the struggle will develop into a conflict between China and the Soviet Union. Eventually the Chinese invasion, it seems, will split into two prongs — a military one controlled from Peking and a peaceful mass-migration seemingly initiated at grass-roots level. Chinese forces will eventually reach the Middle East, but will then be stopped by foreign (possibly Russian) troops previously invited into Iran by the post-Imperial regime. Mrs Dixon appears to place this event in the year 2000.[9] The peaceful migration, however, will gain such momentum that the Chinese will eventually reach the Franco-German border (according to Mrs Dixon, in 2037). A sharing of the world's resources, and a mingling of its races and cultures, will then ensue.

During this time the USA — which will meanwhile have suffered major financial and social setbacks and drastically, though temporarily, reduced its sphere of direct influence in the world — will assist the Russians militarily against the oriental assault. At the same time, however, the millions-strong 'peaceful arm' of the Chinese invasion will (paradoxically, perhaps) assist Western Europe by non-violent means to counter Soviet influence in its own area.

Meanwhile it is curious to find that neither de Sabato nor Jeane Dixon makes any reference to the cataclysmic series of events predicted by Cayce[2, 3, 14] for the world at large, and for the USA in particular, for the same period (not that Cayce, for his part, predicts the Chinese invasion either). True, de Sabato mentions earthquakes in Italy and upheavals off Dakar, and Mrs Dixon envisages a great earthquake in Jerusalem. She also predicts that a comet (presumably Halley's) will crash into one of the earth's oceans during the mid-eighties, causing tremendous earthquakes and tidal waves — and some kind of world-wide religious conversion into the bargain. The Great Pyramid, too, presages an unspecified spiritual or celestial event of enormous psychic impact for November 1985[28], while astrophysicists Gribbin and Plagemann[16], not to mention Kinsman's psychics[23], anticipate major earthquakes at Christmas 1982, thanks to a temporary imbalance between the planets in the solar system. An even more potent and genuine planetary line-up is, it seems, in store for May 5th in the year 2000[14], though

---

[a] But compare the 'Almond Tree' prophecy for 1986 (p. 23). Mrs Dixon likewise narrows down the first clashes to a date during the eighties.[9]

conventional scientists are prone to discount the gravitational and magnetic influences of such configurations as insignificant.

Yet Cayce's proposed scenario is literally so earth-shaking that, if prophetically valid, it is difficult to understand how any other major psychic could have failed to foresee it. Following the destruction of Los Angeles and San Francisco by large-scale earthquakes, large parts of the American west coast will, it seems, be either submerged or separated from the mainland, while new land will appear in the Atlantic in the area of the Bahamas — allegedly part of the former Atlantis, the rediscovery of whose records will eventually transform our view of man's ancient history.[2,3] Goodman's psychics date these events to 1980-85[14], while Kinsman's tend to pinpoint mid-1982 as a starting-date.[23]

Subsequently both Vesuvius and Pelée will erupt, New York will be devastated by earthquakes, severe disturbances will occur in the polar regions, and much of Japan and the Northern European plain (some areas of Britain no doubt included) will disappear beneath the waves. Moreover, within three months of the eruptions mentioned, the sea will start to make enormous additional inroads into the Western United States, eventually covering — if it can be believed — much of the area to the west of the 100th meridian, or over one-third of the total area of the USA. At the same time some south-eastern states will likewise suffer major inundations; the Great Lakes, through accelerated geological changes already known to be in progress, will start to discharge via the Chicago River and Mississippi Basin into the Gulf of Mexico; and land will appear off Tierra del Fuego at the southern tip of South America. Goodman's psychics elaborate further on this, predicting world-wide geological disturbances, the re-joining of Africa and Europe at the Straits of Gibraltar, the appearance of new land in the North Sea and off the west coast of South America, and severe economic and social difficulties generally.[14] Cayce himself recommends, not surprisingly, a return to individual and family self-sufficiency. And most of this by the year 1998.

But the worst is yet to come. For in the year 2000 the spinning earth will suddenly topple and undergo a dramatic polar shift. Following the inevitably cataclysmic effects of this abrupt change of axis, the world's entire climatic pattern will be changed. Perhaps this dramatic event explains Cayce's further prediction that the 'upper parts of Europe' will be changed 'in the twinkling of an eye', for an exact 180° shift would result (thanks to the earth's orbital geometry) in the southern hemisphere's current ice-age climate[27] being suddenly transferred to the northern hemisphere (superimpose the south polar ice-limits on a map of the north polar region, for example, and it will immediately be seen that they take up more or less the same position as in the middle of the last ice-age). But then the rising of new land in the North Atlantic (mentioned earlier) would have an almost equally catastrophic effect on Northern Europe, since it would have the result of obstructing the warming waters of the Gulf Stream.

According to Goodman's psychics, it will be a full thirty years before civilisation starts to recover from these cataclysmic events, and some centuries before it will become apparent that the long-promised millennium has finally dawned. In the meantime Jesus of Nazareth will have returned, and the earth will also have been visited by the long-suspected extra-terrestrial aliens . . .

The fact that the extraordinary geological events listed are, apparently, largely unforeseen either by de Sabato or by Jeane Dixon does not, of course, necessarily mean that Cayce and his commentators are wrong. It is conceivable that psychics see only the kind of events to which they are attuned. Their visions are largely spontaneous, and prompted by their own particular spheres of interest. It is quite understandable that Cayce, as an American, should have been more concerned with American events than de Sabato — though this still fails to explain Mrs Dixon's evident unawareness of Cayce's cataclysm. Nevertheless, it seems wise not to dismiss the latter's revelations out of hand. He has, it is true, been wrong in the past. His forecast of new land in the Bahamas area, actually dated for '68', was validated only in the sense that one Dr J. Manson Valentine, of the Miami Museum of Science, decided deliberately to invoke the Fourth Law by diving in search of it in that year on the strength of Cayce's 'readings', and discovered the unexplained underwater ruins that have since become a matter of common knowledge.[14, 28] Cayce, it seems, is, like anyone else, at the mercy of the First and Second Laws of prophecy, as well as of the Seventh Law (that of Prophetic Foreshortening). To the extent that he has made his predictions, however, and that readers subscribe to them, they will also tend to be self-fulfilling, under the terms of the Fourth Law. And so some kind of cataclysm is still possible.

That a mere prediction could actually affect the earth's geology may, of course, seem too fantastic for words. Yet Cayce, like other psychics — and not least the biblical prophets — frequently points a direct connection between mental attitudes and physical phenomena. Goodman coins the word 'bio-relativity' to describe the possible link.[14] Technically, one imagines, it could be said to operate even where people merely adjust their lifestyles and the siting and design of their buildings to meet the dangers of living in quake-prone areas, or where techniques are employed to predict and defuse — or at least avoid provoking — major earth-movements. The more literal interpretation, however, belongs to a different order of reality entirely. Certainly the human psyche has powers over the 'real' world whose extent, we may be sure, is as yet hardly even suspected. But whether it is sufficient to provide — like Gribbin and Plagemann's planetary line-ups — the admittedly minute trigger-effect which is all that is needed to transform a mere geological imbalance into a major cataclysm is a matter for debate.

Yet we should bear in mind the operation of the First and Second Laws. Neither Cayce's predictions of geological upheavals nor de Sabato's and Jeane Dixon's of overwhelming Chinese invasions will necessarily occur literally as forecast. It is even conceivable that both may prove to be opposite sides of the same prophetic coin, encoded symbols for a *psychic* upheaval of major proportions that will overwhelm man's whole way of life and cast of thought unless he takes steps to defuse it beforehand, and ultimately resulting in a dramatic 'polar shift' — i.e. a total re-orientation of the psyche to the world, of man to himself and the rest of the universe. Indeed, it is in the nature of prophecy to operate on several levels at once, so that it is even possible that *all* these psychic and physical events will occur simultaneously — Chinese invasion, geological upheavals and all. For prophecy is seldom a matter of either/or. It continually amazes by its power to reconcile seeming opposites and contradictions. There seems to be more than a good case, in fact, for proposing an Eighth — and final — Law of prophecy, as a kind of rider to the already-existing Law of Self-Fulfilment:

If it can happen, it will; if it can't happen, it might.

We should have, presumably, to call this the *Law of Non-Existent Impossibility*.

And nowhere is this law more applicable than to the apparent contradictions inherent in the various prophecies of events at the very end of our present century. For the nineties, according to de Sabato, will see 'the great crisis', the time during which only the 'still small voice' of inner wisdom will stand between man and self-destruction.[40] This Armageddon-like scenario is reflected in Lindsey's 'seven-year countdown', which appears to begin during the same period.[30] Jeane Dixon herself envisages the main Chinese war lasting from 1999 to 2037, while her 'Antichrist' is leading the world's youth further and further astray, assisted by an American tyrant originally given power on the strength of his earlier peace-making skills.[9] The Great Pyramid, for its part, appears to predict a total collapse of world-civilisation commencing between 2001 and 2007, only partially alleviated between 2022 and 2028, and not finally overcome until 2052-2058.[28]

Yet at the same time there are signs of the emergence of a new, spiritual philosophy and way of life. Cayce places this as early as 1998, the Great Pyramid in 1999, and Mrs Dixon apparently at about the same time, when a great flaming cross will, she says, be seen in the eastern sky — though due allowance needs, as usual, to be made for her Christian preconceptions. Astrologically, meanwhile, the New Age of Aquarius is seen as dating from 2010 or shortly thereafter.[27] De Sabato likewise sees the dawning of a new era at some time between 1993 and 2023, with the beginnings of a consequent new, millennial era of peace and prosperity apparent by 2021 at the latest.

Indeed, the Second Coming, he predicts, will itself take place between 2003 and 2031, apparently in the form of an extra-terrestrial human visitation from another planet, subsequently to be followed by others.[39] The Great Pyramid appears to concur, with only slight variations, placing its latter-day messianic advent at 2034-9.[28] Cayce dates the same event at 1998, though the Law of Foreshortening may possibly have been at work here, as elsewhere in Cayce's predictions. Such datings seem to square acceptably with the rabbinic tradition that the Jewish festival of the 'Blessing of the Sun' held on April 8th, 1981 — an equinoctial festival which occurs once every twenty-eight years — will be the last before the coming of the Messiah.

Meanwhile, Nostradamus's 'grand roy deffraieur' of 1999 could, as mentioned earlier, turn out to be either an extra-terrestrial tyrant or a 'redeemer king'. It is worth noting that science-fiction writer Arthur C. Clarke likewise expects extra-terrestrial contacts in the 2030s and actual encounters in the 2090s — though he seems to suggest that the prophetic Law of Foreshortening tends to be reversed at the rational, scientific level. The events he mentions, in other words, could well occur much earlier than predicted.[6]

Armageddon, then, or Golden Age? Kingdom of Heaven, or hell on earth? The apparent contradictions do not necessarily rule out either possibility. As prophetic fulfilments have repeatedly revealed in the past, both sides of the predictive coin can present themselves either simultaneously or consecutively — or, of course, both. And in neither case will events, in any case, turn out as expected — unless, of course, the Fourth Law is deliberately invoked after the style of the first-century Essenes.

As for subsequent events, the Fifth and Seventh Laws (of Diminishing Accuracy and Prophetic Foreshortening) will continue to apply as ever. Clarke's gravity-control and suspended animation may arrive in the 2050s, and space-time distortion in the 2060s — though both could well appear, in his case, ahead of time, as well as turning out to have as much a psychic as a physical basis. The same considerations could apply to interstellar flight in the eighties, immortality (sic!) in the nineties and astronomical engineering in the early twenty-second century.

The Pyramid's predictions of the arrival of further messianic 'light-bringers' between 2134 and 2499 may prove equally well-founded, as may de Sabato's vision of a truly 'prophetic' Golden Age starting between 2162 and 2191, during which another inhabited planet will be discovered. This age, he suggests, will enter its final, 'apocalyptic' phase between 2534 and 2561, when the sky will turn orange, and man — by now separated into geographical areas corresponding to particular choices of life-ethos — will be 'purified' by natural disasters, linked to present-day nuclear experiments. Following the end of this age in around 2737, the 'end of the world' proper will follow in around 2800 — though this will, in effect, represent the beginning of a new universal order entirely.[39]

Apparently indifferent to much of the above, the Great Pyramid predicts a great transformative age between 2989 and 3989, during which a human élite will achieve immortality and succeed in penetrating entirely new dimensions of consciousness (the one no doubt being a function of the other), followed by a further such age for the rest of humanity between 7276 and 8276 — astrologically, the Age of Sagittarius.[27, 28] In terms of this same astrological view, an age of destruction will then occur, lasting from the ninth to the eleventh millennium, with an entirely new cycle of earthly existence initiated in 12,800 — though Cayce's polar shift, if it occurs, could well interfere with astrological calculations of dates beyond the end of the present century.

Yet apparent contradictions and non sequiturs should no longer surprise us. Thanks to the strange, almost magical nature of prophecy, man will inevitably undergo the future that he himself has created — warts, contradictions and all. He can, if he wishes, allow that future — compounded as it largely is of his own disorganised, barely cognised fears and wishful thinkings — to run rough-shod over him, taking pot luck as to what it will do to him in the process; or he can take his destiny consciously into his own hands and, by exorcising the great, unfulfilled predictions, wipe the slate clean for a new exercise in prophetic creativity. In this way he can not only ensure that the power of the ancient predictions can never again be misappropriated, as it has so often been in the past, by mere megalomaniac power-seekers and 'progress'-fanatics. He can also go on to manifest, if he cares to apply his mind to it, a new heaven and a new earth transcending even the former vision.

'Your sons and your daughters shall prophesy,' proclaims the ancient biblical prophet Joel; 'your old men shall dream dreams and your young men see visions; I will pour out my spirit in those days even upon slaves and slave-girls.'[a] And where there is a vision, as the Fourth Law itself guarantees, there is a future.

The alternative is likewise clearly spelt out by the Bible. As the Authorised translation has it, 'Where there is no vision, the people perish.'[b]

[a] Joel 2:28-29   [b] Proverbs 29:18

19
Time for Action

And so where does our investigation lead us? What are we to do with our rich prophetic inheritance? Shall we continue to allow it to rot and ferment in the depths of the collective psyche, letting loose a whole succession of ill-conceived monstrosities upon an unsuspecting world, just as it has done for at least the last two thousand years? Or shall we address ourselves to taming and applying it intelligently by deliberately cooperating with the Fourth Law of prophecy — an awesome task that has not been attempted since the Essenes last did so to such shattering effect in first-century Palestine?

The answer seems plain. Our future is too important to be left to the mere throw of the prophetic dice. In the light of the results so far, only fools would persist in playing Russian Roulette with the Laws of Prophecy.

But mastering our prophetic inheritance demands a determined effort to analyse and understand it. The foregoing chapters, indeed, represent just such an attempt. We need, too, to know just what the outstanding prophecies demand of us. Only then can we decide how best to satisfy those demands, and so arrive at an eventual plan of action. That, then, must be the burden of our final chapters. The Golden Age, we may be sure, will not happen by accident.

Basically, it could be said that the prophecies — with the biblical predictions at their basis — make up a kit of parts for constructing humanity's house of the future. The Laws of Prophecy, for their part, are the tools for putting them all together. But it needs to be remembered that the Essenes have already used some of those materials in constructing what was, in effect, the house's ground-floor. Those materials, therefore, cannot now be re-used. It is not for us, after all, to dismantle what has already been put together. In constructing the upper storey, and so completing the house, we shall consequently have to limit ourselves to the materials that are left.

On the other hand, those materials will need to be used fully, for if any pieces are left over in our prophetic backyard they are liable to be used by vandals as tools for breaking into the once-completed house, or even as

firewood for setting light to it. Moreover, until that backyard is fully cleared
we shall be unable to start work on turning it into the garden-paradise of our
own devising which is to be the culmination of all our dreams.

Our task, then, is to complete, not to destroy.[a] And in doing so, we shall
need to tailor our blueprint closely to the materials still available. Objective
Number One must therefore be to compile an inventory . . .

As we saw in chapters 11, 12 and 13, the Essenes of the first century, trusting
in sudden Divine intervention, and taken aback by the death of Jesus, failed to
apply much beyond the Passover of AD 33 their policy of deliberate fulfilment
which had proved so successful up to that date. Inevitably, therefore, our kit
of unused prophetic materials corresponds to a major extent with the residue.
In summary, this comprises the prophecies relating to

    (i) the assumption of political power by the revived Messiah,

   (ii) the ultimate forty years of Divine Wrath,

  (iii) the triumphant return of the Son of Man and

  (iv) the inauguration of the final millennial Kingdom.

Superimposed upon those prophecies we also have the additional expectations aroused by the Essenes' Pentecost Declaration and Little Apocalypse
— and notably the vision of a cloud-borne Second Coming, preceded by the
virtual self-destruction of the former World Order without the need for any
active intervention on the part of the Forces of Light.

Such, then, must inevitably be the basic plan of the new World House, as
detailed fully in the chapters already mentioned and in the scriptural texts to
which they refer. Its features, however, have been subject to a certain amount
of embellishment by later seers and prophets, and insofar as it is possible to
incorporate such additional features without doing violence to the original
design it will probably be wise for us to do so. When dealing with such
prophetic constructions, after all, one can never be quite sure that a given
modification may not have received official planning-permission.
Prophetically, in other words, it may by now have achieved sufficient
'life-force' to be viable in its own right.

Our basic plan of action, then, falls naturally into four phases, as tabulated
above. As we shall go on to see, it seems likely that the fulfilment of all these
phases is now either in the offing or within our active capability in the near
future — mind-boggling though that claim may at first seem, especially to
Christians of the *deus ex machina* variety. By working closely with the Fourth
Law of prophecy, therefore, there is every chance that we shall finally succeed
in our task, where the ancient Essenes, trusting to the operation of largely
unknown forces, lamentably failed.

---

[a] Compare Jesus at Mt. 5:17.

We, like Peter in two at least of the gospel fishing-stories, must commit ourselves to the waters of destiny and *go to meet the Messiah.*[a]

Inevitably, then, we need to take up the story again where the Essenes left it — in the darkness of the Garden Tomb. For though it may be objected that the originally-planned triumphal entry into Jerusalem was abandoned by the Essenes at the time of the Pentecost Declaration, the fact remains that this particular series of prophecies was never fulfilled and so, like the rest of the undischarged predictions, still hangs like an ever-building thundercloud over our heads, ready to burst upon us in a storm of unprecedented fury as soon as circumstances permit. To that thundercloud our initiative must serve, as it were, as a kind of lightning-conductor, designed to spare the building of human destiny by itself defusing the situation.

The required scenario, therefore, is plain. Referring to our earlier analysis, we can even tabulate its main features for easy reference. Those of Phase One, for example, will run as follows:

(a) The restored Messiah must reappear on Jerusalem's Mount of Olives at the time of a great earthquake.
(b) He must enter Jerusalem from the east, escorted by a procession of rejoicing followers dressed in shining white.
(c) Visiting the tomb of his spiritual ancestor, King David, he must emerge in suitably-perfumed royal robes as the great monarch returned.
(d) Supported by a popular rising, he must proceed with his followers to the Temple Mount, there to be enthroned, anointed and crowned King of the New Israel.
(e) In token of his power, the Cloud of the Divine Presence must descend upon him amid thunders and lightnings.
(f) Then, while the Messiah himself remains — albeit under Divine protection — in the thick of the subsequent fighting and turmoil, his immediate followers must go underground for the duration of the ensuing forty-year Time of Wrath.

But what, it may be asked, does all this have to do with us? Surely such things are a matter of Divine, not human intervention?

Transposed to our own times, the Essenes, it now seems clear, would with hindsight have argued otherwise. If the Messiah is to appear, then he must be produced. And producing the Messiah is, as it was before, inevitably just as much a function of humanity as of Divinity.

If our modern seers are to be believed, moreover, that Messiah is already with us. No special act of will, in consequence, will now be necessary. Born

[a] Mt. 14:22-36, Jn. 21:1-13

in 1962, he will be just thirty in 1992, the time pinpointed by Jeane Dixon (whose dating-record, it has to be said, is a remarkably good one) for the beginning of her 'Antichrist's' mission to 'capture the youth of the world' from his headquarters in Jerusalem. He will start his reign, in other words, on attaining the age of full Jewish maturity — the age, moreover, at which David likewise attained the kingship and Jesus himself commenced his messianic mission.

It is, of course, inevitable that the New David will be seen in an equivocal light — much as Nostradamus himself appears to see him in his celebrated '1999' prophecy (see page 16). There are doubtless many Jews — upon whose support the necessary popular rising will of course depend — who will be willing to regard him as their long-awaited Messiah. Some Muslims may take a similar view. At the same time there are multitudes of Christians, long dazzled by a rabidly other-worldly messianic image, who will — like Jeane Dixon herself — be affronted at the suggestion that a mere man could ever fulfil that awesome role and project on him all the functions of the Antichrist. And there are even greater multitudes of relatively disinterested, if bemused, observers who will be content to watch what happens and judge by the results, much as Jesus himself appears to have recommended.[a]

What is important, however, is that the new Messiah should himself believe in his identity and mission sufficiently to inspire others with that same belief — just as Jesus and John the Baptist did before him. They, too, were pilloried as sacrilegious upstarts in their day, and their latter-day counterparts should expect nothing less — even regarding it, perhaps, as potential evidence of the rightness of their cause.

Christ or 'Antichrist', however, the new leader must have the courage to step forward and play out his role to the full if the great prophetic plan is to go forward. And his task will require considerable attention to detail.

It is axiomatic, for a start, that he must already be in Jerusalem, and preferably in residence on the Mount of Olives, before the expected earthquake. His initial followers, too, must either have joined him there or have been recruited locally beforehand. In order to offer a potential 'defusing' of Nostradamus's '1999' prophecy, it is additionally advisable that he should have travelled to Jerusalem by air, rather than by any other form of transport.

Goodman's psychics[14], it will be remembered, predict a succession of major earthquakes in the Middle East between 1985 and 1990, and if they are correct the Jerusalem earthquake would no doubt be part of the series. Mrs Dixon, who also predicts the quake, sees it, not unnaturally, as marking the end of the long-running Arab-Israeli conflict, and as an event with far-reaching political repercussions.[15] While she herself fails to date it, the fact that the beginning of her 'Antichrist's' takeover in Jerusalem is dated to

_a_ Mt. 7:16-20

1991-2 could well suggest that this will also be the year of the earthquake. Meanwhile, in the light of the so-called 'Prophecy of the Flowering Almond Tree' (page 23) and the Great Pyramid's apparent prediction of crucial spiritual developments in November 1985 (notionally dating from the 30th of that month[28]), this year may well be seen as the beginning of the run-up period.

The New David would therefore be well advised to aim to arrive in Jerusalem by 1985 — and certainly no later than the dramatic arrival of Halley's Comet in early 1986, with all the important consequences for religious faith which Jeane Dixon associates with it.[a] Nostradamus, after all, seems specifically to link cometary arrival and transfer of 'imperial' headquarters at II:41.[b]

Among the immediate tasks of the latter-day Messiah-to-be will be the location of the original 'tomb' in the former Garden of Gethsemane. This, if it still survives, will take the form of a man-made grotto somewhere on the lower western slopes of the Mount of Olives, and directly opposite the Temple Mount. The Grotto of the Agony is, of course, one likely site, as is the Cave of Gethsemane, while a further possible site could lie beneath the Franciscan church of Dominus Flevit. Of these, however, the second, with its olive-press, is possibly the most likely choice and may thus — in view of its acquired biblical associations, at least — serve as a suitable starting-point for the ensuing operation.

In the meantime the new world-leader must prepare himself for his role. He must study the scriptures and the Dead Sea Scrolls, immerse himself in current Jewish messianic expectations, thoroughly survey the general locality and familiarise himself with all the major prophecies and the best in New Age religious thought. In short, he must create in his own mind a crystal-clear idea of the vision which he has to fulfil. For only in this way can that vision be guaranteed to come into manifestation.

If, in the interim, events conspire to permit the Israeli authorities to start work on rebuilding the ancient Temple, that will, of course, be all to the good. But the prophecies do not suggest that this is a prerequisite for the new messianic initiative, and so the expected earthquake can cheerfully be left to clear the site for rebuilding operations in its own way and at its own time.

What is vital, however, is that the New David should then be prepared to act. Possibly he will be warned by a series of premonitory tremors. But at all events he must appear with his followers on the mountain almost in the same moment as the great earthquake strikes. Modern techniques of earthquake-prediction could possibly help in arranging for this.[14] The manner of his

---

[a] Note that the comet's 'fly-by' is actually due to start as early as 1985. 1986 merely marks its closest approach, following its swing around the back of the sun.   [b] Compare chapter 1, page 17.[5]

appearance, moreover, is fully laid down by the prophecies.

It is tempting to assume that the Messiah should appear in the self-same shroud in which his former body was laid to rest in the tomb. That relic, after all, actually seems to be available[54] — possibly the sole surviving artifact capable of directly linking the two messianic initiatives across the centuries. Yet it is clear that the original Essenes saw its role as being over as soon as the body of Jesus was removed. Instead, the risen Messiah must re-appear in the full panoply of David — armour, sword, sceptre and scented royal robes — as detailed in Psalm 45. True, they must also have envisaged some kind of anonymous cover-all to enable him to re-enter Jerusalem without raising the suspicions of the authorities — and we have already suggested that this function was to be performed by the familiar Essene robes. This disguise may be unnecessary in our own day, however, and so it may be possible for the New David to ride into Jerusalem in all his resplendent majesty.

Note the word 'ride', however. In Jesus' case, it would have been sufficient to be borne into the city on a portable throne, since he had already once ridden into the city as Psalm 45:4 requires, and specifically on a donkey as predicted at Zechariah 9:9. That royal entry having since been dismissed by most Jews as fraudulent, however, it would seem advisable for the new Messiah to repeat it, donkey and all — the sole occasion when our new initiative will presume to re-use a prophetic idea already applied by the Essenes. Riding into Jerusalem, after all, necessarily involves riding *something* — and the donkey is, even today, a recognised form of local transport.

The processional route will, of course, lie directly across the Kidron ravine, as close as possible to the Temple Mount. In the immediate aftermath of the great earthquake, the procession's sudden appearance will inevitably have a dramatic effect upon those who see it emerging from the flying dust and the smoke of a hundred burning buildings. Agog, and scarcely believing their eyes, they will watch as it makes its way directly into the Temple enclosure via the now walled-up Golden Gate in the eastern side of the Haram es-Sharif. If the earthquake has failed to unblock this gate, it follows that explosives may have to be used.

At this point, it was suggested earlier, the procession should make its way to the ancient tomb of David in the steep slopes overlooking the Kidron valley south of the Temple Mount — the original site of the former Zion. But this area lies well outside the present city walls, and visiting it would involve a considerable and — to the now-massing spectators — probably incomprehensible détour, even if the ancient sepulchre could be located in the first place. The suggestion was in any case made simply in order to satisfy the presumed need to symbolise King David's resurrection as foreshadowed by Psalm 22:29 and Jeremiah 30:9. Centuries of accumulated tradition would now make this symbolic act dependent on visiting the tourists' 'tomb of David' in the south-western part of the city — a lengthy procedure which will, of course, be out of the question at this critical juncture.

Consequently the New David will have simply to be acclaimed as such as he enters the Haram es-Sharif by the Golden Gate. This act on the part of his jubilant supporters will in fact more than make up for his failure to visit David's tomb, since long centuries of Jewish tradition maintain that the future Messiah will indeed enter Jerusalem via this very gate.[11]

It is possible, of course, that there will be some resistance on the part of the forces of law and order at this point — though quite probable that, in the earthquake's aftermath, they will be more occupied elsewhere in the city with urgent rescue-work and the prevention of looting. Certainly armed violence should by no means be seen as a necessary feature of the popular rising which must accompany the Messiah's triumphant arrival on the site of the ancient Temple. True, he must duly be enthroned and anointed with oil (in token of Psalm 45:6-7) amid the rubble of the Dome of the Rock, close to the site of the former Holy of Holies. But the kingdom of which he must go on to be crowned king (in accordance with Psalm 21:3) is to be a *world*-kingdom — the *new* Kingdom of Israel (= 'rulers with God'), not the mere, political state of the same name. It is possible, of course, that a vastly relieved Jewish people will eventually make him a present of that, too, but — as we shall see — his immediate task will be to found not a new political order, but a new spiritual one, in preparation for an even greater Kingdom that will encompass both.

The Israeli authorities need have no immediate qualms, therefore. The plan outlined in the original Essene *War Rule* allows all of six years for the winning-over of Jerusalem and the re-establishment of the Temple worship[52], and a seventh for the laying of further plans for world-conquest.

The great coronation-ceremony, then, must proceed beneath the persistent pall of smoke which will no doubt, for the onlookers, serve as a terrifying reminder of the Divine power and wrath. Any after-tremors of the earthquake will no doubt add even more to the overwhelming effect of the occasion. There is no way of knowing, indeed, how far nature will contribute to the event in other ways. Nor, for that matter, should those organising the ceremony be over-shy of using artificial effects of their own devising. The smoke of incense would no doubt add to the power of the occasion. And if thunder and lightning there are to be, then there is no reason why they should not provide them, perhaps using the facilities provided by the underground workings with which the area is riddled — much as Jesus, in his own day, left nothing of the kind to chance. What is important, after all, is *that* the prophecies should be fulfilled, not necessarily *how*. Effect, in this case, is all, provided that it is convincing.

True, it is not absolutely necessary that the expected Cloud of the Presence should be a visible phenomenon at all. Conceivably it would suffice for it to take the form of a psychically-sensed aura of power engendered by the awesome nature of the event and the collective belief of those present. Belief, certainly, is a vital ingredient in the process. The whole messianic initiative, as Jesus himself observed repeatedly, is, in essence, an act of faith. And if that act can alter our world, then it is very largely because that world itself is compounded of our beliefs and illusions.

Nevertheless, one senses that the Essenes themselves would not, with hindsight, have been satisfied with such intangibles. Belief sometimes needs a physical crutch. Various commentators have suggested that, even during the Exodus itself, the semi-legendary Cloud of the Presence may, like the equally-legendary pillar of fire and smoke which accompanied the long march, have been some kind of technological phenomenon. Certainly, therefore, the use of such special effects should not be ruled out on this occasion. The world's news-media can be counted upon to do the rest.

Once crowned, the New David's first task must, of course, be to recall his people to their ancient Covenant (as presaged by Psalm 22) in view of the imminence of its fulfilment. Next, he must take a wife, in fulfilment of Psalm 45:9-17.[a] And finally he must proceed to his new headquarters — described in the same psalm as a 'palace panelled with ivory' — there to be welcomed by the celebratory sound of stringed instruments and dancing.

The world-mission which must then follow will, as Jeane Dixon correctly anticipates, have as its object the winning-over of the youth of the world. Mrs Dixon is understandably uneasy about this, however, in view of her traditional Christian background. Her original vision of the New David took the form of a kind of latter-day Moses[28], destined from his birth in 1962 to spread to all people love, knowledge and the light of 'serene wisdom', and she accordingly identified him as the Messiah-to-be.[15] Later, however, she became worried by the extraordinary similarity between his early life and that of Jesus of Nazareth. This was being brought about, she felt, by some kind of 'unnatural planning', while his 'wavelength' was not that of the familiar, Christian, Holy Trinity. Neither of the last two observations is, of course, in the least surprising in the light of what we now know about the nature of the original Essene initiative (the former, indeed, seems specifically to confirm the approach of the present volume); but Mrs Dixon, being naturally unaware of all this, was to deduce as a result that the New David was some kind of devilish caricature, rather than the genuine article. In fact, he was the long-prophesied Antichrist.

Naturally, then, she now views him as a danger to the world, and in particular to its youth. Yet it is to them that the mission of the New David must inevitably be directed. For it will involve the spreading of an entirely new view of the universe and of man's place in it — a view which we shall go on to examine in detail in our final chapter — and it follows that such a view is

***

[a] The symbolic echoes of the Passover, anticipating Yahweh's 'marriage to His people' in the coming Golden Age, will not, of course, escape the Jewish onlookers.

incapable of being adopted by those whose views and outlook are already fixed. Those of middle-age and over, in other words, will tend to be prevented by a kind of philosophical future-shock from even understanding what the new form of consciousness is about, let alone adopting it. They will be like caterpillars who refuse to believe in butterflies, let alone that they will ever turn into them. As the physicist Max Planck once observed, a new idea is generally adopted not because the aged representatives of established wisdom accept it, but because they die. And Jesus, too, pointed out that only those who are like little children can hope to enter the promised Kingdom of Heaven.[a]

The new mission to the youth of the world, then, will be an international movement dedicated to spreading the already developing ideas and values upon which the New Age is to be founded. Those ideas and values will not necessarily be the traditional Christian ones. No doubt that is why Mrs Dixon foresees the invasion of Europe by what she calls a 'false oriental philosophy' between the years 2020 and 2030. For the wisdoms of all ages and cultures will be called upon to surrender their most precious secrets, and the collective human psyche will add to it yet further wisdoms that have so far never even been expressed.

It is for the soul of man that the New David will have to fight, and for a vision which runs counter in almost every way to the established religions and philosophies of the great world-powers of the day. He may well have to pursue his struggle amidst a time of turmoil such as the world has never seen. Inevitably, he and his followers will at times be the target of murderous onslaughts. Yet they will not need to reply in kind. Merely by giving to the blows they will succeed in escaping most of their force.

The massed forces of the Old Age, however, will be unable to check their headlong onrush. In large measure they will go on to destroy each other in a massive, mutual venting of long pent-up aggression, much as the Essenes' original Pentecost Declaration foresaw. From time to time, it is true, one party or the other may claim the Messiah's support, but in the event they will succumb, while the vision and its bearers survive, much as Psalm 23:4-5 seems to prefigure.

But this is to anticipate the events of our story. First, the new Messiah must identify himself. In this, sincere belief, steadfast purpose and total commitment to the coming Kingdom will be all. Not everybody will thank him for it. Yet, in response to Yahweh's celebrated call at Isaiah 6:8, 'Whom shall I send? Who will go for me?' it is for him to answer, 'Here am I; send me.'

With the coronation of the New David in the year 1991-2, Phase Two of the

[a] Mt. 18:3

latter-day messianic plan is due to swing into action. Its details, like those of Phase One, can be tabulated for easy reference on the basis of the scriptures listed and referred to in chapter 12. Tailoring our scenario to the so-called Little Apocalypse of Matthew 24, they will run as follows:

(a) The buildings atop the Temple Mount will be totally devastated.

(b) Wars will rage world-wide.

(c) Famines, epidemics and earthquakes will become widespread.

(d) The representatives of the messianic cause will be hated and even persecuted.

(e) False prophets and would-be Messiahs will pervert the truth.

(f) News of the new messianic initiative will be spread to all nations, to the almost uncontrollable anger of their governments.

(g) The Temple Mount will be desecrated by the feet of foreign forces, and Jerusalem's inhabitants put to flight.

(h) Sun and moon will be darkened — conceivably by clouds of volcanic dust in the upper atmosphere.

(i) The earth will 'reel to and fro', eventually in some sense turning over completely.

(j) The stars will fall from heaven[a] (presumably a reference either to one or more comets colliding with the earth, or to the disappearance of the familiar constellations following the earth's 'toppling') and a great sign in the shape of a sword will appear in the sky.[b]

Once again, then, the devastation of Jerusalem is the starting-point. Thereafter, the picture closely mirrors the predictions of Cayce, Jeane Dixon and de Sabato. With the long Chinese war, the massive geological disturbances of the nineties and the shifting of the earth's axis in around the year 2000, all hell will truly be let loose. Famine and pestilence will be the almost inevitable result, and will further threaten those who survive until the very continuance of man's existence on earth may well be threatened. No wonder that the Great Pyramid predicts a total breakdown of civilisation for twenty years, starting towards the latter end of the period from 2001 to 2007.[28]

Not that there is any suggestion that these events will be somehow *caused* by the messianic initiative of Phase One. Psychic links between man and his universe there undoubtedly are, but in this case there is no question of deliberate instigation. On the contrary, the inception of the plan as a whole at this time will be a direct function — just as it was two thousand years ago — of the fact that Phase Two is clearly about to happen of its own accord. The tail will, to an extent, be wagging the prophetic dog. Moreover, if Goodman's concept of 'bio-relativity' is valid[14] — as virtually all the prophets

---

[a] Compare the 'Prophecy of the Flowering Almond Tree' on page 23.   [b] Curiously enough, if the earth *were* to turn over completely, the Southern Cross would become visible in the northern hemisphere. Can such a cross, one wonders, be interpreted as a 'sword'?

seem to suggest — acceptance of the new teachings may actually tend to *mitigate* the effects of the larger catastrophes, if only by encouraging those involved to adopt lifestyles more consistent with the times. That need, indeed, is already becoming apparent, as we begin to sense in the events of our own day something of the fury of the coming storm.

And amid all these events the messianic initiative of Phase One will continue. The New David can hope still to be alive, well, and pursuing his task of fulfilling, or 'folding up' the prophecies in 1998, as predicted by Cayce (who seems to imply that he will by this time be in Egypt). That, after all, is the year which, according to the Essenes' *War Rule* and Jeane Dixon's dating of the beginning of his mission, should mark his final re-establishment of the Divine Covenant in Jerusalem and the first extension of his mission abroad. Such a date is also well within de Sabato's tolerances for the beginning of what he terms the 'Progressist' or 'Gradualist' period of the Golden Age. Perhaps that is why Mrs Dixon foresees the appearance of a great cross in the sky in 1999 (see (j) above), leading to what she sees as a distorted kind of 'Christian unity', and why the Great Pyramid seems to foresee the establishment of the new 'Kingdom of the Spirit' from the same year. 1999, after all, appears to mark the beginning of the third millennium (i.e. the 'third day') after the birth of Jesus of Nazareth. Meanwhile, Nostradamus's '1999' prediction could simply mean that the new 'redeemer king' is to undertake an air-trip to France (hence the verb *viendra* — 'will come') during the summer or autumn (i.e. July or October, depending on whether his 'sept mois' should be counted from the modern New Year or the former Spring Equinox).

Throughout (and not least in this last prediction) there are continuing prophetic rumblings of dire events hammering out their grisly counterpoint to the messianic initiative. As events go from bad to worse, it is more than likely that anxious, weary groupings and nations, only too glad to place all their burdens and responsibilities on other people's shoulders, will increasingly tend to offer the New David temporal power and even military command. The temptation for him to accept and play the dictator will be considerable. He may even be turned into a god, much as subsequently happened to Jesus himself. It cannot be emphasised too strongly, however, that it would be fatal for him to agree to anything of the kind. The temporal expectations, at least, may well have been part of the original Essene plan, but the effect of the Pentecost Declaration was to remove from the Messiah all direct responsibility for military and political matters during the interregnum leading to the establishment of the new, millennial dispensation. Indeed, under the original plan itself, his word was to be his sole weapon even when the Kingdom finally dawned,[a] and his role was to be the Prince of Peace.[b]

In the event, it is possible that misguided feelings of pity may get the

[a] Isa. 11:4 [b] Isa. 9:6

better of him. He may even make the supreme error of siding with one side or
the other in the fighting. If he does so, his mission will almost certainly be
foreshortened. True, he may hope to see his own grandchildren, in fulfilment
of Psalm 128:6. But Mrs Dixon sees him making a sharp 'left turn' before his
ultimate goal is reached — a turn, moreover, which will also mislead most of
his followers. Nostradamus likewise seems to refer to the event at VIII:77 —
though to get at its true meaning we should be wise to start by reconstituting
the seer's deliberately garbled language into an approximation of modern
French, taking full account of ancient spelling conventions. Referring to the
version cited in chapter 1 (p. 16), the 'correct' wording of the quatrain appears
to be as follows:

L'antéchrist très bientôt annihilé,   The Antichrist being very soon set at
Vingt et sept ans, sans durer, a sa guerre.   nought, his struggle lasts no more
Les hérétiques morts, captifs, exilés.   than 27 years. The heretics dead,
Sang, corps humains, eau rougie, grêlent   captured, exiled. Blood, human
       les terres.   bodies and reddened water deluge
       the lands.

To the extent that this version is valid, then, and that the quatrain itself is
applicable at this historical juncture, it would seem that the year 2018-19 may
see the end of the new Messiah's mission. If so, and if the Catholic
Nostradamus's word 'hérétiques' applies to his followers, their fate is
unlikely to be a pleasant one. Israel, as de Sabato suspects, may itself be all but
extinguished. Those who follow the errant Messiah in his 'left turn' will in
fact not last out the full forty years of the time of troubles, and the rest of the
world will be left leaderless and comfortless for the remainder of the period.
The satanic forces of reaction will be allowed their fling. True the Great
Pyramid appears to foreshadow an improvement in conditions between 2022
and 2028. But it is not until 2031-2 — the end of de Sabato's period of
messianic inauguration — that the full forty years of 'Divine Wrath'
following the Messianic take-over will be spent (always assuming, once
again, that there will be little, if any, foreshortening). Only then, in other
words, will Phase Three of the great plan eventually begin, and the new
Messiah, the true Son of Man, reveal himself.

The idea may, of course, seem to contradict what has gone before. If the
New David was indeed the predicted Messiah and is now dead, how can the
new Messiah be the true one? How, for that matter, can a Messiah who is
dead have been genuine in the first place, in view of the scriptural promises
that he would live for ever?

The answer lies, as ever, in the Essenes' original plan. The former initiative
is, after all, merely the completion of that started in the first century by Jesus
the Nazarene. It is still part of the First Coming, not the Second. But the New
Advent represents a new order of reality entirely — that represented by the

final accession of the Son of Man at the end of the ultimate war between Light and Darkness. Thanks to the operation of the Fourth Law of Prophecy on the Essenes' Pentecost Declaration, that ultimate messianic role can now never be fulfilled by a mere, mortal man. The age-long expectation of millions has long-since scotched the possibility. Indeed, in view of the impossibly ideal conditions foreseen for the world over which he is to rule, it is doubtful whether it was ever on the cards anyway. The Ultimate Messiah is a figure who rides on the clouds, who makes the winds his messengers, the flames his servants. He is an immortal archetype, a god-like super-being, a Heavenly Messiah. And in order that he shall be born it is necessary that the former, earthly Messiah shall die.

The king is dead. Long live the King.

And so perhaps it is appropriate that Nostradamus's word for the earthly predecessor of the Ultimate Messiah is not 'Antichrist' but '*Ante*christ'. In this, of course, he is merely following normal French practice. But the word seems strangely indicative of the true role of the soon-to-be-revealed New David. For, like Moses to Joshua, like John to Jesus (= Joshua), he is to be the forerunner, the prefigurer of things to come. His task is to be the proto-Messiah, the earthly herald of the new, supreme entity, the harbinger of the true Second Coming.

20
Apocalypse

Satisfying the requirements for Phases Three and Four of the prophets' messianic plan for Planet Earth is, on the face of it, an impossibility. Consider, for a start, the demands of the ancient prophecies relating to Phase Three, as outlined in chapter 12:

(a) Some kind of symbol of the coming Messiah must appear in the sky.
(b) All the world's peoples must see it at once.
(c) The dead must be revived to experience these events.
(d) The elect of the New Israel must be identified and restored to their homeland.
(e) A 'new spirit' must fill the hearts of the faithful, and new visionary abilities arise within them.
(f) The Son of Man must set himself up in the New Jerusalem, there to pronounce judgement upon the universally submissive nations of the world.

Then superimpose on this list the further requirements of the Pentecost Declaration — long sanctioned and strengthened now by centuries of prophetic expectation:

(g) The Son of Man must approach the 'Ancient in Years' in the clouds and be presented to him.
(h) He must be given absolute and everlasting authority over all nations.
(i) He must return to earth on the clouds of heaven to exercise that authority, using the winds as his messengers, the flames as his servants.

Such demands, it seems, can amount to little more than science-fiction. And when to these are added the requirements of Phase Four, the whole thing starts to appear totally ludicrous, in practical terms at least:

(a) The new Son of Man must rule not by force, but by instruction.
(b) Universal peace and plenty must ensue.

(c) Man must be released from all his former limitations.

(d) The blind must be made to see, the deaf to hear, the lame to run, the dumb to speak, the deformed to stand straight.

(e) Death itself must be abolished.

(f) Day and night must cease to have any meaning: time, in effect, must come to an end.

Agreed, the imagery is poetic, idealistic, even beautiful. But as a description of any conceivable future world-order it seems totally out of touch with reality. Well might the Essenes have seen such a transformation as totally dependent on some kind of Divine intervention. For, indeed, they had no choice in the matter — and neither, on the face of it, do we.

But we should not forget the Eighth Law of prophecy: *If it can happen, it will; if it can't happen, it might*. Reality is sometimes stranger than fiction. And the key to the vision's fulfilment may well lie in the word 'conceivable' in the preceding paragraph.

For it seems to be a law of human experience, repeatedly proved by history itself and mirrored in the Fourth Law of prophecy, that what we can fully conceive will eventually come to birth. The words themselves possibly give a clue to the nature of the process. That conception is, in essence, a process of psychic fertilisation, the germination of an idea which then slowly accumulates form around it. The idea becomes embodied, as in nature, through a process of combined analysis and synthesis. The body grows and develops to its full term until suddenly, and with only a brief period of premonitory convulsions, it bursts forth ready-formed into the world of reality.

Such may well be the case with the ideas and concepts listed above. The events tabulated under Phase Three of the messianic plan may well come to pass, as may the new world described under Phase Four. To us it may still seem inconceivable.

Yet the truth is that it has already been conceived.

We do not have to go outside Jewish tradition to discover the key to unlocking the mystery. For one of the ancient Jewish teachings recounts that the original Adam of the mythical creation-account was not merely the first physical man. His soul, it was said, actually contained and comprised the souls of all men since. As well it might, in view of the fact that the word *Adam* means simply . . . Man.

The tradition was in due course to become embodied in part of the secret lore of the Pharisees — that of the *Adam Kadmon*, or Archetypal Man. This 'original Adam', it was taught, was the initial man-thought in the mind of God, anterior even to the creation of the world. It was a thought of which all men since are merely partial, physical manifestations, and to the fulfilment of which all subsequent creation was designed to lead. Hence the celebrated Jewish phrase which describes man as 'last in creation, first in thought'.

Ultimately, it was taught, the *Adam Kadmon*, or Divine man-thought, would achieve its supreme and final manifestation in Perfect Man — a being who would, almost by definition, once again contain and comprise the souls of all men. And so the First Adam — the *Adam Kadmon* created before time began — would at long last become the Last Adam, the crown of all creation, at whose advent time would finally cease.

During the course of the centuries this elegant, even moving concept became, almost inevitably, associated with that of the messianic initiative. Among esoteric scholars, at least, the messianic advent started to be seen in terms of the fulfilment of the Adamic promise. The Messiah would be human, but also more than human. In some imperfectly-understood, mystical way he would not only lead the human race, but somehow encompass and embody it, rather after the style of the Hindu *Purusha*.

The idea surfaces in several of the accounts relating to the Jesus-initiative. John's Gospel, for example, sees Jesus himself as the incarnation of the primeval *logos*, or man-thought, in all its perfection.[a] The apocryphal *Gospel of Peter* (one of the sixteen not sanctioned by the early Church) contributes, at IX/34, a fanciful description of Jesus' emergence from the tomb, in which he is supported by two men whose heads reach the very sky, while his own stature actually 'overpassed the heavens'.[20] This account too, then, sees Jesus in terms of the infinitely-tall Heavenly Messiah — i.e. the pre-existent *Adam Kadmon*. And St Paul who, if in some ways deluded, was certainly thoroughly familiar with such esoteric Pharisaic concepts, often refers to the ascended Jesus, to whom he elsewhere refers specifically as the 'Last Adam'[b], in terms of this same idea. It is present at Ephesians 4:10, where he is described as 'filling the universe', while at 4:16, as elsewhere, the faithful are described as his collective 'body'. The theme is taken up again at 1 Corinthians 6:15 — 'Do you not know that your bodies are limbs and organs of Christ?' — and elaborated considerably in chapter 12.

Perhaps such developments were inevitable, once the Essenes' Pentecost Declaration had broached the idea that Jesus had himself become transformed into a heavenly Messiah. Henceforth there was no escaping the conclusion that the ultimate Second Coming, following the Time of Wrath, would mark the advent not merely of a man, but of a Superman — a semi-divine being who would, in some miraculous way, embody the souls of all humanity, the hopes of all mankind.

Thus, Daniel's celebrated vision of 'one like a man coming with the clouds of heaven' now has to be reinterpreted. For 'one like a man' means nothing more or less than a human entity. Daniel's term *bar enash* — an Aramaic

[a] Compare Jn. 1:1-14   [b] I Cor. 15:45

orientalism often translated 'son of man', but merely, like *ben adam* throughout the book of Ezekiel, meaning 'man' (as opposed to, say, 'son of elephant') — has henceforth to be taken to mean not merely man singular, but Man collective. And, seen in that light, an extraordinary realisation results.

That vision has already been fulfilled.

Many thinkers have already come to the conclusion that the celestial events of Christmas 1968 were of extraordinary, even overriding importance in the evolution of the human psyche. Not all of them have realised, however, that the power of prophecy may have had something to do with it. Yet that conclusion is almost inevitable when one considers the facts.

For Christmas 1968 was the time of Apollo 8 — that first, tentative, three-man voyage around the back of the moon. For the first time, it could be said, earthbound man's umbilical cord had been finally cut, and he could look back 'from outside' to take in at a glance his ancestral planet. As astronaut Russell Schweickart was to put it on another occasion, the earth suddenly seemed 'so small and so fragile, such a precious little spot in the universe, that you can block it out with your thumb. You realise that everything that means anything to you — all of history and art and death and birth and love, tears and joys, all of it, is on that little blue and white spot out there which you can cover with your thumb. And you realise from that perspective that you have changed, that there is something new, that the relationship is no longer what it was.'

Things had changed indeed. For the first time, man had seen his world as *smaller than himself* and, by the same token, himself as more than world-sized. Thanks to the mere, crude effects of spacial perspective, he had at last caught a first-hand glimpse of what he could become if he really put his mind to it. A single planetary being, even a transcendental entity. Distance had truly lent enchantment to man's vision of himself — and vision has an odd way of becoming reality.

But there was even more to it than that. The mission of the three astronauts had, unsuspected by them, opened yet further doors of human perception. 'As they rounded the barren lunar globe for the tenth and last time (I quote from my own book *The Cosmic Eye*[a]), and the resplendent half-earth once again rose from behind that now familiar curved and rocky horizon, what they saw coming up to meet them was somehow strangely familiar.

'An image straight out of the racial memory. A god out of the world of the archetypes.

'It was none other than the rounded form of the Great Mother, Earth herself, clad in the same flowing robes of shimmering blue and white that had

[a] By courtesy of Thule Press.

been those of mother-goddesses of earth and sea and sky throughout man's history — and not least his most recent mother-goddess, the Virgin Mary herself . . .

'Freeing himself from the maternal embrace, infant man had dared for the first time to hide behind the back of the celestial armchair — only to discover, as every child does, that mother is none the less there for being unseen, and ready to welcome him back with open arms.

'It is scarcely surprising, then, that the theme of the hour was to be essentially that of the return to the womb. Almost as though in anticipation of the fact, the three-day return-journey to Earth started on Christmas Eve. And so the homeward flight coincided with the immemorial northern festival of the rebirth of light from out of the winter darkness. In astronauts Borman, Lovell and Anders the three wise men, in pursuit of their star, were once again to discover an earthly nativity . . .'

And the child that was reborn was, of course, Man himself. A single entity who could, almost for the first time, look back on something that 'he' had done and experienced collectively. Moreover since identity is, to a large extent, a function of memory, that collective realisation was, perhaps, the first of a long series of steps towards the forging of a true, collective identity — an identity wholly consistent with the idea of the Ultimate Messiah.

Coming, as predicted, 'with the clouds of heaven', Man had indeed approached the Ancient of Years and been presented to him — for whether you picture the Ultimate Reality in terms of a transcendent Sky Father or an immanent Earth Mother is purely a matter of cultural convention, a trick of perspective, and no more misleading in the one case than in the other. Furthermore, he had done so by making the flames his servants and the winds his messengers — for it was the now-familiar thunderous ignition of combustible gases that had blasted the great rocket out into space in the first place, and the 'air-waves' (= winds) that had subsequently broadcast the fact to the world at large. As a result, moreover, people all over the world did see it simultaneously — for the experience was relayed world-wide via television. Thus, it was truly a first-hand, not a second-hand experience: the whole of humanity had shared in the astronauts' initiation. And if the Essenes' theory of reincarnation is valid, the fact that a world population-explosion was in train at the time presumably meant that the vast majority of the 'dead' were actually alive at the time to witness and so participate in the experience.

Extraordinary as it may seem, then, several of the requirements of Phase Three of the prophetic plan had been directly fulfilled by Apollo 8 (albeit transformed, as usual, by the operation of prophetic laws One and Two), and were to be further supplemented by subsequent space-missions. It was they which, in the event, unwittingly supplied the long-awaited sign of the coming Messiah in the sky. As a result, the world would never be quite the same again. Though perhaps he did not yet fully realise it, man had been given the key to a whole new order of consciousness and thus of existence. He had gained potential access to a planetary kingdom in which he could eventually go on to exercise mind-boggling powers, thanks to the prospect that all individual human minds and wills could eventually be merged into one vast, world-wide megapsyche . . .

Tom Bearden has described the likely result in the admittedly improbable event that the brains of all human beings could be directly linked by the enforced wearing of skullcap radio-transmitter/receivers.[46] At a stroke, most of man's major problems would be solved. Since all would have instant, universal feedback, there would no longer be any feeling of 'us' and 'them'. No longer would human beings regard each other as enemies to be competed against. No longer would nations even need to exist as such. Every human being would become a 'mancell' of the greater body which is Man himself. A normal, healthy body, after all, does not go to war against itself. As Bearden puts it, 'This is indeed absolute and perfect democracy; not only is each mancell *participating* in his government, he *is* his government . . . poverty, war, crime, hunger, fear, intolerance and misery are gone . . . The gigantic expansion of consciousness and intelligence is indescribable. Any mancell can recall anything from total linked memory and think it directly, complete with all its shadings and ramifications . . . *With linkage, insight is immediate and unbelievably multidimensional. The entire capability and dimensionality of the species is brought to bear, and such insight is incomprehensible to our present understanding.*' Just as the consciousness of a human being, in fact, exceeds that of each cell of which his body is made up, so the new, collective consciousness might reasonably be expected to exceed the old.

Not that we have come that far just yet, however. Nor is Bearden's 'skullcap' idea likely to catch on in the foreseeable future, even if it were feasible. Anything of the kind would have to be voluntary, not compulsory. Yet just such a process of universal, instantaneous linkage is already in train. Via satellite telecommunications-links — dependent, once again, on man's newfound space-technology — thinking man is rapidly being moulded into what, from outside, might well appear to be a single planetary organism. His ever more rapid world-wide transport system contributes even further to the effect.

But, as yet, the view from outside — essentially, once again, the view from outer space — is necessary to appreciate this fact. Perhaps that is why it has taken space-flight to make man fully aware of the vision. If it is to become translated into physical, down-to-earth reality, a deeper linkage is necessary than that provided by mere conscious communication. Yet that process, too, is now in train. Increasingly, the world's spiritual groupings — and the young within them particularly — are totally re-aligning the very roots of their consciousness, rather like the baobab tree with its proverbial 'roots in the air'. The Findhorn Foundation, in Moray, Scotland, is a case in point. More and more they are coming to see, not mind as a function of themselves as individuals, but themselves as functions of Universal Mind, as the body of Christ on earth, even as organs of consciousness grown for the universe's own evolutionary purposes by Planet Earth herself. That greater entity — whether we call it Universal Mind, Divine Will or Planetary Awareness — they are then allowing, through meditation and attunement, to express itself on whatever level directly through them and their actions. As a result, extraordinary processes of 'coincidence', synchronicity and manifestation are revealing themselves, in apparent confirmation of the thesis. At the psychological level, similarly, there are moves afoot — thanks particularly to 'healing' groups basing themselves on the work of the great Swiss psychologist C. G. Jung — to allow the hitherto largely suppressed substratum of the world-wide collective unconscious to come to the surface and express itself through the potent language of symbol.

Perhaps inevitably, therefore, these developments have been parallelled, and in many cases accompanied, by a strong 'back-to-the-earth' movement and an almost world-wide ecological crusade. Loyalty and faithfulness to Gaea, the Earth Mother, in all her aspects and at all her levels, has already become the watchword of thousands of young people all over the planet.

And it is perhaps significant that all these developments, totally consistent as they are with the ultimate coming of the collective Son of Man, seem to have come into prominence in the late sixties, at almost exactly the same time as the crucial Apollo 8 mission. A new world-order was, it seems, even then in the act of being created. And so it was absolutely appropriate that the returning astronauts, broadcasting from deep space to the waiting and listening earth that memorable Christmas Eve, should have made the highlight of their transmission the reading of the familiar Genesis creation-account: 'In the beginning God created the heaven and the earth' . . .[a]

The end, truly, as it was in the beginning.

Not that that new entity, that ultimate Messiah, that glorious central figure of the Second Coming, will be in any meaningful sense God Himself. The entity which, according to the Great Pyramid, will achieve initial world-sovereignty between 2034 and 2039,[28] will simply be what the Essenes always imagined him to be — Man at last come fully into his own through attunement with the Ultimate Reality. In place of the one-man messianic tyranny apparently envisaged by the Old Testament prophets, what will emerge will be a kind of world-wide 'theocratic anarchy' curiously similar to the priestly council envisaged by the Qumran Essenes, and totally in tune with the Mosaic expectation of a 'kingdom of priests' and 'holy nation'.[b] God's kingdom will, in effect, be a second Garden of Eden ruled over by a

[a] Gen. 1:1[18]   [b] Ex. 19:6

Second Adam — but, in this case, man *en masse*, working as a single entity.

The Prime, Creative Reality itself, however, is something with which man will never realise his total oneness until he has learnt to become one with his planet, one with his star-system, one with his galaxy, one with the universe, one with spacetime itself. And each of these steps will in turn depend upon his having gone one step beyond his current physical limits. Space-flight and soul-flight will, in other words, go hand in hand. And only then, once the long trek is over, will man finally discover that it was never really necessary in the first place . . .

Perhaps it is these further stages in the evolution of the human psyche that are represented by de Sabato's further stages of the Golden Age dated to 2163-2191 and 2533-2561 respectively,[39] or by the Great Pyramid's indication of man's entry into new dimensions of being entirely between 2989 and 3989, and between 7276 and 8276.[28] That total, ultimate re-integration may even have to wait until the beginning of earth's new precessional cycle in 12,800 AD.[27]

The Second Coming, then, will simply mark the emergence of a new archetype into the collective human consciousness. In Jungian terms, it can be seen as the Archetype of the Self. Surfacing out of the collective unconscious into the collective conscious, it will become part of the collective memory, and thus in itself a guarantee of collective identity. Yet it will also manifest, inevitably, at the individual level. There are some who will reflect it more clearly and more passionately than others. These, in their turn, will therefore have a role to perform as leaders or teachers. The imminent New David will be one such, his role being to prefigure and give substance to the new vision, to provide the physical springboard which such a quantum jump of con-sciousness demands. Other leaders, too, will no doubt follow, for the Fourth Law of prophecy has a way of operating in a continuous cycle until the prediction concerned is finally exorcised. There is, on the face of it, no reason why the former David should not himself reincarnate again and again to pursue his redemptive task. The Pyramid itself hints at just such renewed initiatives, while de Sabato's forecast of a series of Christ-like visitations from another planet starting between 2003 and 2031[39] is also consistent with the idea, if in an unconventional way.

But the new archetype will at the same time be a very old one — indeed, for man, the most ancient of all. It is both the A and the Z of the evolution of the human psyche, just as the First and Last Adams represent, in Jewish esotericism, the beginning and the end of the human story. That is why, in the Revelation of St John, the Ultimate, Cosmic Christ can say, 'I am the Alpha and the Omega, the first and the last, the beginning and the end.'[a] It is also why, in the same book, as in the Garden of Eden, there is no Temple and no need for religion, for man is once more attuned to his Creator.

The great twentieth-century Catholic theologian Teilhard de Chardin takes up this same theme in his suggestion that the whole of humanity is now converging, via what he calls 'planetisation', upon 'point Omega' to embody collectively the future Christ. This process he terms 'Christogenesis'. 'The only subject,' he writes,[47] 'ultimately capable of mystical transfiguration is the whole group of mankind forming a single body and a single soul in charity.' And again, 'To co-operate in total cosmic evolution is the only act that can adequately express our devotion to an evolutive and universal Christ.' But that tendency, he suggests, is already with us: 'it is quite evident that the passionate awareness of a universal quasi-presence is tending to be aroused, to become correctly adjusted and to be generalised in human consciousness.' Increasingly, 'the world is seen to be suspended, by its conscious side, from an Omega point of convergence, and Christ, in virtue of his Incarnation, is recognised as carrying out precisely the functions of Omega.'

The further implications of the matter, consequently, are clear to Teilhard. 'To be the alpha and omega, Christ must, without losing his precise humanity, become co-extensive with the physical expanse of time and space.' Moreover, the concept of Omega itself necessarily involves, ultimately, 'an escape from Space and Time.' The eventual result, for man, may thus be 'a phenomenon perhaps outwardly akin to death', but at the psychic level it would be 'in reality a simple metamorphosis and arrival at the supreme synthesis. An escape from the planet, not in space or outwardly, but spiritually and inwardly . . .'

Teilhard's insights, inevitably, are coloured by Christian preconceptions regarding the deity of the eventual universal Messiah. Yet his vision is otherwise remarkably similar to the one we have outlined. And certainly it is more than capable, if in a way which the prophecies' authors can never have expected (such are the workings of the first two Laws of Prophecy), of taking care of all the apparently impossible requirements of Phases Three and Four of the messianic plan as outlined above.

It is inevitable, for example, that the eventual formation of the new, collective human entity will result in a drastic reduction in psychosomatic illnesses of every kind, while the entity itself can, almost by definition, never suffer from blindness, deafness, lameness, dumbness or deformity — for it will have almost infinite numbers of eyes and ears, arms and legs, and will by its very fluidity always be able to take up whatever shape and role is demanded of it by circumstances. By the same token — failing the extinction of the entire human race — it will be totally immortal, as the prophecies have always demanded. Though individual cells of its body may die, the organism as a whole will for ever be totally unaffected.

And so true man (i.e. the 'Son of Man') will finally, if in a slightly unexpected sense, be restored to his ancient inheritance of lordship over his planet. As the world-wide New Israel, he will exercise his universal rule from the Temple of his own collective body amid the glories of the New Jerusalem — which, for centuries now, has been prophetically transformed from an earthly city into a heavenly estate, and thus into an extraterrestrial vision destined to redescend upon the earth (the view from 'out there' lies, as ever, at the centre of the process). Being a world-wide entity, he will indeed know neither day nor night, any more than the former British Empire ever knew sunset. People of all nations, whether or not they are physically, as some claim, the descendants of the Lost Ten Tribes of Israel, will make up the cells of his body, thus completely transcending their former national limitations. All nations, in short, will become subject to the new Messiah's authority — indeed, nationality as such will become largely irrelevant. And so Pangea[a], the earth's original, single continent will, in effect, also be its last.

As it was, once again, in the beginning.

With the freeing of the human psyche from its age-long internal and external wars and tensions (the two, psychologically, are of course largely functions of each other), man's energies will then be freed to transform his planet into the Garden of Eden which, in reality, it always was. Man (Adam) and Life (Eve), no longer hiding themselves from each other behind symbolic fig-leaves, will at last be reunited. And as the as-yet largely untapped reservoirs of his unconscious mind are progressively released, he will learn to exercise extraordinary powers which have hitherto been attributed only to psychics and magicians. His world, in consequence, will be transformed, and even the universe itself — thanks to his continued use of the power of prophecy — will be eventually transmuted, just as St Paul himself foresaw.[b]

'When anyone is united to Christ,' wrote the immensely insightful Pharisee on another occasion[c], 'there is a new world; the old order has gone, and a new order has already begun.'

Yet there is a curious corollary to all this. Those human beings who refuse to accept the new archetype will, naturally enough, not partake of it. Only those who accept it will make up the New Man, the Second Adam or Ultimate Messiah. The rest, inevitably, will therefore not enter the promised Kingdom. But then, strange as it may at first seem, it is only the future Son of Man who ever will — since all those who enter the New Kingdom will, by definition, be co-rulers, members of his body, the collective Christ. Even if that supreme entity eventually succeeds in attracting those still outside the fold, it will only ever be by incorporating them into himself. Hence, no doubt, the symbolism of the Last Supper.

That redemptive mission, presumably, will for ever be the function of any Messiah, as long as there are human beings untouched by the new initiative.

a 'Whole-Earth'   b Rom. 8:21   c 2 Cor. 5:17

It was the function of Jesus the Nazarene in his day, and will be the purpose, too, of the New David whose task it is to set the whole new, prophetic process in motion. Upon him and his associates much will therefore depend.

Their script is now written, subject only to last-minute editing and stage-directions. The stage itself, albeit as yet in darkness, is almost ready. Down in the pit, the subterranean orchestra is already tuning up. The last-minute, walk-on parts are even now being filled. Most of the main actors, one suspects, have already taken up their roles. Soon it will be time for them to come on stage, ready for the curtain to rise.

The time for action will have come.

This hour is not the end of anything,
But just the pause
Before the massive wheels of circumstance
Grip firmly once again,
Iron to iron
Pulling to Jerusalem.

Author unknown

Reference-bibliography

All scriptural quotations are taken from the New English Bible unless otherwise indicated: see page-footnotes.

1. Agee, D., *Edgar Cayce on ESP* (Paperback Library, New York, 1969)
2. Anon., *Earth Changes* (A.R.E. Press, Virginia Beach, 1963)
3. Carter, M. E., *Edgar Cayce on Prophecy* (Paperback Library, New York, 1968)
4. Carter, E. H. and Mears, R. A. F., *A History of Britain* (Clarendon, Oxford, 1948)
5. Cheetham, E., *The Prophecies of Nostradamus* (Spearman, 1973)
6. Clarke, A. C., *Profiles of the Future* (Gollancz, 1962)
7. Cross, C., *Who Was Jesus?* (Hodder & Stoughton, 1970)
8. Cruden, A., *Complete Concordance to the Old and New Testaments* (Lutterworth, 1930)
9. Dixon, J., *My Life and Prophecies* (Frederick Muller, 1971)
10. Esslemont, J. E., *Bahá'u'lláh and the New Era* (Bahá'i Publishing Trust, 1974)
11. *Fodor's Guide to Israel, 1979* (Hodder & Stoughton, 1979)
12. Gascoigne, B., *The Christians* (Granada, 1978)
13. Glass, J., *The Story of Fulfilled Prophecy* (Cassell, 1969)
14. Goodman, J., *The Earthquake Generation* (Turnstone, 1979)
15. Greenhouse, H. B., *Premonitions: A Leap into the Future* (Turnstone, 1972)
16. Gribbin, J. and Plagemann, S. H., *The Jupiter Effect* (Macmillan, 1974)
17. Head, J. and Cranston, S. L., *Reincarnation in World Thought* (Julian Press, New York, 1967)
18. *Holy Bible* (King James Version)
19. Holzer, H., *The Prophets Speak* (Manor Books, New York, 1975)
20. James, M. R., *The Apocryphal New Testament* (Clarendon, Oxford, 1953)
21. Joyce, D., *The Jesus Scroll* (Angus & Robertson, 1973)
22. Keller, W., *The Bible as History* (Hodder & Stoughton, 1974)
23. Kinsman, F., *Future Tense: A Prophetic Concensus for the Eighties* (Pendulum, 1980)
24. Kittler, G. D., *Edgar Cayce on the Dead Sea Scrolls* (Paperback Library, New York, 1970)
25. Langley, N., *Edgar Cayce on Reincarnation* (Paperback Library, New York, 1967)
26. Leek, S., *Reincarnation: The Second Chance* (Stein & Day, New York, 1974)
27. Lemesurier, P., *Gospel of the Stars* (Element Books, 1977)
28. Lemesurier, P., *The Great Pyramid Decoded* (Element Books, 1977)
29. Levi, *The Aquarian Gospel of Jesus the Christ* (L. N. Fowler, 1964)
30. Lindsey, H., *The Late Great Planet Earth* (Lakeland, 1970)
31. Marx, K., and Engels, F., *Manifesto of the Communist Party* (1848)
32. Mascaró, J. (tr.), *The Bhagavad Gita* (Penguin, 1962)
33. *New English Bible* (Oxford & Cambridge University Presses, 1970)
34. Peake, A. S., *Commentary on the Bible* (Nelson, 1962)
35. Powell Davies, A., *The Meaning of the Dead Sea Scrolls* (Mentor Books, New York, 1956)
36. Rampa, T. L., *Chapters of Life* (Corgi, 1967)
37. Read, A., *Edgar Cayce on Jesus and his Church* (Paperback Library, New York, 1970)
38. Rutherford, A., *Pyramidology* (Institute of Pyramidology, 1957)
39. Sabato, M. de, *Confidences d'un voyant* (Hachette, 1971)

40. Sabato, M. de, 25 *ans à vivre?* (Pensée Moderne, 1976)
41. Schonfield, H. J., *The Authentic New Testament* (Dobson)
42. Schonfield, H. J., *The Passover Plot* (Hutchinson, 1965)
43. Schonfield, H. J., *The Pentecost Revolution* (Macdonald, 1974)
44. Schonfield, H. J., *Those Incredible Christians* (Bernard Geis, New York, 1968)
45. Spangler, D., *Links with Space* (Findhorn Publications)
46. Steiger, B., *Gods of Aquarius* (W. H. Allen, 1977)
47. Teilhard de Chardin, P., *Let Me Explain* (Collins, 1970)
48. Tomas, A., *Beyond the Time Barrier* (Sphere, 1974)
49. Vacca, R., *The Coming Dark Age* (Panther, 1974)
50. Vaillant, G. C., *Aztecs of Mexico* (Pelican, 1965)
51. Vermes, G., *The Dead Sea Scrolls in English* (Penguin, 1968)
52. Vermes, G., *The Dead Sea Scrolls: Qumran in Perspective* (Collins, 1977)
53. Vermes, G., *Jesus the Jew* (Collins, 1973)
54. Wilson, I., *The Turin Shroud* (Penguin, 1979)
55. Woldben, A., *After Nostradamus* (Spearman, 1973)
56. Yerby, F., *Judas, My Brother* (Heinemann, 1969)
57. Young, R., *Analytical Concordance to the Holy Bible* (Lutterworth, 1939)
58. Zebrowski, G., *Macrolife* (Futura, 1980)

Index